Caribbean Folklore

Recent Titles in
Greenwood Folklore Handbooks

Campus Legends: A Handbook
Elizabeth Tucker

Proverbs: A Handbook
Wolfgang Mieder

Myth: A Handbook
William G. Doty

Fairy Lore: A Handbook
D. L. Ashliman

South Asian Folklore: A Handbook
Frank J. Korom

Story: A Handbook
Jacqueline S. Thursby

Chicano Folklore: A Handbook
María Herrera-Sobek

German Folklore: A Handbook
James R. Dow

Greek and Roman Folklore: A Handbook
Graham Anderson

The Pied Piper: A Handbook
Wolfgang Mieder

Slavic Folklore: A Handbook
Natalie Kononenko

Arab Folklore: A Handbook
Dwight F. Reynolds

Caribbean Folklore

A Handbook

Donald R. Hill

Greenwood Folklore Handbooks

GREENWOOD PRESS
Westport, Connecticut • London

Library of Congress Cataloging-in-Publication Data

Hill, Donald R.
Caribbean folklore : a handbook / Donald R. Hill.
p. cm. — (Greenwood folklore handbooks, ISSN 1549–733X)
Includes bibliographical references and index.
ISBN-13: 978–0–313–33605–8 (alk. paper)
1. Folklore—Caribbean Area—Handbooks, manuals, etc. 2. Caribbean Area—Social life and customs—Handbooks, manuals, etc. I. Title.
GR120.H55 2007
398.209729—dc22 2007026932

British Library Cataloguing in Publication Data is available.

Library of Congress Catalog Card Number: 2007026932
ISBN-13: 978–0–313–33605–8
ISSN: 1549–733X

First published in 2007

Greenwood Press, 88 Post Road West, Westport, CT 06881
An imprint of Greenwood Publishing Group, Inc.
www.greenwood.com

Printed in the United States of America

The paper used in this book complies with the Permanent Paper Standard issued by the National Information Standards Organization (Z39.48–1984).

10 9 8 7 6 5 4 3 2 1

Copyright Acknowledgments

The author and the publisher gratefully acknowledge permission to excerpt material from the following sources:

"Slowpoke Slaughtered Four", edited by John Bierhorst, from *Latin American Folktales,* edited by John Bierhorst, copyright © 2002 by John Bierhorst. Used by permission of Pantheon Books, a division of Random House, Inc.

Excerpts from William S. Pollitzer and David Moltke-Hansen, *The Gullah People and Their African Heritage.* Athens: The University of Georgia Press, pp. 112–114. © 1999, 2005 by the University of Georgia Press, Athens, Georgia.

Excerpts from *Life in a Haitian Valley* by Melville J. Herskovits, copyright 1937 by Alfred A. Knopf, a division of Random House, Inc. and renewed 1965 by Frances S. Herskovits. Used by permission of Alfred A. Knopf, a division of Random House, Inc.

Excerpts from Frank J. Korom, *Hosay Trinidad: Muharram Performances in an Indo-Caribbean Diaspora.* Philadelphia: University of Pennsylvania Press, 2002: 6–7. Reprinted by permission of the University of Pennsylvania Press.

Excerpts from the book *A Treasury of Afro-American Folklore* by Harold Courlander. Copyright © 1976, 1996 by Harold Courlander. Appears by permission of the publisher, Marlowe & Company, A Division of Avalon Publishing Group, Inc.

Every reasonable effort has been made to trace the owners of copyrighted materials in this book, but in some instances this has proven impossible. The author and publisher will be glad to receive information leading to more complete acknowledgments in subsequent printings of the book and in the meantime extend their apologies for any omissions.

Contents

Preface

I have studied Caribbean folklore for 40 years, but until I took on this project, I did not realize just how much material there is on the subject. A quick flight over the Internet yields these startling results. At this writing, "reggae" gets over 64 million—yes, 64 million—hits in Google ("classical music" is millions behind with 53 million hits!). "Salsa" is mentioned on 53 million sites, although most of those references are to the sauce and not to a style of music. "Caribbean music" gets just under half a million hits. "Creole" rings in with over 13 million sites, and "Santería" comes in with more than 1.3 million. "Caribbean religion" brings many fewer hits: 13,700. "West Indian folklore," which is mostly about the English-speaking islands, generates only a little over 1,500 hits; but, strangely, the larger topic, "Caribbean folklore," which presumably encompasses all island cultures, including the Latin Caribbean, produces only 944 hits. "Fernando Ortiz" (coupled with "Cuba"), who lived until the mid-twentieth century and was the most accomplished researcher on Afro-Cuban culture, generates 154,000 hits, and a search of "Roger Abrahams" (coupled with "folklore"), the very-much-alive folklorist of the English-speaking Caribbean, receives over 14,000 hits.

This unscientific survey of the field demonstrates several points about Caribbean folklore. Many people have written about or are interested in some aspect of Caribbean folklore. Their interest is usually based on a specific example or genre of folklore and not a broader topic; people like "reggae" or "salsa," not "Caribbean music." Similarly, scholars have tended to focus on folklore of one language group in the Caribbean, such as the English-speaking or Spanish-speaking Caribbean. They usually focus on one group, such as I did with my work on Carriacou, Grenada, which has a population of between 5,000 and 7,000 people. Finally, some scholars focus on one folklore genre, as is the case with Judith Bettelheim's Caribbean-wide interest in festivals and masquerading. But with a couple of exceptions—such as Harold Courlander's *A Treasury of Afro-American Folklore* (1996), which covers all the Americas; John F. Szwed and Roger D. Abrahams' *Afro-American Folk Culture* (1978), the major bibliography of written resources encompassing all the Americas to the late 1970s; and Abrahams and Szwed's *After Africa* (1983), which features a wide range of folkloric descriptions from British sources through the nineteenth century—there have been few studies of Caribbean folklore as a whole.

This handbook is an attempt to unite the aforementioned disparate studies; it concerns Caribbean folklore and Caribbeanesque cultures in North, Central, and South America, where different languages are spoken and people with Caribbean connections mix with others who have no such cultural links. I do not slice off the Spanish-speaking Caribbean from the English- or French-speaking Caribbean, although all but a few of the sources included here are in English. It includes every type of folklore I could think of, from folk religion to music to everyday life to material culture to festivals to folktales and other oral traditions. It covers Caribbeans at home and abroad and it considers folkloric notions of what foreigners, especially tourists, may think about the Caribbean and its folklore.

Men play African-style Wari on handmade board in Castries, St. Lucia, 2001. Photo credit: Don Hill.

With such a broad conception of folklore and the area in question, this handbook is a guide, not an encyclopedia. This is the place to start one's quest; it is not a definitive source. Sadly, I am already aware of many "I-wish-I-included-thats" and "why-didn't-I-mention-her-research," exclusions that others and I will discover plenty more of, I am sure. This book is merely a sign along the route toward Caribbean folklore and not a destination that an encyclopedia of Caribbean folklore in all its linguistic, geographic, and sub-disciplinary scope would be. But it is hoped that the student or general reader—maybe a young person far more Internet savvy than I—will read something here and, with a few mouse clicks or a library visit, open up a whole new area of folklore research in the Caribbean that I have overlooked.

Each chapter is organized in such a way as to stand alone or in concert with the others. That is, the book may be read from beginning to end, or the reader/researcher may go directly to the chapter or even the section within a chapter that best suits his or her needs. In Chapter 1, the Introduction, I take up the subject of Caribbean folklore as a whole. I present my rationale for using such a broad definition of *folklore,* for combining the Latin Caribbean with the rest in a volume that might have included only the islands where English is spoken, and for including so many peoples and places outside the Caribbean.

Ferguson "Sugar Tamarind" Adams, famous twentieth-century drummer from Carriacou, 1970s. Photo credit: Don Hill.

Chapter 2, "Definitions and Classifications," should be useful both to a novice and to a person interested in a specific aspect of Caribbean folklore. I begin this chapter by reviewing folklore concepts as applied to the Caribbean. Both Caribbean people and Caribbeanists tend to see folklore in conventional terms, such as "oral tradition," "folk music," or "folk festivals." I have added to these basic categories "Creole languages," "vernacular culture," "everyday-life studies," and "Caribbean religions," among others. The terminology explained in this chapter comes from the disciplines of folklore, cultural anthropology, ethnomusicology, linguistics, and literature. I also define concepts that come out of the Caribbean experience, such as "Creole," "bush medicine," particular musical styles, and festivals.

Chapter 3, "Examples and Texts," includes illustrations of folklore from the area. The chapter is divided into sections, beginning with the topic of oral traditions. Here one will find discussions of myth fragments and folktales. In the section on language, I quote from a rich sample of Gullah words with African origins and list a few Caribbean proverbs. The largest section in this chapter is the one on customs, which explores incidents from everyday life, an example of outsider art, foodways, a complicated type of divination, a cooperative labor practice from Haiti, folk architecture, and how rural Caribbean people once organized space. The section on music, dance, and song is self-explanatory, although I blur the lines between folk and popular genres. Therefore, examples throughout this volume range from traditional music transmitted orally in face-to-face settings to mass media–transmitted popular and classical music that has some connection with what is referred to as roots music. Finally, the last section in Chapter 3 is on seasonal festivals and other events. Here I have included extracts from writings on the nineteenth-century Cuban "Day of the Kings," the Trinidadian "Hosay," and the Haitian "Rara" carnival.

People who have studied Caribbean folklore have used a discrete kit of theories and techniques. Those ideas are the subject of Chapter 4, "Scholarship and Approaches." Crossing right through almost every folkloristic study of the area is an ethnographic approach; that is, writing down, recording, or filming a folk event. Ethnography has its roots in travelers' accounts and in the creation of folklore and anthropology as disciplines in the late nineteenth and early twentieth centuries, especially in the theories of Franz Boas and Bronislaw Malinowski. Coming from Boas and others was the sense that folklore was a kind of alternate history. Many folklore scholars, especially Fernando Ortiz and Melville Herskovits, have focused on the African component in Caribbean folklore. Afrocentrism, a version of their historical approach, has been taken up by a range of scholars who have more or less zeroed in on Africa as a fountainhead of Caribbean folklore. Other scholars use descriptions of festivals, icons found on artifacts, or other techniques to establish African or other historical affinities. Performance-centered approaches to Caribbean folklore became firmly established in the work of Roger Abrahams and his students, who have looked at word and action interplay, connections between performers and audiences, and the functions of folklore performance. Everyday-life studies, while not directly applied to Caribbean folklore, may be inferred in the ethnographic monitoring of customs on a daily basis by ethnographers. In recent years, folklorists and anthropologists have put themselves into the story and have sought to describe personal and subjective understandings of the element of folklore they study, whether by actively taking part in a ritual or simply by describing how one goes about doing fieldwork as a part of the ethnography. Finally, linguists have studied what are, in my opinion, the most intriguing languages anywhere in the world: Creole languages, which are made up from bits and pieces of African and European (or other) languages found in the Caribbean.

Chapter 5, "Contexts," traces how folklore finds its way into mainstream and literary Caribbean culture. In the eighteenth and nineteenth centuries, slave narratives and travelers' accounts were widely read and contain glimpses of the folk culture of those times. There are a few ethnographic or other objective studies written over the last 50 years that are quite literary, and a review of these leads into an extended examination of Caribbean fiction, written both by authors who remained at home in the islands and by expatriates. An appeal of Caribbean fiction is its folkloric allusions, used by writers to add color and make points metaphorically. The Caribbean's theater is much less prominent than its literature but no less interesting. The use of folklore in international film is interesting but not especially common. But probably the greatest impact Caribbean folklore has had on world popular culture is in music and, to a lesser extent, dance and international festivals. In this chapter, music is covered in detail. Finally, tourist folklore is taken up along with art—including painting, plastic arts, and design—which is mostly marketed to tourists or other non-Caribbean people.

The remaining sections of this handbook consist of a glossary of terms that are used more than once in the chapters and have some special Caribbean significance; a bibliography of works on Caribbean folklore; a guide to Web sites that relate to our topic; and an index. None of these sections covers all possible sources, and all are meant to push the reader to his or her library or computer to research the words, books, or topics in greater depth.

I would like to thank the editors at Greenwood for their considerable help in preparing this volume; the late Dan Crowley for guiding me toward the Caribbean; Roger Abrahams, whose early research inspired my own work; and Susanna Fout and the other students of my experimental Caribbean Folklore course, who read early drafts of this handbook.

One

Introduction

The narrative of Caribbean culture consists of the lives of Creoles, Asians, American Indians, and others. Collectively, these people create and re-create lifeways that are permeated by a serendipitous body of folklore. What is that folklore? What are the circumstances that have brought such different peoples together to create it? Why do Caribbean people and researchers see significance in Caribbean folklore?

The study of folklore has its roots in the documentation of the ebbing traditions of European peasantry at the onset of the Industrial Revolution. Its sister discipline, cultural anthropology, began in earnest half a century later with field-oriented studies of rapidly changing societies throughout the world that were being colonized by European powers. Thus, while definitions of folklore originated within a scholarship interested in the remnants of European peasantries, American anthropologists focused on the cultures of peoples at the edges of the European diaspora, especially Native Americans. At the time, both folklorists and anthropologists called the colonized, Third World people "primitives." That label was incorrect because it implied that the people were somehow lesser human beings. They were not primitive in any biological or mental way, but only in their technology, particularly technology that facilitates conquest.

The Caribbean presents a special case for folklore study. Its culture does not fit the folklorists' or the anthropologists' models for the types of societies they should study. Caribbean people were not European peasants, although some yeoman farmers in the Spanish-speaking Caribbean had roots in that tradition, as well as with Africans and Native Americans. Most people in the region had some African roots, although very few established African-like societies. The crops produced by Caribbean peoples on plantations filled the needs of an economically expanding Western Europe and North America, not Caribbean needs. Therefore, Caribbean people were not "natives," and though many were the descendants of people who had been enslaved, neither were they "primitives" in the way that anthropologists liked to refer to "their people"—the isolated, indigenous people and cultures that continued to exist, relatively untouched by this industrial age in the far corners of the colonized world.

The raw materials necessary for industrializing Great Britain and the Low Countries—cotton, coffee, indigo, and especially cane and its products (molasses, sugar, rum)—were grown and processed by West African slaves well into the late nineteenth century. These slaves were taken to the islands from ports in Africa to the Caribbean and the Americas through notorious sailing routes, known as the Middle Passage. After more than two centuries of importing human cargo from Africa, there existed in the Caribbean a variety of settlements. Europeans owned estates, were merchants or colonial officials in towns, or were part of a rural peasantlike group of yeoman farmers. Mostly it was people from Africa who worked the estates, some as house servants. Free Africans lived in towns. In a few places in the Caribbean area, slaves escaped into the mountains or upriver, where they formed "maroon," or runaway, populations. With various degrees of success, these people have sometimes maintained African-like cultures almost to the present day. A few Africans and more people of mixed descent—typically the children of a white estate owner and a slave woman—also owned estates and slaves. Rural people in the larger islands, such as the guajiros of Cuba and the jibaros of Puerto Rico, were yeoman farmers of mixed Native American, European, and African descent. These farmers lived away from the colonial power centers.

After slavery was abolished (between 1834 and the 1880s, depending on the laws of the local island's mother country), wage-labor migrations from India, China, Indonesia, and Mediterranean Europe resulted in a further mélange of peoples, cultures, and folklore throughout the region. Since most of the people who came or were brought to the Caribbean were not "primitives" or "peasants" in the classical European use of those terms, Caribbean cultures defied categorization by either folklorists or anthropologists.

However, by the 1960s, folklorists moved away from the definition of folklore as the study of remnant peasant populations. They developed broader, omnibus definitions of folklore that see folkloristic processes embedded in all cultures and in the human condition. In concert with the folklorists, anthropologists—as they saw their constituency of isolated, foraging bands and so-called tribal villagers vanishing before their eyes—began to study those societies as they morphed into the modern world, rather than imagine them as they once were. Anthropologists also took greater interest in other, modern societies that received immigrants from technologically simpler societies.

Indian musicians and dancers in Trinidad, postcard, early 1900s.

With their distinct yet overlapping histories, folklore and anthropology began to move into the Caribbean, but with slightly different agendas. Because of its historical tie to European populations, and to societies influenced by those populations in the Americas and elsewhere, folklorists have tended to focus on folklore in industrialized countries such as Europe, the Americas, or Asia. Because of their links to humanities departments and especially to literature, folklorists in a

Caribbean setting tended to study oral literature and performance of folk drama, as in the case of the work of Roger Abrahams.

On the other hand, some anthropologists, like myself, began to focus on non-European people within the Western world, including the Caribbean. Following our mentor, Melville Herskovits (or, in my case, my mentors' at Indiana University mentor), we were interested in the African connection to Caribbean folklore. And as nonideological Afrocentrists, we either saw "Africa" in Caribbean culture or "synchronized" Africa in Caribbean culture. In the Caribbean setting, folklorists studied "folklore" while anthropologists studied traditional, especially African-influenced, "culture." Nevertheless, by whatever name one calls it, folklore or culture, both the folklorists and the cultural anthropologists were ideological children of Franz Boas, who helped create both modern disciplines in the United States.

Almost from the beginning of recording technology, folk music has been recorded in the Caribbean by academics, even before the discipline was named "ethnomusicology." In addition to recording folktales, Elsie Clews Parsons—whose training was in sociology but who was primarily interested in folklore and anthropology—recorded songs, as did anthropologist J. Alden Mason. Intrepid field recordists followed their lead, including Alan Lomax, Zora Neale Hurston, George Gaylord Simpson, Harold Courlander, and many others.

In cataloging Caribbean folklore, my approach here is to merge these three streams—folklore, cultural anthropology, and ethnomusicology—and add to them ancillary studies from other disciplines whose efforts fit into the emerging broad definition of folklore. When all these approaches are taken together, they cut a wide path through Caribbean lifeways that is often overlooked or underplayed by traditional academic fields, such as conventional history, economics, or literature, whose scholars look for "great men" (rarely "great women") and "important events" and miss the humanity that is just beneath their noses.

The topics chosen for study by folklorists and anthropologists have ranged widely and have focused more on some topics and less on others. For example, music, dance, festivals, and spoken performance and storytelling have received more attention than cuisine, folk architecture, or everyday activities. Some of the folklore topics neglected by academics have been taken up by literati, first by outside observers such as Lafcadio Hearn in the late nineteenth century and Joseph Mitchell in the early twentieth century and today by Caribbean authors such as Earl Lovelace and Edwidge Danticat. Throughout the last two centuries, an active English-language press in the Caribbean has given rich, descriptive accounts of the events of the day, whether of a notorious murder trial or the arrival of a famous visitor to an island. Together with academic research, a large body of Caribbean folklore is emerging in print and on the Internet, though it is scattered and seemingly disjointed due to the different disciplinary interests of the people who have gathered the folklore. The job of this handbook has been to sift through these different sources and present a structure, not a "theory," of how all this information may be comprehended in a fashion that is interesting and shows a way for a reader to find out what he or she wants to know about Caribbean folklore.

While sticking to works in English, I have stressed a unity in Caribbean folklore—not a linguistic or cultural unity but a unity of the circumstances under which Caribbean folklore came into being and currently exists. I have always felt that dividing the Caribbean into a Latin American component and a West Indian component, with the Dutch and the French sometimes lumped with the West Indian branch, is an improper distinction. Today, there are many folklore studies and historical documents in English translation from the Spanish, French, and Dutch Caribbean. There are also original English-language studies that take up topics from countries where English is not the primary language. Therefore, it is no longer necessary to divide the Caribbean by language in that old and once-conventional way.

Not only have I used an inclusive approach to what folklore is, who has studied folklore, and what societies to look at for Caribbean folklore, I have also extended the geographic area beyond the strict boundaries of the Caribbean Sea and the islands included therein. In the United States, I cover the Gullah culture of the sea islands of South Carolina and Georgia and the Creole culture of New Orleans and southern Louisiana. Elsewhere in North America, I include Caribbean immigrants who have settled in New York, Montreal, southern Florida, and elsewhere. I touch on Caribbean populations in Mexico, Central America, and South America. And following a tradition in anthropology and folklore, I include Guyana, Surinam, and French Guinea as part of the Caribbean cultural area.

All these peoples and places create Caribbean or Caribbean-like folklore because their circumstances of life reflect similar forces. Their cultures, whatever else they contain, include an ever-shifting mix of African and European influences in settings outside of Africa or Europe. That mix, if not in the Caribbean itself, maintains direct or indirect connections to the Caribbean. While Caribbean culture, as reflected in its folklore, is not the only place in the world where Africans and Europeans met in circumstances of colonialism and exploitation, it is the type case for understanding this process anywhere in the world. I think it is the best locale where folklore tells us so much about the contemporary predicament of many people in the world today, in this era of globalization and transnational cultures. Therefore, the importance of Caribbean folklore transcends its particulars.

With all these strands of folklore in so many places, one may still see characteristic tags that mark Caribbean folklore. For all its breadth, Caribbean folklore is like a call-and-response melody, a song with a lead voice and a chorus. Caribbean folklore weaves in and out to with a warp and weft that are constantly changing. Caribbean folklore is a short, ever-changing melody, not a Mahlerian symphony. It is that constant variation that is important, not the fixed design. Because of this characteristic, Caribbean folklore tends not to have the depth of Asian, African, European, or Native American folklore, built up over thousands of years. Instead, Caribbean folklore is scarcely several hundred years old, and its short history makes it seem shallow. By "shallow" I do not mean "not profound"; I mean that it has a facade that makes it seem pedestrian whereas in fact it is always changing, always adjusting, always different, always new. It is made up of fragments, pieces, shreds, and patches, just as modern life is for many of us.

If Caribbean folklore is fresh and lacks an ancient history, it is wider than indigenous cultures of the continents from where it came. It holds pieces from all those areas, like a kaleidoscope with bits of glass (but not the entire glass), in ever-shifting patterns. It is combinations of the ancestral lore, remembered in fragments, and fit and refit to new settings. It exhibits bricolage, the chance fusion of different traits fused into a new lore for some new purpose. For this reason, it seems to reflect the contemporary world very well, more so than grand old traditions.

Two

Definitions and Classifications

CARIBBEAN

For the purposes of this book, the Caribbean "culture area" is broadly defined to include all the islands between the Bahamas and Trinidad in the Caribbean, together with certain mainland countries in the Americas where there reside minorities who share cultural features with the peoples of the Caribbean. The mainland countries are Mexico (especially Vera Cruz state), all of Central America (centering on the people who live near the Caribbean coast), and the non–Native American populations of Guyana, Suriname, and French Guiana. I will also touch on "Caribbeanesque" populations (such as the Creoles of Louisiana) and "transnational" Caribbean people (*transnational* refers to people whose family members live in two or more countries). The major transnational Caribbean populations outside the region are in the North American northeastern cities (from Quebec to Washington, D.C.), Florida, Great Britain, the Netherlands, and France.

WEST INDIES

Sometimes the "West Indies" is a synonym for the "Caribbean," but here the more usual definition will be used; that it, the West Indies will be defined as the islands and/or countries in the Caribbean except for the islands where Spanish is spoken. The West Indies, then, are the islands where English, Dutch, French, or Papiamento is spoken as the major language. The West Indies consist of the

Bahamas, Jamaica, Haiti, the Cayman Islands, and the islands of the Eastern Caribbean. In a stretch, Bermuda, out in the Atlantic, could also be considered part of the West Indies.

GLOBALIZATION, TRANSCULTURALISM, SYNCRETISM, AND TRANSNATIONALISM

Because of its 400-year-old international population, the people of the Caribbean were one of the first to experience globalization. Today, globalization refers to the increasing international contacts in economic activity. Of course, culture and folklore, also become global. Trinidad's Carnival, for example, is celebrated in over 100 cities throughout the world. It seems wherever there is a "Trini" (a person from Trinidad) there is Carnival as well as their special folk customs, blended with the customs of the country where Trinidadians reside. This is an example of what Cuban folklorist Fernando Ortiz called "transculturalism" or the mixing of very different cultures. Syncretism is North American anthropologist Melville Herskovits's term for how particular cultural traits from different cultures combine to form something new. The classic example he used for syncretism is the combining of African gods with Catholic saints in Afro-American religions such as Santería, a Cuban religion that fuses the Yoruba gods, or Orisha, with Christianity. Transnationalism is the result of globalization whereby a group of people, with their own special culture and folklore, are spread out over several countries or continents and continue to act as a unit. The possibility of transnationalism was very difficult in earlier eras of immigration when transportation and communication were not so fast or as relatively inexpensive as today. Since most of the Trinidadian-style Carnivals are scheduled at different times, it is possible to attend a lot of them. Masqueraders and singers move from country to country and from Carnival to Carnival to perform.

FOLKLORE

Some folklorists steer clear of formal definitions of folklore, preferring to study the beliefs and activities of people engaging in ordinary activities that are not usually examined by other disciplines, such as vernacular music as opposed to popular or classical music, jokes circulated via e-mail as opposed to situation comedies on television or comic opera, or common speech as opposed to written language or formal rhetoric. Although any definition of folklore will have its detractors and its exceptions, beginning with a classical definition of the scope of the field helps to delineate categories of belief and behavior that are the focus of folklore studies. Folklore, in its broadest sense, may be defined as traditional beliefs and behaviors that circulate within a group of people in different versions based on a perceived model. Generally, folklore is learned and transmitted verbally or by example within a "face-to-face" setting, although the key to understanding folk communication is that the source of folklore is ephemeral or "in the moment" and not fixed, unlike a recording or written material that is referred to over and over again as a standard. Folklore is held in the head and not in some permanent, accessible medium. However, information from newspapers, e-mail, and even digital sounds, that "pass through" one person to another before returning to a fixed medium, in settings that may not be face-to-face, may also be considered folklore.

The most-researched area of Caribbean folklore is the collection of folktales. A good start in the study of Caribbean folklore is the research of Elsie Clews Parsons, a pioneer in the collection of Caribbean folktales in the first half of the twentieth century. Her archive, "Elsie Clews Parsons Papers," is at the American Philosophical Society in Philadelphia (http://www.amphilsoc.org/library/mole/p/parsons.htm).

FOLKLIFE

Folklore includes the study of everyday life, or folklife. Folklife consists of the "total lifeways of any human community, including its artifacts, art, craft, architecture, belief, customs, habits, foodways, costume, narrative, dance, and song, among other cultural expressions" (Primiano 1977, 322). Folklife also includes vernacular language, vernacular religion, magic, life-cycle and community rituals, "body language," and the cultural use of space. Folklife is everyday life for all human beings.

For this work, both folklore as oral traditions and folklife as the rest of traditional culture will be considered to be folklore, folk culture, or vernacular culture.

VERNACULAR

The term *vernacular* originally meant a dialect of a language, or situational or local uses of speech as opposed to standard or formal language. The word has entered into the folklorists' lexicon in recent decades, however, to refer to local versions of material culture and customs. *Vernacular* is a partial synonym for "folklife-plus-language." One might define much of early Haitian painting and craft as "vernacular art," meaning art produced by people without formal training. That term avoids the unfortunate phrase "primitive art," since such art is not primitive but rather unschooled or naïve.

EVERYDAY LIFE

The academic study of everyday life reaches beyond folklore. Berger and Del Negro have identified three strands of everyday life studies (2004, 4–8). Neo-romantics such as Kirshenblatt-Gimblett have defined folklore as " 'the aesthetics of everyday life' " (in Berger and Del Negro 2004, 4). These folklorists have sought to glorify or at least create a record of the mundane activities of ordinary people. Others have looked closely at festivals, rituals, and other vernacular performances and tied them to ordinary life, either as a way of removing oneself from the hum-drum of daily existence or as a way to highlight that existence. A third approach to everyday-life studies is to show how people in powerless positions reinvent the mass-media-transmitted culture that is presented to them by governments and major corporations. This phenomenon is readily seen in Carnival and in folklore intended for tourist consumption. Many formerly colonial societies readily accept popular culture from industrial societies in their Carnival, but then they twist and bend what is received to create a local and often rebellious response to the very culture they seem to accept so openly.

THE FOLK COMMUNITY

Through the first half of the twentieth century, both folklorists and American cultural anthropologists shared an ideal of a small folk community. As Robert Redfield defined the "little community," folk communities were distinctive, small, homogeneous, and self-sufficient (1989, 4). Folk communities were people who lived in small towns and interacted mostly with each other but who also had contact with larger cultural units, such as a city or nation. The culture that originated in the little community was the "little tradition," while the formal culture—including philosophy, art, classical music, literature—that entered into the little community from the outside and influenced it was the "great tradition." Folklore was the little tradition of little communities in the world of great overarching civilizations, such as the Euro-American great tradition or the great traditions of south and east Asia. For folklorists, the "folk" were the "lower stratum" in a society that contains literate people (Green 1997, 321–22). In Europe, the folk were the remnants of the peasant culture of the preindustrial age. However, the "primitive" communities were "little communities" that existed in parts of the world where so-called tribal political systems existed before the colonial era.

Cultural anthropologists make no such distinction and see folk tradition as being the folklore of any "little" or folk community. For many anthropologists, any community may be a folk community, since folklore has more to do with a type of face-to-face communication that may exist within any group, even if that group, for much of the time, is part of a literate society and communicates through literate methods. Thus, folklore scholars have moved away from the Redfieldian concept of a little community that exists in a set place with a stable population. They now see a folk community as a group of people who get together for a purpose, such as a bowling team that meets twice a week, but who go their separate ways the rest of their time. Other than at Wednesday-night bowling, they may never see each other. Alternatively, a folk community may be the human nodes on an e-mail list, some of whom frequently write and others who just read the e-mails. By removing the criteria of the daily, "face-to-face" interaction, a folk community may consist of all sorts of real or virtual groups who "meet" in fact or in cyberspace, for some collective purpose.

The culture of the Caribbean is more than a fusion of European culture, which has its own folk component, with African (and sometimes Chinese, south Asian, and Native American) traditions. It is a dynamic culture that continually adds new and revises old folk traditions. While most folklore studies have focused on Afro-Caribbean culture, here the entire spectrum of Caribbean culture will be covered. Although most of this culture comes from the grass roots, people of all stations participate in making folklore.

CREOLE

Most people from the Caribbean are Creoles. The term *Creole*—Criollo in Spanish—is a complicated one, with many overlapping definitions. It refers to a people, the culture of those people, or to vernacular languages. There is no agreement on just who "Creoles" are. They are sometimes considered people born in the Caribbean whose ancestors came from Europe, Africa, or either continent. Another definition, once common in the French-speaking Caribbean, is that Creoles were people of French descent born in the Caribbean. In the nineteenth century, these people were often elite families who jealously guarded their French heritage. Today, most people who identify themselves as "Creole" are of African or partly of African descent who were born in the Caribbean. The inference is that Creoles are different from the indigenous people of the Caribbean and from other minorities in the area, such as the Chinese (although many Chinese are "Creolized"), south Asians, maroons (people of African descent who rebelled against slavery and set up their own communities in Jamaica, Suriname, French Guiana, and elsewhere), whites who do not fit the older definition of what a Creole is, and others. This Creole mixture of people created a folk culture that is the primary, but not exclusive, focus of this handbook.

ETHNIC IDENTITY AND FOLKLORE

An ethnic group is a community of people who share a culture and are seen as distinct from other communities with whom they interact. Ethnic identity is by no means fixed; it tends to change through time as people are defined by outsiders or define themselves in various social settings. That is, one's ethnic identity may shift or be layered. For example, a Caribbean person may identify him- or herself as a Creole, a Trinidadian, or a West Indian. In colonial days, many middle-class Caribbean people identified with the mother country, so that they were Spanish rather than Puerto Rican, or British rather than Vincentian. If a person born in Trinidad is living on that island, he or she may be identified as a Creole, white, or Indian (that is, a person whose ancestors came from old British India). If that person travels to another island, the person would be labeled a Trinidadian. In the United States, if that person were a Creole, he or she would most likely be identified as a West Indian or, in white American, as a black person. Even though the identity may shift, it is assumed that the characteristics of group members remain more or less distinctive vis-à-vis other groups. The point here for folklore studies is that traditional behavior or ideas may serve as markers for ethnic identity.

In the Caribbean, music is often a clue to self-identity or to the classifying of some person who is different. Being knowledgeable about or liking a particular folk dance, such as the rumba, may help in defining a Latino (larger identity) or Cuban (more specific identity). Language or accent may also help to classify people; for example, Cubans tend to pronounce Spanish differently from Puerto Rican people, and the accent of Trinidadian English is different from that of Jamaicans. Moreover, one Jamaican community will talk with a very different accent and even use a different vocabulary than other Jamaican communities. Someone whose identity is closely related to a speaker—say, a Trinidadian speaking to a Jamaican—will readily identify the island of origin of the person with whom he or she is talking. On the other hand, an American not originally from or otherwise associated with the West Indies may not be able to distinguish between a Jamaican accent and a Trinidadian accent and may classify both as West Indians. Dress, religion, and personal mannerisms all may be used as ethnic markers. One should always remember, however, that identity might shift. A Trinidadian may speak with a broader accent when speaking to a fellow islander but may have a less recognizable accent when speaking to an outsider.

CULTURE

Folklore is part of what anthropologists call "culture," the shared beliefs, activities, customs, behaviors, and traditions of a people that are handed down from one generation to the next and that constitute the major means by which a people adapt to their physical environment and to other people. The part of culture that is not folklore consists of the formal processes by which children learn to become adults in school or in settings that utilize a body of formally acquired knowledge. The folklorist's concept of folklore is very close to what the anthropologist refers to as traditional culture, except that the former was once applied to European-influenced customs while the latter refers to customary beliefs and behaviors among any group of people, although most cultural anthropologists worked outside Europe. The approach used here is that the division between a "folk" and a "primitive" culture is untenable, since the processes of communicating information from one generation to the next is identical in any traditional setting, regardless in what part of the world the behavior takes place or what group of people is involved.

In the Caribbean, folklorists have tended to focus on oral traditions. Cultural anthropologists have zeroed in on ethnography, the documentation of cultural traditions, of a community, or of some aspect of a community. Both folklorists and anthropologists have joined musically trained scholars in ethnomusicology, the study of the localized music. Therefore, Caribbean culture has not been studied under a single discipline or theory, and there is no set body of scholarship or literature that one can point to as constituting Caribbean folklore as opposed to some other body of work that is not Caribbean folklore.

The study of Caribbean folklore has criss-crossed many fields. Researchers, often unbeknownst to others working on different islands but doing similar work, have looked at Caribbean oral traditions (from mythology and dogma to narrative, folktales, proverbs, ballads, contemporary song lyrics, and jokes), informal language, periodic rituals and festivals (from life-cycle rites to annual festivals such as Carnival and special events), material folk culture (craft, outsider art, bricolage, costumes, and folk architecture), foodways, dance, and cultural notions of the use of space and gesture. The remainder of this chapter will consist of a review of Caribbean research in each of these areas.

TRADITION AND ORAL TRADITION

Tradition is an important concept for folklorists and anthropologists. It is the notion that culture, especially folkways, is the essential patrimony of a people. It is their learned inheritance—not their DNA or genes, but shared customs, ideas, and notions of what is right and what is not right—that every group of people have and that they transmit through the generations, generally but not exclusively in face-to-face encounters where the culture is communicated from a knowledgeable person to a learner. This communication occurs when the learner observes or hears people express their knowledge about their culture, whether openly or unwittingly. Cultural knowledge or traits—the word *trait* is one that cultural anthropologists used two generations ago—are bits and pieces put together uniquely by each individual. Collectively, the individuals in a culture pass to the next generation the traditions of their society, always altered by a person's experiences even though they are often thought to be unchanged.

Oral tradition is just that—tradition communicated orally. A "Man-of-Words," as Roger Abrahams has called the oral performance style of West Indian men (1983), is someone who communicates in traditional ways through a variety of contexts. For example, a man may be known as a good talker and communicate through "broad talk" in the course of his everyday life (21), using a lot of Creole words and in a vernacular style that may be emulated by others. Sometimes, folk communications may be perpetuated in more structured circumstances. In the Caribbean not so long ago, adults would tell folktales to kids for fun and as a didactic device. In the early 1970s, I recorded folktales when I was conducting fieldwork in Carriacou, Grenada. They were told at wakes and at other settings. Today, in most places in the Caribbean (with the exception of Haiti, where such traditions persist), it is more likely that storytelling takes place in a formalized performance, with the teller of tales performing on an auditorium stage for an audience that may or may not be familiar with the storytelling tradition.

BELIEF

Anthropologists define belief more broadly than folklorists do. For a cultural anthropologist, belief means taking a statement as true whether or not there is empirical evidence for the assertion. Belief is often of a religious nature, and in recent centuries, in the Judeo-Christian world, belief has come to refer to faith in the unknowable; that is, in statements that cannot be proved empirically. Beliefs, then, range from the existence of God to miracles (a supernatural intervention that may not be scientifically verified) to magic (manipulation of supernatural forces for private or sometimes public gain) and "luck" (good fortune that cannot be explained in the normal course of events).

Folklorists have sometimes used the unfortunate word *superstition* to refer to belief. Superstition is false knowledge, something that is thought to be true but is not true. Superstitious beliefs express a cause-and-effect relationship, or at least have an empirical referent in which the cause or referent is false. Some folklorists humorously assert that "superstition" is belief held by someone else, not me: I have beliefs, not superstitions. This is just the folklorists' way of stating that although they are saddled with the negative term *superstition*, they do not look down on people who hold to superstitions. In other words, everyone holds to some belief or other, regardless of how folklorists label them. Therefore, most of us, in one way or another, are superstitious. Sometimes a superstition is a compulsion that quiets the mind and avoids a catastrophe. For instance, I double-check the stove every day when I leave the house. I know I have turned it off, but I want to be sure. If I leave the house and have not driven too far, I will return and check the stove again. If I have gone a long distance before I realize that I did not double-check, I worry about it all day until I return. Beliefs that are not proved in empirical reality or cannot be so proved are the glue that holds societies together. Superstitions or beliefs proved false may nevertheless be important traditional behavior.

Therefore, the issue is whether people hold a belief as true and how that belief coheres within some traditional system of knowledge. Belief may be true; it is just that the proof is not apparent. Traditional medicine—in the English-speaking Caribbean this is called bush medicine—is a form of belief. So are ideas associated with rites of passage (rituals that mark transitions in one's life), such as the Caribbean belief of burying the caul after the birth of a child so that the child might have good luck. Magic is belief and, anthropologically speaking, so are notions about God.

In modern societies where formal science plays an increasingly significant role in understanding the world around us, it is important to realize that most of us, even scientists, go about our daily lives based on belief. We also, of course, have a naïve understanding of science to govern our lives. For example, it may be that fluoridated toothpaste reduces dental cavities, but I have never read any scientific study that proves that to be the case, and I would be willing to bet that virtually all the readers of this sentence could say the same thing: we *believe* that fluoridation reduces cavities but we have no proof. Only the scientists who have studied the issue have the proof. On the other hand, we have naïve scientific knowledge—maybe I should call it trial and error—that it is not a good idea to walk in front of a moving truck.

Anthropologist Bronislaw Malinowski thought that belief reduces anxiety. However, it is more than that. Belief may be the bedrock of a system of knowledge. Artistic endeavor, including folk craft, reveals knowledge that sometimes codifies traditional belief and presents a kind of reality that gives a human understanding to the world "out there."

MYTH

Anthropologists see myth as the keystone of folk belief. Myth is a folk narrative sometimes circulating in oral tradition that deals with the supernatural origin of the world and a people's place in it. Myths may be set in a distant past, before the natural, empirical world came into being. Alternatively, myths may describe a world that is timeless and ongoing, a world that exists in, around, behind, above, and below this world. According to Malinowski, myth in small societies was a charter for belief. In so-called tribes, myth was a sacred story told in pieces that explained how a particular people came to occupy the land they live in and their right to be there. Often, single elements of the myth would be related in folktales, proverbs, and other short segments. Bits of a myth may show up in people's names, in place names, or in proverbs. If a myth is told as a narrative, every storyteller has his own version of the myth, and people from different villages or different cultures would have different versions, often ones that favored them and not their enemies in the "once-upon-a-time" world of myth.

Myths were told as stories and played out in rituals, with the central characters being human or animal but also having a supernatural bearing and supernatural powers. They are different from the humans and animals of this world in the way they look and in their magical abilities. They are like humans in their faults. In rituals, humans play these characters in skits that give life to mythic events.

In simple, relatively self-contained horticultural societies, myth was used to explain the culture, especially the placement of kinship groups vis-à-vis each other. The verbal articulation of belief holds family and larger groups together as a cohesive unit. Myth was the centerpiece for such people. It was these societies—now rare as globalization washes over all human groups—that were the core of twentieth-century ethnography and the major interest of anthropologists one or two generations ago. People with traditional, fulsome myths are disappearing and are being sucked into the "global village."

Modern societies are pluralistic. They contain a mix of people from many different backgrounds, including the recent descendants of people from preindustrial societies in which myth was more explicit. Today, ideas about how the world came to be compete with each other. Myths become fragmented, a patchwork of different beliefs formed by individuals, families, ethnic groups, and governments into new sacred and secular world views. Grand mythic elements are now circulated in popular literature, film, classical and popular music, and nationalistic ideals fostered by political leaders. The age of myth has not passed, but the nature of mythmaking has changed.

Caribbean countries share the fragmentation of myth with the industrialized world. Some mythic components have their origin in the cultures of Western Europe, and those, most often studied by folklorists and students of popular culture, tend to dominate formal cultural institutions, especially in the entertainment industry. The hobbits, Harry Potter with his mystical powers, characters in a Steven Spielberg film, and the stories from the Disney Corporation tend to popularize new myths whose roots lie in medieval Europe. However, most Caribbean islands have mythic traditions that they share with West Africa, Asia, or Europe, or are rooted in the Caribbean experience. These beliefs were once expressed in traditional stories but now are spread through a vigorous literature and in music. Reversing the dominant trends coming from the metropolis, Caribbean literature and music not only speak to Caribbean peoples but also are popular in many countries outside the Caribbean, as they have become a fixture in global popular culture.

Reenactments of slavery in songs and in plays; the return to Africa via magical flight; the Hindu festival of lights (Diwali); tourist and local notions of a tropical paradise perpetuated through depictions in sight and sounds of sea, surf, sand, and sex: are all Caribbean myth fragments that have current circulation.

BRICOLAGE

Bricolage is a term that was first used in a scholarly context by French anthropologist Claude Lévi-Strauss:

> In its old sense the verb 'bricoler' applied to ball games and billiards, to hunting, shooting and riding. It was however always used with reference to some extraneous movement: a ball rebounding, a dog straying or a horse swerving from its direct course to avoid an obstacle. And in our own time the 'bricoleur' is still someone who works with his hands and uses devious means compared to those of a craftsman. The characteristic feature of mythical thought is that it expresses itself by means of a heterogeneous repertoire which, even if extensive, is nevertheless limited. It has to use this repertoire, however, whatever the task in hand because it has nothing else at its disposal. Mythical thought is therefore a kind of intellectual 'bricolage'—which explains the relation which can be perceived between the two. (1966, 19)

Lévi-Strauss first applied *bricolage* to myth. A myth is made up of bits and pieces—motifs is what Stith Thompson would call them—that are stitched together in a unique way each time a story is told. The meaning of bricolage has been expanded to refer to the ability of taking anything at hand and using it for some purpose other than its normal use. For example, I sometimes use a shoe with a hard sole as a hammer. Bricolage contrasts with *craft* in that a craftsperson uses a known, fixed set of traditional tools to do a job that has been done before and will be done again; for example, the tools a carpenter uses.

The idea of bricolage is "made" for Caribbean folklore. Over the last 400 years, the people of the Caribbean have built a satisfying culture from many other cultures, just as Old and New World crafts have been converted, through bricolage, for other uses. Caribbean folklore reflects this helter-skelter nature. Caribbean people's oral traditions, their language, their festivals, and their material culture all reveal a combination of disparate elements, contributing to a folklore that is always adapting, always under modification, always surprising, and always interesting.

FOLKTALE

A folktale is a traditional oral story or narrative. In classic folklore studies, folktales are considered false, although in an African and Caribbean setting, some folktales may be considered myth fragments and, therefore, some people may consider them true as well as explanatory and didactic. Formerly, many scholars adapted the Aarne-Thompson folktale index to classify tales (1964) or the geographically wider and much larger Motif index compiled by Stith Thompson (1955). The problem with this classification of tales is that it is very Eurocentric, and so tales from other parts of the world—the Caribbean included—are not represented as richly as those from Europe or from areas of the European diaspora. Of course, the Caribbean is part of the European diaspora but it is also part of the African and Asian diasporas.

In the decades since Stith Thompson topped off his life's work by completing Aarne's index, folklore interests have shifted away from their geographic distribution to the performance of folktales or to the textual analysis of folktales. A few scholars have continued to expand the index and added many examples of folktales from outside the European-influenced areas. In addition, the index remains a good way to orient oneself when looking for examples of stories in various parts of the world or how widely they are spread.

The folktale index is divided into five major headings, with many subheadings: Animal Tales, Ordinary Folk-Tales, Jokes and Anecdotes, Formula Tales, and "Unclassified" Tales (Aarne and Thompson 1964, 19–20). In the section on ordinary folktales, in the subsection entitled Religious Tales, "The Singing Bone" is one of my favorites. A boy kills his brother or sister and buries the sibling in the ground. From the bones of the dead, a shepherd makes a flute, which reveals the shameful deed (Aarne and Thompson 1964, 780; hereafter cited as A-T). This tale is extremely widespread and is well represented in Caribbean folktales.

Like all folktales, those from the Caribbean are formulaic. They were sometimes named after the opening part of the formula, which North Americans know as "Once upon a time." The parts of the Caribbean influenced by Afro-French customs are called "krik-krak." A storyteller begins a tale by saying "Krik!" while his listeners shout "Krak!" In the Bahamas, they are called "old stories," and in Puerto Rico they include the "Juan Bobo" cycle of numskull stories ("Juan Bobo" gets over a hundred hits on Amazon.com). Traditionally, they were told to children and adults in communal settings.

The Caribbean area is full of animal tales (A-T, 1–299). Many of these are derived from the Akan (Ghana) cycle of tales about a trickster spider, Anancy.

Anancy stories are related to the Brer Rabbit trickster tales from the southern part of the United States (Harris 1955). At this writing, there are about 250 hits on Amazon.com for books or story readings on CD for the word "Anancy." Many of these are literary adaptations of the tales for children; the folk versions can be scatological and raucous.

The largest category in the Aarne-Thompson index is Ordinary Folk-Tales. These include four subheadings: Tales of Magic, Religious Tales, Novelle, and Tales of the Stupid Ogre. Tales of Magic (A-T, 300–749) has seven sub-categories, among which are Supernatural Adversaries, Magic Objects, and Supernatural Power or Knowledge.

In the Caribbean, many stories fit within the broad category of tales of magic. Unlike the old notion that folktales are prose tales that are not taken as true, magic tales may be thought to be true by some Caribbean people. I once spoke to a man who claimed to have been accosted along a dark, lonely road on Union Island, in the Grenadines, one night by lajabless, a supernatural woman with one cloven foot who entices men to a bad fate. Another person told me about an experience he had in Haiti when a neighbor transformed herself into a loogarou. The loogarou is similar to a soucoyant from the eastern Caribbean or ole higue from Guyana and Jamaica. At night, she changes her skin and becomes a vampire, with fire coming from her eyes.

Carnival characters, displayed as individuals or groups of characters that play roles, are something thought to have supernatural powers. Devil masquerades in Trinidad's Carnival are an Afro-Creolization of the "good" Chinese dragon, turned into a menacing character. Small children might fear the dragon, who acts out a story line with his imps as they move through town.

Aarne and Thompson populate their Religious Tales section (750–849) with stories concerning God, Christ, St. Peter, and other characters from Christian tradition. Among these are "God Repays and Punishes," "Truth Comes to Light," "The Man in Heaven," and "The Man Promised to the Devil." Such stories are told in the Caribbean but are considered humorous and false. There are other sorts of religious tales that would perhaps not be classified as folktales at all, but are part of Caribbean religious traditions. There are stories about Yoruba and Hindu gods as well as supernatural tales related to the Christian and Muslim traditions that are interpreted locally. Just as Christians would not like biblical stories to be called folklore, with the implication that the tales therein are false, so it is with believers in localized accounts that stem from the grand religious systems of West Africa, the Middle East, and India. In the Yoruba tradition, as syncretized and reinterpreted in the Caribbean setting, there are countless stories about the activities of the Orisha that inhabit humans during possession and request favors from believers (Bascom 1980). Classic Hindu tales are also told in Trinidad and Guyana. In Jamaica, the Rastafarian faith—based on a special vision of the Christian Bible—has its own, sometimes individualistic, way of understanding truth.

Novelle, or romantic, tales (A-T, 850–999) are short stories that sometimes have a moral. Many of the Caribbean tales are of this type, especially in the Spanish-speaking islands. Jokes and anecdotes (A-T, 1200–1999), as everywhere, are common in the Caribbean. Riddles are word puzzles in which the answer to the verbal play is usually a single word. In the Martiniquean movie *Sugar Cane Alley*, the old man Medouze, tells young José many riddles. Proverbs are traditional sayings that make a moral or didactic point. For example, the Haitian sense of family is conveyed in this proverb: "It's your own people who tell you the truth" (Ibekwe 1998, 64). Folktales in Aarne-Thompson's last main category, Formula Tales (2000–2399), are also known in the area.

A different way to look at folktales of the Caribbean is to understand them in terms of performance style. This approach to folktales focuses less on the story or content of the tale and more on the way it is told, especially the interaction between the raconteur and his or her audience (Abrahams 1983). Still another approach to the folktale is to discover its deeper meaning in terms of its cultural context. Short-story writers and novelists use folktales as a device on which to hang their narrative.

MAGIC, SORCERY, AND WITCHCRAFT

Magic is the manipulation of supernatural forces, usually for private gain but sometimes, as in divination, for a public purpose. Sorcery is the use of spells or materials to magically cause good or harm to someone. Sometimes the words *sorcery* and *witchcraft* are used interchangeably. For many anthropologists, witchcraft or sorcery is supernatural manipulation by a member of society with the intent of causing harm to a person or to the group as a whole. In small, preindustrial communities, accusations of witchcraft are a technique that leaders have used to reveal a social problem that is thought to be caused by a witch. If the accusation is seen as accurate, the witch may be brought back into the group, as a member in good standing, through exorcizing the supernatural source of the problem from the witch. If the issue is not resolved, then a bad fate may befall the accused witch.

In the Caribbean, it is not possible to separate witchcraft from sorcery. *Obeah (obi), wanga,* and *brujería* are some of the terms used for magic, witchcraft, and sorcery. In Haiti and in the eastern Caribbean, wanga, or obeah, is thought by ordinary people to be black magic; that is, magic that is prepared and used against someone. A client may visit an obeahman to buy a substance or formula that will be used to magically cause harm to an intended victim. Everyone knows about the so-called voodoo doll, into which the obeahman or his client sticks pins. Since the doll represents the victim, each time a pin is stuck into the doll the victim suffers. This fictional example of magic would be obeah if used by an obeahman. However, obeah is a form of sorcery in which the magic used by the obeahman may be for good or evil (Henry 2003, 202–10). The word *obi* and much of the magic used by obeahmen have their origins in Benin (once a Fon kingdom), although in the Caribbean obeah has added magic from elsewhere in Africa, Asia, and the United States.

Brujería is a generic name for witchcraft in Cuba and elsewhere in Latin America (Ortiz 1995). More than obeah, brujería forms a magical system and is a syncretization of various African magical systems. In the United States, magical substances used in brujería, and statues that depict the Orisha or Catholic saints, may be purchased in botanicas (Latin herbalist shops) that dot the neighborhoods where immigrants live.

BUSH MEDICINE

Potions and "dream books" may be purchased in botanicas. Dream books are usually published in the United States and contain lucky numbers associated with dreams, numbers that are lucky for buying lottery tickets or have magical or curative qualities used in bush medicine, the West Indian phrase for the pharmacopeia of folk cures. Both amateurs and professionals use bush medicine, especially when Western doctors are rare or too expensive. Sometimes the bush doctor is an old woman who searches the countryside for special herbs and other traditional medicines. Alternatively, a cure can come to a person in a dream. Traditional healers like Ebenezer Elliott ("Pa Neezer") ministered to people of all classes and ethnic groups in Trinidad (Henry 2003, 202–10). In the Spanish Caribbean, the bush doctor is called a *curandero*.

VERNACULAR RELIGION

Vernacular, or folk, religion is the local interpretation and practice of religion, whether or not that religion has a national or international liturgical authority. Christianity, Islam, and Hinduism are found in the Caribbean in versions more or less similar to what is found in other parts of the world. Their followers collectively represent the majority of the religious people of the islands. Nevertheless, very large minorities follow vernacular religions or mix local beliefs with an international religion. This means that many beliefs in vernacular religion are held in oral tradition and in undocumented or only partly documented rituals.

Some Afro-Caribbean religions or rituals that have supernatural or religious qualities combine different African faiths (such as Fon, Yoruba, and Congolese religious systems), while others are syncretized with Christianity. Vodou (Haiti), the Big Drum Dance (Carriacou, Grenada), Kumina (also known as the Bongo Nation, Jamaica), the Maroon Nation (Jamaica), and Abakuá (Cuba) are some of the mostly African religions or rituals. Lucumí and Santería (based in Cuba) and the Orisha (formerly Shango in Trinidad) combine Yoruba religion with Roman Catholicism. The Spiritual Baptists (once derisively called the Shouters), the Converted (St. Vincent), the Shango Baptists (Grenada), Revivalism (also known as Pocomania, Jamaica), and the Rastafarians include notions from Protestant Christianity along with several West African religions.

Vodou is the name given to the Afro-Haitian religion, based on Fon (Benin) and Congo spiritual beliefs but also including ideas from many other African religions, as well as Christianity. There is no definitive practice of Vodou, and locally it is quite varied. At the core of Vodou faith are the loa, or gods, that possess people in religious ceremonies held in a hounfour, or temple. The leaders are the

Buru drummer George Matthews, Clarendon parish, Jamaica, 2000. Photo: Kenneth Bilby.

houngan (male) and mambo (female). Vodou includes some of the same deities as Lucumí and Santería, where they are called Orisha.

Lucumí is the name used in Cuba for the most African form of Yoruba religion in Cuba, as well as the name for Yoruba people themselves. Santería is the name used for this religion when the Yoruba gods are depicted as Catholic saints; that is, the characteristics of a god are fused with those of a particular saint. Believers in Santería/Lucumí run all the way from Catholics who attend mass but treat saints as if they had the attributes of African gods to individuals who fully participate in Lucumí rites—and everything in between. The Orisha is the name given to Yoruba gods. Each god has its own favorite color(s), musical rhythm and dance style, foods, and so forth. The Orisha enter into the heads of dancers and possess ("mount") them. They request favors or provide advice. Obatala is the creator god and Eleguá is a trickster god that is the intermediary between humans and other gods. Eleguá is also the guardian of the crossroads. Yemaja is the goddess of the sea and Shango is the god of thunder and lightning. Ọshun is the goddess of love and marriage. Ogun is the god of iron and ironworkers. The gods join humans in rituals when they mount a person's head and, for a time, take over the person's thoughts and movements. Gods communicate in this and in other ways to the people and advise them how to conduct their lives.

Kumina seems based on Congolese culture and, to a much lesser extent, Ghanaian beliefs. It revolves around a rhythm (riddim) that induces possession (myal) by the spirits of the dead, spirits from the sky, and spirits from the earth. It has influenced the Nyabinghi, a Rastafarian ceremony. The Maroon Nation in Jamaica is influenced by many Ghanaian religious ideas and consists of two different groups, one in the western Cockpit Country, whose leader was Cudjoe, and another in the eastern Blue Mountains, whose leader was Nanny. They are the descendants of enslaved people who escaped and fought wars with the British before signing a treaty in order to retain their independence (Bilby 2005).

The Big Drum Dance of Carriacou, Grenada, brings together the dances of many different African Nations into a single ritual that honors their ancestors (McDaniel 1998). Unlike most other Afro-Caribbean religions, there is no possession in the Big Drum Dance. The ancestors look down from heaven on the ceremony and are pleased or displeased. The ancestors communicate with living people through dream messages. The dance occurs for wakes that take place three, nine, and forty nights after the death of an individual and annually after that until the person is entombed with a marble tombstone. It is also performed at community maroons (not to be confused with the Maroon people of Jamaica and elsewhere), when requested by an ancestor in a dream, or when someone launches a vessel or opens a shop, as well as on other occasions.

Abakuá is a male secret society that centers in the cities of Havana and Matanzas in Cuba. Derived from a similar secret society from Calabar (southeastern

Painting of 18th-century Jamaican Maroon leader and National Hero, Nanny, by Jamaican "intuitive" artist Evadney Cruickshank, ca. 2003. Courtesy of Wayne Cox. Photo: Kenneth Bilby.

Nigeria), it functions as a folk crime/legal/vigilante justice system in poor neighborhoods of those cities.

The Rastafarians emerged in Jamaica in villages and in the slums of Kingston in the 1930s, as a Christian-like group based on the veneration of Haile Selassie. Throughout the world, Haile Selassie (Ras Tafari, the Emperor of Ethiopia), who was overthrown in 1935 by the Italians, was considered a great leader for speaking out against Italy and Mussolini before the League of Nations. Before being overthrown by the Italians, he led the only continuously independent country in Africa. Some people in Jamaica considered Haile Selassie to be God. Marcus Garvey, the revered Jamaican nationalist, was said to have foretold the coming of the Messiah (Selassie) to help poor black Jamaicans. The Rastafarian religion coalesces around Selassie and Garvey, and it originally appealed to poor young men as colonial authorities attempted to suppress the religion. In the 1960s, the faith gradually gained legitimacy. Today, it combines very many Jamaican folkways, including ritual components from Kumina (from which Nyabinghi may have developed), natural (ital) food, use of marijuana (ganja) as a sacred herb, and special music fused from a variety of sources. The "Rastas" believe (their word for "belief" is "knowledge") that they have been cast into Babylon and that through spiritual practices they will be returned either physically or spiritually to Africa (Ethiopia), their true home. By spreading their sense of an egalitarian community, their music, their organic food, their crafts, their use of marijuana as a healing substance, and their special speech, they have had a major impact on youth culture throughout the world.

Many people of Asian Indian descent in Guyana, Trinidad, Guadeloupe, Jamaica, and several other islands arrived in the Caribbean in the nineteenth century to replace former slaves as agricultural workers. Some practiced Hinduism; others were Muslim. Today, Hinduism has lost some of its features that existed in India, such as the caste system, but it has retained Diwali and folk plays based on stories from the Ramayana, an ancient Sanskrit sacred text that relates the birth and adventures of Rama, the seventh incarnation of Lord Vishnu.

There are also Muslims in the Caribbean. They fall into two loose groups, the descendants of Muslims from India and Afro-Caribbean people who converted to Islam, especially since the late 1960s. Their major festival in Trinidad is Hosay, which commemorates the death and martyrdom of Husayn, son of Fatima, who was daughter of the Prophet Mohammed.

MUSIC AND DANCE

The constant flux and remixing of vernacular music and dance in the Caribbean has been a wellspring for the rest of the world for over 100 years (Hill 2004, 363–73; and Manuel et al. 1995). Dance, of course, is always associated with music and, as is the custom in West Africa, music is usually associated with dance. Musical styles that are for contemplation only are rare in Africa and in the Caribbean. Important exceptions are the griot (troubadour) tradition in the western Sahel, Latin poetic songs, lullabies, and contemplative calypso in the Caribbean.

In the nineteenth century, the vernacular Cuban rhythm called the habanera made its way into Bizet's *Carmen*. That same rhythm, as modified in Argentina, became the rhythm of the tango early in the twentieth century. Soon thereafter, that same rhythm was used by composer and jazz bandleader W. C. Handy as one melodic strain in one of the first important blues songs, "St. Louis Blues." Then, successive waves of related dance rhythms came out of the Caribbean and South

America: rumba, calypso, chachacha, pachanga, salsa, merengue (meringue), reggae, and dancehall.

The habanera is one example of a group of rhythms called clave. Clave is the basis of much of Caribbean music. It usually has two beats followed by three beats or vice versa and is a synthesis, a kind of "reduction division" of complicated two- and three-beat West and Central African rhythms. It shows up in many Afro-Caribbean musical styles, from rumba to reggae. Clave is delightfully made visible in the body movements of Caribbean dancers.

Understandably, the richest vein of folk music and dance in the Caribbean comes from the largest islands, the Greater Antilles (Hispaniola, Cuba, Puerto Rico, Jamaica). Although the music of Cuba is the most varied, folk music from Haiti, a country that shares the island of Hispaniola with the Dominican Republic, is the most significant historically. Taino Indians, an Arawak subgroup who had replaced the indigenous Ciboney on the island, were enslaved by the Spanish in the sixteenth century, and most died after 50 years of occupation, disease, or the grueling conditions (Averill and Wilcken 1998, 881–95). The French took the western part of Hispaniola from the Spanish. African slaves, imported by the French, brought West African cultures to the island, including music and dance, although they may have borrowed some musical concepts from the Tainos, such as the chac-chac, or rattle. Different African groups tended to live in different parts of Haiti, so the Vodou religious rituals that developed varied from place to place within the colony. The greatest influences on the ritual music and dance of Haiti came from Dahomey (now the country of Benin) and Congo. There are two major groups of nations of loa, the Rada (which includes the Rada and the Nago nations) and the Petro (which includes the Petro, Ibo, Kongo, and Gede nations), each with their own music and dance styles. The Djouba nation is found in both the Rada and the Petro groups. The drums in Vodou rituals—the ogan, boula, segon, and the manman—play rhythms from simple to complex respectfully. Different loa have different rhythms, and breaks in the rhythms mark possession of a dancer by a loa. Singing is tailored to the particular drum pattern and to the loa who may possess a dancer.

Secular songs and dance are influenced by Vodou music (Frank 2002, 109–13; Wilcken 2002, 114–23). Urban Haitian music consists of styles brought by rural immigrants to the city as well as staged and popular music and dance seen in the mass media. The latter is derived from the folk music and is aimed at the urban middle class and tourists. In the United States, specifically New York City and Miami, dance troupes have been quite popular among both Haitian émigrés and North Americans.

Haiti has two very different Carnivals, each with its own dance and music styles. Rara Carnival music performed on Vodou instruments, plus bamboo and metal horns, scrappers (a serrated edge that is rubbed with a stick or piece of metal), and frame drums. This music is played in parts of the island during Lent as the bands wind themselves down the roads with a shuffling movement. Many bands converge on Easter Sunday to close the Rara Carnival. The urban Carnival music is played mostly on European instruments. Until the mid-twentieth century, many kinds of balls and other events persisted. They performed the same world dance styles that were popular among elite people of an earlier era, such as the waltz and the mazurka, but in a heavily Afro-Creolized way. In recent times, konpa bands with electrified instruments have replaced these French-style orchestras. The popular Haitian music and dance style, the meringue, which was probably influenced by the Cuban son early in the twentieth century, has gone through many changes since the 1920s. Unlike the ritual dances for Vodou, the meringue is a couple's dance. The Dominican merengue is very similar to the Haitian meringue.

Rural Cuban folk music germinated during the first 250 years of Spanish rule, when the enslaved indigenous population mixed with runaway African slaves (cimmarones, or maroons) and Spanish Creoles to form a vibrant and varied guajiro culture of peasants. Prominent in their evolving music were variants of Spanish punto, décima, seis, tonada, and zapateo that originated in Iberia when the North African Moors controlled much of Spain and Portugal. These styles, especially prominent in western Cuba but found all over the island, consisted of formulaic poetry performed in singsong fashion over a string instrument accompaniment. In eastern Cuba, the changüi developed during the same span of centuries. It is an African-influenced form of call-and-response music, with a lead singer and a chorus responding to the lead's voice. Changüi is also a dance.

As Haiti was falling to liberated slaves around 1800, some of the French and mixed-race estate owners fled, with their slaves, to the nearby eastern tip of Cuba where they set up new plantations. From this migration came two related forms of musical performance. The first was a ballroom dance accompanied by a salon string orchestra, most likely made up of slaves, called the orquesta tipica or orquesta Francesa (or charanga). This was similar to the dance orchestras that were still popular in urban Haiti through the mid-twentieth century. In eastern Cuba, the orquesta Francesa performed contradances for elite functions. Contradances are a group of dances related to North American square dances and to European and Caribbean quadrille dances. These spread out of Europe beginning in the late eighteenth century and flooded over all the Caribbean, where they continue to be danced today. The other configuration in eastern Cuba was the tumba Francesa ("French drum"), a drum assemblage that played Afro-Creolized dances for the slaves, some of which were similar to contradances and quadrilles.

The orquesta tipica and tumba Francesa both influenced the development of the danzón in the late nineteenth century. Created by middle-class Creoles of mixed race in Matanzas and Havana, the danzón incorporated different contradances into one dance for individual couples. Sometimes the danzón was played by a charanga, a brass band that incorporated the earlier orquesta Francesa and that eventually replaced the latter as the name for ballroom, string, and flute orchestras. Early in the twentieth century, the changüi, together with other folk genres, influenced the development of the son in eastern Cuba that became the rage as a national song style by the 1920s, when it gained popularity in Havana. It was said to represent the spirit of Cuba, since it blended the melodic forms and instruments from Spain and West Africa, played over a clave rhythm, into a single style. At about the same time, the rumba, which was a vernacular dance that sprung from tenement (solar) yards in Havana and the docks of Matanzas, was transformed into a popular dance craze. Middle-class Cubans as well as the elite began to incorporate more Afro-Cuban cultural arts, especially music and dance, into their sense of "being Cuban." Intellectuals, Fernando Ortiz among them, glorified Afro-Cuban culture. By the end of the twentieth century, most Cubans recognized the qualities of their folk arts in defining the essence of being Cuban, a place of Creole culture that blends African, Spanish, and indigenous folk, popular, and elite culture into a whole.

In central Cuba, many African slaves lived on huge estates called latifundia. Some were descendants of people who were brought in chains to the island centuries ago, whereas others arrived in Cuba in the second half of the nineteenth century. On the latifundia and in towns the enslaved and free Africans

This is an early twentieth-century Cuban postcard. It shows a solar (barracks housing) enclosing a yard, where rumbas were performed.

were sometime permitted to form cabildos (clubs) in which both African rites and Catholic observances were performed and often intermixed. This is where the Lucumí/Santería religion was established, though in many different ways, depending on both the cabildos where the rites were practiced and the era in which they were performed (Brandon 1997). From these folk observances came drums for music and dance. Other musical instruments and vernacular spirituality added to the Cuban's sense of identity and well-being. Drum rhythms, versions of the rumba, and the batá and other types of drums all came from the cabildos and fed Cuban popular and elite culture alike.

By the late 1920s, popular versions of Cuban folk music and dance had spread to the Americas, to Europe, and eventually "back" to Africa, where Africanized versions of rumba that came about in the 1950s continue to be popular. Other Cuban music and/or dance styles that spread about the world include the bolero, chachacha, the mambo, and the pachanga. Cuban music, especially the son, danzón, and bolero gained influence in the Caribbean as well. The danzón was widely popular from Mexico to South America and had an influence on the Puerto Rican danza. Early in the twentieth century, the son influenced the merengue in the Dominican Republic and, later, was one ingredient in the emergence of salsa, a pan–Latin American big-band music and dance. The bolero, a romantic ballad with guitar accompaniment, has been the classic vehicle for a stereotyped Latin romanticism.

The history of vernacular music in Puerto Rico parallels and follows that in Cuba. In the nineteenth century, the danza was influenced by the danzón. The Hispanic folk-music complex of décima and seis was similar to that found in Cuba, except, perhaps, more varied. Afro-Puerto Rican styles consist of two major styles, the bomba, a centuries-old drum-based topical music still found in the district of Loíza Aldea, and the plena, an urban topical music and dance that developed in the city of Ponce in the early twentieth century (Vega Drouet 1998, 932–41). The plena is broadly similar to the son and calypso.

The music of Jamaica differs from the music in rest of the Greater Antilles. Into the seventeenth century, the Spanish controlled Jamaica. When the island was taken by the British in the mid-1600s, enslaved Africans escaped or were set free, becoming the maroons. The island remained under British control until independence in 1962. Of the many kinds of maroon dances, the most important is the Cromanti dance, in which the ancestors intercede with God (Nyangkipong) for ordinary people (Lewin 1998, 902). Maroon ritual dances are named after putative African nations from whom they are thought to have originated. Maroon drums include the goombay, or frame drum, a tambourine without metal shakers. Jamaican sailors who worked on British vessels introduced this drum into Africa a couple of centuries ago. The frame drum today is widely played along coastal West Africa.

Kumina is another drum-based ritual, and there were others. The Pocomania or Revivalist music is Afro-Christian. The participants sing Protestant hymns that are changed into rhythmically complex music that triggers possession. The Rastafarians have borrowed from traditional Jamaican music, especially Kumina, as well as secular Jamaican mento and North American popular music to create a drum-based spiritual music. Mento is a secular music and dance that used Western instruments as well as the African-originated rumba box and other instruments. The melodies in mento come from many sources, including British folk and popular songs, calypso, and locally composed topical songs.

In the 1960s mento gave way to ska and rock steady and eventually reggae, the most persistently popular musical style to come out of the Caribbean that probably even surpasses the Cuban craze in the first half of the twentieth century. Reggae is also associated with several different dances, with either couples dancing or individuals dancing alone. Reggae comes in many versions, from roots (spiritually oriented, especially based on Rastafarian themes) to slackness (with risqué lyrics). Dancehall is a high-tech version of reggae, played on huge sound systems, first developed by Jamaicans in the 1950s but now considered one of the roots of all modern DJ systems throughout the world. Like most Caribbean islands, Jamaica has its own version of the contradances, called the quadrille.

The most influential vernacular music from the eastern Caribbean comes from Trinidad. The first European power to control Trinidad was Spain, which, wanting to enhance the economy of the island in the late eighteenth century, wrote laws that encouraged Catholic (mostly French) estate owners from elsewhere in the Caribbean, to relocate to Trinidad with their slaves, in order to develop agriculture (Hill 1993, 12–13). Although the island was ceded to Great Britain in the early 1800s, much of the rural population was Afro-French. Throughout the nineteenth century, British and Afro-British, Asian Indian, Amerindian, Venezuelan, and indentured Africans filled out the human mosaic that became the population of Trinidad.

Each of these groups brought their music to the island, and two basic musical amalgams developed: Creole, which became dominant, and Asian Indian. Creole rituals centered on the Orisha and Spiritual Baptist ceremonies. Carnival (kalindas; leggos, or road marches; calypsos, and many other styles), quadrille dance music, children's songs, ballads, funerary music (hymns, bongos, and drum music), Christmastide parang, and soca are the forms of vernacular Creole music in Trinidad. The Asian Indian music has also yielded many styles, including music for festivals (tassa drumming for Muslim Hosay parades, Hindu chants for Divali) and chutney (originally ribald music for groups of women at weddings but now Creolized and performed in the manner of calypso and soca).

Carriacou, a small island in the Grenadines about 120 miles north of Trinidad, is a good example of a place that offers music and dance similar to the rest of the Lesser Antilles. The Big Drum Dance is one of the oldest creole dances in the islands (McDaniel 1998 and Hill 1998). A three-drum set plays Creole and Nation dances in a sequence to invoke the pleasure of the ancestors. There is no possession in the dance. The nations and dances bear a family resemblance to those mentioned from Haiti and Jamaica. In the very recent past Carriacou had three types of quadrille dances: the lancers, the quadrille proper, and the Albert quadrille. All three were set dances with a caller and four couples going through six or more different dances. The lancers configuration was made up of fiddle, guitar(s), cuatro (a four string instrument, not the eight or twelve stringed Puerto Rican cuatro), and triangle. Bass (drum), fiddle, and triangle accompany the other two types of quadrilles. Carriacou had game songs for young people. One is the pass play, in which a boy danced, touched a girl who took up the dance and touched a boy who continued.

Carriacou is located in the Grenadines between the larger islands of St. Vincent to the north and Grenada to the south. This region is where the Spiritual Baptist faith incubated as migrants from the area left for Trinidad to influence Trinidad's version of the religion. Much of the music of the Spiritual Baptists—the varieties of hymns—is performed outdoors in church rites. These include "prayer meetings," when people sing staid and rousing hymns all night long. Through the 1970s Carriacou was one of the best places in the Eastern Caribbean to observe old-fashioned Carnival, as it may have existed on many islands from the late nineteenth century through the first fifty years of the twentieth century. That traditional Carnival was filled with its small masquerade skits, singers, stick fighters complete with drummers and singers, and wandering string bands. Since the 1950s, the Carnival of Trinidad has set the pattern for virtually all pre-Lenten Carnivals in the English-speaking Caribbean.

Moving north through the Lesser Antilles we will make only three more stops, St. Lucia, Martinique, and Guadeloupe. St. Lucia's culture mixes Afro-French and Afro-British customs. Martinique and Guadeloupe are French départements (overseas states, like Hawaii is a state of the United States). St. Lucia is rich in folk music and some of it originates in jwé (play) where débòt (a drum dance) is performed (Guilbault 1998b, 942–51). It also has the kwadril (quadrille) as well as calypso. Perhaps the most interesting entertainment in St. Lucia is the spectacle of the La Rose and La Marguerite societies. These are friendly societies that compete against each other in their dress and in their music, which consists of chants accompanied by a tambourine, baha or bamboo trumpet, chac-chac (maracas), scrapper and guitar. They also have a ritual that is Yoruba based—the kélé—with drums and singing.

People from Martinique originated or adapted vernacular dance and music from the French Caribbean, styles that also have an international following. In the nineteenth century, the beguine was a drum based music (bélè or, in English,

Belair dance in Dominica, early twentieth-century postcard.

belair) that was related to similar dances through the Lesser Antilles (Desroches 1998, 714–921). By the late 1800s, in Saint Pierre, this folk beguine gave way to an orchestral form, with clarinet lead. This form of beguine resembles New Orleans Jazz, the original jazz, which also has a French and Creole base. Another popular dance is the Mazouk, a Creolized form of the Mazurka. The Kadans is a more Afro-Creolized dance with many subtle rhythms that was brought to the island by Haitian refugees. Zouk, a diminutive of the word Mazouk, was another re-Afro-Creolized music that brought together many musical strains from nearby islands.

In Guadeloupe, musical performance was divided into two broad groups, the bamboulas where enslaved Africans performed and the soirée, dances for the estate owners and their families and friends (Guilbault, "Guadeloupe," 1998a, 873–80). Much of the current music is based on drum-based rhythms, whether or not actual drums are present. Léwòz was originally an outdoor musical style played on the gwoka (big drum). Also popular are the quadrille and zouk.

INFORMAL LANGUAGE AND VERBAL ARTS

A Creole language is one created out of two or more unrelated languages that are spoken in a given location, usually in the original context of colonialism. A standard language is the language used by people with some formal educa-

JÉNÈZ 1 2

Istoua kréyasion an

1 1 Nan konmasman, Bondié kréyé siè1 la ak latè-a. [2]Min latè pat gin fòm, li pat gin angnin sou li. Fènoua té kouvri toupatou. Léspri Bondié tap plannin sou dlo ki té kouvri tout latè.

3 Bondié di: Sé pou limiè fèt.

Epi limiè té fèt. [4]Bondié ouè limiè-a té bon. Bondié mété limiè-a you bò, li mété fènoua-a you lòt bò. [5]Bondié rélé limiè-a lajounin, li rélé fènoua-a lannouit. You lannouit pasé, you matin rivé: sé té prémié jou-a.

6 Bondié di ankò: Sé pou gin you vout nan mitan dlo-a pou séparé dlo-a an dé.

7 Bondié fè vout la séparé dlo-a an dé, you pati anro vout la, you lòt pati anba-l. Sé konsa sa té pasé. [8]Bondié rélé vout la siè1. You lannouit pasé, you matin rivé: sé té dézièm jou-a.

9 Bondié di ankò: Sé pou dlo ki anba siè1 la sanblé you sè1 koté pou koté ki sèk la ka parèt.

Sé konsa sa té pasé. [10]Bondié rélé koté ki sèk la tè. Li rélé pil dlo-a lanmè. Bondié gadé sa-l té fè-a, li ouè-l bon.

11 Bondié di: Sé pou tè-a pousé tout kalité plant: zèb, plant ki bay grinn, piéboua ki bay foui ak tout grinn yo.

Sé konsa sa té pasé. [12]Tè-a pousé tout kalité plant: zèb, plant ki bay grinn, piéboua ki bay foui ak tout grinn yo. Bondié gadé sa-l té fè-a, li ouè-l bon. [13]You lannouit pasé, you matin rivé: sé té touazièm jou-a.

14 Bondié di ankò: Sé pou limiè parèt nan siè1 la pou séparé lajounin ak lannouit. Ya sèvi pou maké jou yo, lanné yo ak sézon yo. [15]Ya sèvi limiè nan siè1 la pou kléré tout latè-a.

Sé konsa sa té pasé. [16]Bondié fè dé gro limiè, pi gro-a pou kòmandé sou lajounin, pi piti-a pou kòmandé sou lannouit. Li fè zétoual yo tou. [17]Li mété yo nan siè1 la pou kléré latè-a, [18]pou kòmandé sou lajounin ak sou lannouit, pou séparé limiè ak fènoua. Bondié gadé sa-l té fè-a, li ouè-l bon. [19]You lannouit pasé, you matin rivé: sé té katriyèm jou-a.

20 Bondié di ankò: Sé pou dlo yo kalé anpil anpil bèt vivan. Sé pou zouazo volé nan siè1 la anro tè-a.

Sé konsa sa té pasé.[*l*] [21]Bondié kréyé gro bèt lanmè yo, tout kalité bèt vivan kap najé nan dlo ansanm ak tout kalité zouazo.

Bondié gadé sa-l té fè-a, li ouè-l bon. [22]Bondié béni yo, li di: Fè pitit, fè anpil anpil pitit, plin dlo lanmè-a. Sé pou zouazo yo fè anpil anpil pitit tou sou tè-a. [23]You lannouit pasé, you matin rivé: sé té sinkièm jou-a.

24 Bondié di ankò: Sé pou tè-a kalé tout kalité bèt vivan, bèt yo gadé, bèt ki trinnin sou vant, bèt nan boua.

Sé konsa sa té pasé. [25]Bondié fè tout kalité bèt, bèt nan boua, bèt yo gadé, bèt ki trinnin sou vant. Li gadé sa-l té fè-a, li ouè-l bon.

26 Bondié di ankò: Ann fè moun. Nap fè-l pòtré ak nou, pou li sanblé ak nou. La gin pouvoua sou pouason ki nan lanmè yo, sou zouazo ki nan siè1 la, sou tout bèt yo gadé, sou tout latè, sou tout bèt nan boua, sou tout bèt ki trinnin sou vant sou tè-a.

[27] Bondié kréyé moun:
li fè-l pòtré ak li.
Li kréyé yo gason ak fi.

[28] Li ba yo bénédiksion, li di:
Fè pitit, fè anpil anpil pitit mété sou
tè-a. Donté tè-a.
Mouin ban nou pouvoua sou
pouason ki nan lanmè,
sou zouazo ki nan siè1 la,
ak sou tout bèt vivan kap maché sou
tè-a.

29 Bondié di: Gadé. Mouin ban nou tout kalité plant ki bay grinn ak tout kalité piéboua ki bay foui ak grinn pou

---

*l*1.20: Sé konsa sa té pasé: *Sé you ansyin vèsion grèk ki bay fraz sa-a la, min tèks ébré-a pa bay fraz sa-a.*
1.1 Jòb 38.4-7; Eza. 42.5; 45.18; Jan 1.3; Kol. 1.16; Eb. 1.10; 11.3; Rév. 4.11. **1.2** Jér. 4.23. **1.3** 2 Kor. 4.6. **1.6** Jòb 37.18; Sòm 33.6; Jér. 10.12. **1.9** Jòb 38.8, 10, 11; Sòm 33.7; 95.5; Jér. 5.22. **1.11** Sòm 104.14. **1.14** Sòm 104.19; Jér. 10.2; Joèl 2.30, 31; Mat. 24.29; Lik 21.25. **1.16** Det. 4.19; Sòm 136.7-9. **1.18** Jér. 31.35. **1.21** Sòm 104.25, 26. **1.26** Jén. 3.22; 5.1; 9.6; 11.7; Sòm 8.6-8; Eza. 6.8; Jak 3.7, 9. **1.27** Mal. 2.14, 15; Mat. 19.4; Mak 10.6; 1 Kor. 11.7; Ef. 4.24; Kol. 3.10. **1.28** Jén. 9.1, 7; Lév. 26.9; 1 Tim. 4.3. **1.29** Jòb 36.31; Sòm 104.14, 15; 145.15, 16.

The opening of Genesis in Haitian Kreyòl. Source: Bib La an Ayisin, Port-Au-Prince, Société Biblique Haïtienne, 1985.

tion or a version of a language understandable to people who also speak dialects of the language. The standard language of the colonizer dominates the official world of commerce, government, formal schooling, and literacy. The language(s) of the colonized people—descendants of slaves, workers, the uneducated, and even the elite when they speak in a casual setting—is more prevalent at home, in the streets, among the working class, and wherever ordinary people congregate. Monique Desroches has written this about the languages of Martinique:

> The island's official language is French, but Creole (Kwéyòl) is used in everyday communication. This type of bilingual society, in which a vernacular tongue remains in active use without an official status, has encouraged the emergence of a parallel culture based on oral tradition. The use of Creole, notably in public contexts, has become a symbol of identification and assertion for the people of Martinique, setting them culturally apart from metropolitan France. (Desroches 1998, 914)

In other words, to understand verbal folklore in Martinique is necessary to understand vernacular language. This statement may be readily expanded to cover the Caribbean region generally. There are scores of Creole languages in the Caribbean, from Creole Guyanais—a French Creole spoken in French Guiana—to Jamaican Creole. Although there is debate as to whether Creole languages exist in Spanish- and Portuguese-speaking countries, certainly vernacular dialects exist wherever standard Spanish or Portuguese is spoken. Each of these Creoles and nonstandard languages opens up a world of oral tradition that is scarcely touched by standard languages.

The Creole language is the vehicle for the expression of folklife. As Roger Abrahams has noted, "'Broad talkers' are the ones who rely primarily on wit and other economical verbal devices, and who commonly use creole as their medium. 'Good talkers' are those who rely on elevated diction and elaborate grammar and syntax, and who speak in the local version of Standard English" (Abrahams 1983, 21). The vernacular is a good language for the pithy phrase, the proverb, the exaggeration, the sexually suggestive utterance, or formulaic folk banter. The standard language is the appropriate means of communication when strangers converse, for school instruction, or for political speechmaking.

Folk plays, speechmaking, and banter are all found in Caribbean folk performances. Jamaican dub and dancehall music is common today, and the poetry of the Spanish-influenced décima and Christmastide speechifying were once widespread. The décima is a highly formulaic folk poetry, often improvised, and delivered in a singsong fashion over set musical riffs played by string instruments. Double-tone calypso was a style of music that reached its peak in Trinidad around World War I. Typically, it consisted of a sung chorus together with a half-spoken eight-line section vaguely reminiscent of a décima. The mummies are an Afro-Creolized British Isle group of plays set in a fictional era of British history (Abrahams 1983 and 2002) and may be related to the Carriacou Shakespeare or speech mas. In the latter mas, Carnival masqueraders dress in jerseys, capes, and wire-mesh masques, and carry whips to strike an opponent who does not deliver speeches correctly. Some of the speeches are based on Shakespeare's "Julius Caesar" (Fayer and McMurray 1999, 53–73). A tea meeting in Nevis and St. Kitts was a seriocomic performance of speeches, singing, comic routines, and back-and-forth banter between a chair, a vice-chair, and an audience (Abrahams 2002). Dub music was one of the ingredients that went into the rap and hip-hop mix that developed in New York City in the 1970s. Dub is a Jamaican invention from the 1960s. It is an instrumental rendition of reggae that is played behind a disc jockey's improvised rhythmic talk or rap. In recent decades, North American rap has infiltrated the Caribbean from New York City and elsewhere in the United States and blended with vernacular music throughout the Caribbean. Together with dub, spoken rap lyrics are often inserted into local musical styles.

NONVERBAL AND OBJECT COMMUNICATION

Forms of nonverbal communication include chronemics, kinesics, paralinguistics, proxemics, and object communication. Chronemics is the cultural use of time, or as a Trinidadian may say, "Anytime is Trinidad time," indicating that some Trinidadians do not operate on a strict nine-to-five schedule. While living in Carriacou, Grenada, it took me a while to become accustomed to the phrases "pass by" and "just now." People kept telling me that they will "pass by my house just now." I thought "pass by" meant to go by someone's house but not enter it or stop, and that "just now" meant they would do this right away. However, "pass by" means to visit at your home, and "just now" means not soon but sometime within the next month or two. Apparently, "Anytime is Carriacou time" also.

Kinesics is a form of cultural communication through face, hand, shoulder, and other body gestures. When I first traveled to the Caribbean, it took me some time to get used to men holding hands, usually just after shaking hands, with no sexual orientation implied. I mastered the Latin greeting of a kiss on the cheek.

Paralinguistics is a form of nonverbal communication through sound, to convey emotion in the language. It can be in the form of grunts or tenseness in speech. The notorious "sucking teeth" conveys profound disgust in the Caribbean, as it does in West Africa.

Proxemics is the cultural use of space. While conversing, people from the Caribbean position themselves closer to each other than North Americans do. They may even touch or place a hand on the shoulder of the person opposite. To my very strict, emotionally subdued, and keep-a-decent-space-from-others upbringing, these customs of familiarity were too close for comfort. I became acclimated to the closeness, however, and now easily fall into appropriate "spacing" when I am with West Indians. I even prefer it to my native ways.

Finally, object communication has to do with cultural information perceived through clothing, body painting, piercing, branding, tattooing, or wearing rings, bracelets, or the like. Object communication conveys style, of which many West Indians from all backgrounds have in abundant quantities.

LIFE-CYCLE RITES

Caribbean "rites of passage"—rituals that mark an individual's movement along life's journey from one socially prescribed social status to another—are packed with folklore. Folk beliefs and practices reveal beliefs about pregnancy and birth, Church confirmation or similar events in the life of a teenager, marriage, and death. Customs relating to marriage and funeral rites can be very elaborate. Many changes have taken place in the Hindu wedding since people from India first arrived as indentured labor in the West Indies after emancipation in the 1840s. The British had outlawed child marriage (although it persisted for a time), and the breakdown of the caste system meant that people from different castes and from different parts of old British India married. Also, bonds between people who arrived in the islands on the same boat became as strong as kinship. But male-centered families and descent traced through the male line persisted, however, as did arranged marriage, although Hindu marriage was not recognized (in Trinidad) by the British until 1946. Elements of the marriage ceremonies remain customary, such as the radically changed women's wedding music, which has become what is called chutney calypso.

In Afro-Caribbean communities, the breakdown of African family and lineage systems was even more severe, but the bonds between people, often from very different cultures, who arrived on the same slave ship, were strong among these groups as well. Although there is great variation throughout the Caribbean, a pattern emerged of three distinct types of unions between a man and a woman. Many grassroots people formed weak bonds across the sexes as lovers. If they had children, the father had varying degrees of responsibility. Many times, as with the Indian community, people lived as common-law partners, a kind of de facto marriage. Only later in life, when one could afford it, did people marry. Such a marriage was a big deal.

A first marriage was arranged on some islands. Often the ceremony, full of interesting folk customs, stretched out over days or weeks and involved a coming together of the families of the bride and groom, since the marriage represented

The flags of the groom's and bride's families "clash" in a "Flag Fight" in a "Joining," part of extended wedding celebrations in Carriacou, Grenada, 1971. The groom's flag always "wins" and is placed on top of the bride's flag. Photo credit: Don Hill.

a union of the families as much as it represented the union of a couple. Traditional or popular music was part of the marriage rites.

In traditional Afro-Caribbean communities the most elaborate rites of passage were (and still are in some places) the funeral rites, which sometimes stretched out over years. In some traditional communities, the Christian belief in an afterlife merges with West African ideas of "living" ancestors to create, in a West African way, a human community of living and dead. Elders are highly respected, and the dead are respected (or feared) even more. Society is made up of both the living and the dead, with ancestors or gods, many of whom were once ancestors, consulted in dreams or possession and placated in rituals ranging from pouring libations on the earth for the ancestors to bathing a stone with the blood of an animal to requesting advice from an oracle through divination A minority of Caribbean people see their ancestors as family members, aggravating at times and comforting at other times. It is no wonder that death is a tricky business. Even though the person who died is gone from this world, everyday life for the living people must be restructured by considering changes brought on by the death. This is why the funerary rites can be long, contentious, and taxing.

PERIODIC RITUALS AND FESTIVALS

In the agrarian Caribbean, crop cycles define breaks in the calendar, and the rituals mark those breaks. Christmas and Carnival are especially noteworthy (Cowley 1996). Celebrations on the islands with strong British influence take place at Christmastide. Jonkonnu is a Jamaican masquerade with music accompaniment. Parang—based on the Venezuelan parranda—is a type of serenading found in Trinidad. Some form of Christmastime serenading is, or was, found on most islands of the eastern Caribbean just as aguinaldos continue to be sung in the Spanish-speaking Caribbean. Carnival originally took place in the few days before the beginning of Lent, when everywhere except Haiti the observance was stopped. Haiti has an additional Carnival, the Rara Carnival, which takes place during Lent and stops on Easter Sunday.

Carnival exists wherever there are Catholic populations. In Europe, Carnivals began as a way Latin Christians could "package" pagan rites and get them out of the way before the restrictions of Lent and the subsequent Easter observance. In the nineteenth century, before emancipation (which took place between the 1830s and the 1880s, depending on the location), Carnival thrived on French- or Spanish-owned estates and in towns. Carnival of the estate owners or townspeople consisted of fancy masquerade balls; the Carnival of the enslaved population consisted of secular drum-based dances, costuming, Africanesque skits, games, and organized activities that mimicked the pleasures of wealthy people. After emancipation in Trinidad, former slaves took to the streets and increasingly controlled the outdoor events in Port of Spain until late in the nineteenth century, when a police crackdown led to a more demure, middle-class Carnival, headed by "colored" Trinidadians, who developed fancy masquerade bands and English-language Carnival music (calypso). In the second half of the twentieth century, Trinidad-style Carnival became the model for celebrations on other islands of the Caribbean, for the tourist industry in the area, and in cities around the world where even a few Trinidadians lived. These celebrations take place at different times in different countries.

Over the last 150 years, very many folk arts have originated in Carnival or have been featured at Carnival. In Cuba, rumba and conga dancing, comparsas (large masquerade bands), and diablitos (little devil masquerades) are important features of Carnival and the Day of Kings, held on January 6 (Bettelheim 2001). The steel drum or pan developed largely as a Carnival instrument, and calypso continues to be the name given to the music of Trinidad's Carnival. Obscure but interesting masquerades have come out of these Carnivals: the moko jumbies or stilt walkers, probably based on West African models, the black-and-white minstrel bands that parody blackface minstrelsy from the United States, the donkey and rider costume called burrokeet, and many more.

Minstrel band in St. Croix, postcard, circa 1920.

Other festive days in the Caribbean that are not associated with Christmas or Carnival include the East Indian Hosay and Diwali.

CRAFT AND BRICOLAGE

The countries of the Caribbean are rich in craft. West African–style drums—such as the ubiquitous set of three batá drums found in Santería—and Iberian string instruments—the guitar and a huge family of Spanish stringed instruments are extremely widespread. Today, while some instruments are factory made, craftspeople continue to ply the age-old trade of instrument maker (see "The Puerto Rican Cuatro Project," http://www.cuatro-pr.org/).

A narrow definition of *craft* is a skill in which an individual makes a useful object, from beginning to end, through a series of steps, generally making one object at a time. The craftsperson makes the object for his or her own use, for friends or neighbors, or for sale. This is contrasted with manufacture, in which an object is made through a series of steps, with one person or a group of people applying a single modification and another person or group continuing the job by applying the next modification, until the object is completed. Manufactured objects are sold worldwide. Craft has historically been associated with preindustrial villages where a blacksmiths, potters, or carpenters ply their skills, sometimes in groups of people called guilds (Europe) or special castes (such as iron workers in Africa). Manufacture is associated with mass production, factories, and application of a common standard to objects that are made.

Nowadays, there is no sharp line between craft and manufacture. The concept of bricolage, previously associated in this chapter to the way myths are constructed, is useful. Drums made from rum barrels (Carriacou), a pan (or steel drum) made from a 55-gallon oil drum (Trinidad), or trumpets made from tin cans (Haiti) are all examples in which a manufactured object is turned into a folk object through the bricoleur's craft—using something made for one purpose and then modifying it through creative ingenuity for some other purpose. Kids in the Caribbean used to make wheeled vehicles by creating a steering mechanism on the end of a long stick. When they turned the handle on one end of the stick, the wheels turned on the other end, as they "drove" down the street.

Boat building, making fish nets, building houses in small, rural communities, cooking, and instrument making are crafts that are still important in some Caribbean societies. The products of these crafts are for the local people, while other craft objects (dolls, toy instruments, baskets, hats, etc.) are sold to tourists. Caribbean people and tourists enjoy some craft products, such as Cuban cigars or guayabera shirts (called "shirt jackets" in English).

OUTSIDER AND TOURIST ART

In the West, art has been contrasted with craft. Art is on "the cutting edge" or is "avant-garde." The artist is a highly trained and skilled seer and takes the person who appreciates art—be it sculpture, painting, classical music, ballet—to where the future is. The artist gives a personal vision and informs the viewer where his society will be. The artist produces for her own satisfaction and speaks to the elite. The craftsperson is supposed to replicate tradition and, therefore, looks back rather than forward. The craftsperson, who may decorate his work, nevertheless produces everyday objects for use and not for contemplation. The artist produces "art for art's sake"—that is, nonutilitarian, pretty, or awe-inspiring works. The craftsperson is competent but not imaginative; the craftsperson is not the "genius" that the true artist thinks she is. The craftsperson makes five dollars an hour and is always employed; the artist may make millions on each piece of work but the art rarely sells.

The sarcasm with which this little parable is written reveals this scholar's romanticized bias in favor of craft as opposed to "art," not an uncommon affliction suffered by anthropologists and folklorists. We feel that the true cultural geniuses are the craftspeople and that the Western concept of "artist," when applied to most societies and most people, is contrived.

A happy medium between art and craft is "outsider" or "naïve" art (once called primitive art, a phrase that, by implication, disparaged the skill of the supposedly primitive artist as compared with the true—read "highly trained"—artist). Whatever name is given to this type of artist, it is bestowed upon someone from a folk tradition who creates nonutilitarian objects for oneself, as decoration on everyday objects (such as a wall or a bus), or for sale to people from a different social class or cultural background. In the Caribbean, the outsider artist is most often a painter—not a traditional occupation—and usually creates paintings for tourists and art collectors. Rather than being trivial, as some local people and tourists view them, outsider artists are in fact arbitrators of their culture to the world beyond their island.

The classic examples of outsider art—that is, outside the mainstream of trained artists and, perhaps, outside mainstream society as well—are the painters of Haiti, one of the poorest countries on earth. While most Haitian artists are outsiders, others are true artists in the Western sense. Taken collectively, they depict their vision of one of the last thoroughly folk societies on earth, a place that has been negatively affected by the modern world (such as repeated invasions from the United States) as well as by certain folk traditions (particularly slash-and-burn agriculture, which has denuded Haitian forests and greatly contributed to massive erosion). The inner strength of the Haitian people as they live out their lives in difficult circumstances is symbolized in the paintings of Hector Hyppolite, Castera Bazile, and Rigaud Benoit (Stebich 1978).

COSTUMES

Folk costume is part of object communication. Today, the eighteenth- and nineteenth-century French Creole woman's outfit—the madras dress and the foulard head tie—brings up feelings of nostalgia for one's land or a sense of shame for the matador or doudou (a well-dressed black or mulatto woman who was kept by mainland, white French officials). "Adieu Madras, Adieu Foulard," the beautiful Guadeloupian song written in the eighteenth century, invokes those mixed sentiments. Some version of that dress is still worn when folkloric concerts are given everywhere in the islands. The dress evokes a sense of island identity.

Costume and traditional design in festive clothing is a symbolic representation of history and relationships between groups of people (Nunley and Bettelheim 1988). Jonkonnu, Hosay, and traditional Carnival costumes tell the folklorist about a people and their history.

Everyday dress is also of interest to the folklorist. Hairstyles come and go for women and men; some of them are based on West African hairdos, while others—the Rastafarian dreadlocks, for example—are more recent and are based on the "look" of the Masai that Jamaicans copied from books, probably in the 1930s. With the rise of manufactured clothing in recent decades, the distinctive

A woman combs a child's hair, Guadeloupe, postcard, circa 1910.

dress from different islands has largely broken down and may now be found primarily in folkloric performances rather than in everyday life.

FOLK ARCHITECTURE AND THE SOCIAL USE OF SPACE

The study of folk architecture in the Caribbean is a fertile topic for future study, because there has not been a lot of work done in this area. Michel-Rolph Trouillot is the author of "The Production of Spatial Configurations: A Caribbean Case" (1983), which reviews French- and Spanish-language studies of the cultural use of space. This article includes a short bibliography of studies, although not necessarily on folk architecture. The leading authority on black vernacular architecture in the United States is John Michael Vlach, who has also conducted fieldwork in the Caribbean (1975). He traces the shotgun house, a house type once found throughout the plantation southern United States and usually built by black Americans, to African antecedents (1986, 58–78). Elvis Presley's first home was a shotgun house. The shotgun house has an entrance on the gabled front, with any number of rooms attached in a line to the rear.

Roger Abrahams, following Sidney Mintz, has written extensively on the use of geographic space in the rural Caribbean, such as the distinction between the "house and yard" (1983, 133–56). Following Abrahams, I have written about the organization of the rooms within the house, the physical placement of the

Jamaican wedding portrait before a wattle and daub house, postcard from the early 1900s.

kitchen, the sense of the yard versus the road in Carriacou (Hill 1977, 22–24) and the distinction between town and country. I have described and illustrated types of traditional houses (African, board, and wall) as they existed in Carriacou in the early 1970s (see chapter 3 of this book and Hill 1973, 251–310).

FOODWAYS

The societies of the Caribbean were created, in part, to provide food (sugar, rum, cocoa, rice, and bananas), drink (coffee, rum), smokes (tobacco, marijuana), and clothing (cotton) for Europe and North America. Caribbean people plant, harvest, cook, consume, and think about what they have consumed (Sanabria 2007, 250–80). The plants that go into Caribbean food are both local and global, as are the Amerindian, European, West African, Asian Indian, Chinese, Indonesian, and other cuisines that are blended together to make West Indian meals. The folklore of Caribbean foodways begins with how the food is produced on plantations for export and in small farms for local consumption. It continues through the processing of that food—harvesting, drying, and grinding corn; planting cane rations, cutting cane, and processing cane into molasses, sugar, and rum; and growing, drying, and rolling tobacco. Preparing, eating, drinking, and smoking Caribbean provisions is often a social activity, full of folkloric elements. Usually, Caribbean women cook and, in some regions, the men eat separately from the women and children.

There is symbolism in food. Cuban American singer Celia Cruz used to yell "Azúcar (Sugar)!" to punctuate a lyric of one of her songs. Jacks Broth is a soup with very small sardinelike fish cooked with ground provisions (yams, sweet potatoes, Irish potatoes) that is thought to make children strong and men sexually active. Arroz blanco y frijoles negro is white rice and black beans, but it is also a symbol for the Afro-Spanish heritage of Cuba.

WORKS CITED

Aarne, Antti, and Stith Thompson. 1964. *The Types of the Folktale: A Classification and Bibliography.* Helsinki: Tampere.

Abrahams, Roger D. 1983. *The Man-of-Words in the West Indies: Performance and the Emergence of Creole Culture.* Baltimore: Johns Hopkins UP.

———. 2002. "Nevis and St. Kitts: Tea Meetings, Christmas Sports, and The Moonlight Night." In *Caribbean Voyage, the 1962 Field Recordings,* Rounder Records, 82161–1731–2. Compact disc notes.

Averill, Gage, and Lois Wilcken. 1998. "Haiti." In Olsen and Sheehy, *South America, Mexico, Central America, and the Caribbean,* 881–95.

Bascom, William. 1980. *Sixteen Cowries: Yoruban Divination from Africa to the New World.* Bloomington: Indiana UP.

Berger, Harris M., and Giovanna P. Del Negro. 2004. *Identity and Everyday Life: Essays in the Study of Folklore, Music, and Popular Culture.* Middletown, Conn.: Wesleyan UP.

Bettelheim, Judith, ed. 2001. *Cuban Festivals: A Century of Afro-Cuban Culture.* Princeton, N.J.: Markus Wiener.

Bilby, Kenneth. 2005. *True-Born Maroons.* Gainesville: U of Florida P.

Brandon, George. 1997. *Santeria: From Africa to the New World.* Bloomington: Indiana UP.

Cowley, John. 1996. *Carnival Canboulay and Calypso: Traditions in the Making.* New York: Cambridge UP.

Desroches, Monique. 1998. "Martinique." In Olsen and Sheehy, *South America, Mexico, Central America, and the Caribbean.*

Ember, Melvin, Carol Ember, and Ian Skoggard, eds. *Overviews and Topics.* Vol. 1 of *Encyclopedia of Diasporas: Immigrant and Refugee Cultures around the World.* New York: Kluwer Academic/Plenum.

Fayer, Joan, and Joan McMurray. 1999. "The Carriacou Mas as Syncretic Artifact." *Journal of American Folklore* 112: 58–73.

Frank, Henry. 2002. "Haitian Vodou Ritual Dance and Its Secularization." In Sloat, *Caribbean Dance,* 109–13.

Green, Thomas A., ed. 1977. *Folklore: An Encyclopedia of Beliefs, Customs, Tales, Music, and Art.* Santa Barbara, Calif.: ABC-CLIO.

Guilbault, Jocelyne. 1998a. "Guadeloupe." In Olsen and Sheehy, *South America, Mexico, Central America, and the Caribbean,* 873–80).

———. 1998b. "St. Lucia." In Olsen and Sheehy, *South America, Mexico, Central America, and the Caribbean,* 942–51.

Harris, Joel Chandler. 1955. *The Complete Tales of Uncle Remus.* New York: Houghton Mifflin.

Henry, Frances. 2003. *Reclaiming African Religions in Trinidad: The Socio-Political Legitimation of the Orisha and Spiritual Baptist Faiths.* Kingston, Jamaica: U of the West Indies P.

Hill, Donald R. 1973. "'England I Want to Go': The Impact of Migration on a Caribbean Community." Ph.D. diss., Indiana U.

———. 1977. *The Impact of Migration on the Metropolitan and Folk Society of Carriacou, Grenada.* Vol. 34, part 2, of the Anthropological Papers of the American Museum of Natural History, 193–391. New York: American Museum of Natural History.

———. 1993. *Calypso Calaloo: Early Carnival Music in Trinidad.* Gainesville: UP of Florida. (Book with CD.)

———. 2004. "Music of the African Diaspora in the Americas." In Ember and Skoggard, *Overviews and Topics,* 363–73.

Ibekwe, Patrick. 1998. *Wit and Wisdom of Africa: Proverbs from Africa and the Caribbean.* Oxford: New Internationalist Publications.

Lévi-Strauss, Claude. 1966. *The Savage Mind.* Chicago: U of Chicago P.
Lewin, Olive. 1998. "Jamaica." In Olsen and Sheehy, *South America, Mexico, Central America, and the Caribbean,* 896–913.
Manuel, Peter, Kenneth Bilby, and Michael Largey. 1995. *Caribbean Currents.* Philadelphia: Temple UP.
McDaniel, Lorna. 1998. *The Big Drum Ritual of Carriacou.* Gainesville: UP of Florida.
Nunley, John W., and Judith Bettelheim. 1988. *Caribbean Festival Arts.* Seattle: U of Washington P.
Olsen, Dale A., and Daniel E. Sheehy, eds. *South America, Mexico, Central America, and the Caribbean.* Vol. 2 of *The Garland Encyclopedia of World Music.* New York: Garland Publishing.
Ortiz, Fernando. 1995. *Los Negros Brujos.* Havana: Editorial de Ciencias Sociales.
Parsons, Elsie Clews. "Elsie Clews Parsons Papers," American Philosophical Society, Philadelphia, http://www.amphilsoc.org/library/mole/p/parsons.htm.
"The Puerto Rican Cuatro Project," http://www.cuatro-pr.org/.
Primiano, Leonard Norman. "Folklife." In Green, *Folklore,* 322.
Redfield, Robert. 1989. *The Little Community and Peasant Society and Culture.* Chicago: U of Chicago P, Midway Reprint.
Sanabria, Harry. 2007. "Food, Cuisine, and Cultural Expression." In *The Anthropology of Latin America and the Caribbean.* New York: Pearson.
Sloat, Susanna, ed. 2002. *Caribbean Dance from Abakuá to Zouk.* Gainesville: UP of Florida.
Stebich, Ute. 1978. *Haitian Art.* New York: Brooklyn Museum and Harry N. Abrams.
Thompson, Stith. 1955. *Classification of Narrative Elements in Folk Tales, Ballads, Myths, Fables, Mediaeval Romances, Exempla, Fabliaux, Jest-Books, and Local Legend.* Bloomington, Indiana: Indiana UP.
Trouillot, Michel-Rolph. 1983. "The Production of Spatial Configurations: A Caribbean Case." *New West Indian Guide* 57, no. 3/4: 215–29.
Vega Drouet, Héctor. 1998. "Puerto Rico." In Olsen and Sheehy, *South America, Mexico, Central America, and the Caribbean,* 932–41.
Vlach, J. M. 1975. "Sources of the Shotgun House: African and Caribbean Antecedents for Afro-American Architecture." Ph.D. diss., Indiana U.
Vlach, J. M. 1986. "The Shotgun House: An African Architectural Legacy." In D. Upton and J. M. Vlach, eds., *Common Places: Readings in American Vernacular Architecture.* Athens: U of Georgia P, 58–78.
Wilcken, Lois E. 2002. "Spirit Unbound: New Approaches to the Performance of Haitian Folklore." In Sloat, *Caribbean Dance,* 114–23.

Three

Examples and Texts

ORAL TRADITIONS

Myth

Humble-o, kou ye?
Humble-o, kou I o?
Vitman, pou nou ale, vitman!
(Chorus then keeps repeating this line).
Nou ka-ale.
Nou vle ale.
Nou ka-ale.
Nou ka-ale.

Translation:

Humble oh, where is she?
Quick, we have to go, quick!
We're going.
We want to go.
Etc.

Spoken:

Krik! Krak!

Well that was a lady have a daughter,
And confirmation will be taking place;
That lady live in Petit Martinique, Carriacou;
And that confirmation will be taking place in Carriacou
Because Petit Martinique have no church in those time.

Well, that poor lady leave the daughter home
And come down to make right to sew a clothes
There was no seamstress in, um-
(Listener: Petit Martinique)
Petit Martinique. Let me one talk!

And when she come now the day appear
That all children will come down from Petit Martinique

To come to Carriacou to land in
Jean-Pierre Bay
To go down town to receive
confirmation
In the Roman Catholic Church.

Well, the first boat arrive; the
daughter did not come.
She wait for the second boat; the
daughter did not come.

(Song)

Krik! Krak!

At that time that girl prove
in family way
And you can't confirm if you
conceive with a child.
She can't come.

The poor mother don't know;
The poor mother don't know if she
conceive;
But she go and make all preparations
before,
And then expecting her with the
boat.

So when the last boat come
And she ain' see the daughter
She take off her kerchief round
she head
And tie she waist and she start
to bawl;

(Song)

Krik! Krak!

Well in those time, in
that time,
The daughter did not come on that
direction at all.
She ain't come with the boat
Because she know that she conceive
with a baby.

Well, the last boat come;
The lady did not see.

Well you know, at those time
We don't have car in Carriacou to
take them to town
They have to walk.
All the candidates form
together
And stepping down to town.

Well when they meet they
going down
They going and pass Belvedere
Cross
Going down town,
Going to the Roman Catholic
Church
To get confirmation
Bishop is there waiting.

Well when they going to cross
You know the road was by
Noblaki [?] Bay
And crossing there
There have a salt-pond there.

There is a man there will take
away all;
Will swallow all the children
All everybody that pass.

Look here!
As soon as they go to cross
That lagoon (Listener: salt-pond)
salt-pond,
All gone!
They take away all!

And is only that one girl
That stay in Petit Martinique;

And that girl come
And she bring a twin,
A boy and a girl.

That is the onliest people
That remain in Petit Martinique.

And all the people that leave
To go and see confirmation
All was swallow by the,
By that man I forget that man name;
He name is Djabloten.
The Devil!

Well, all right, no confirmation;
Nobody in Petit Martinique did not
confirm
On that day because they all gone,
They did not reach town.

And that girl remain in Petit
Martinique
She make twin and,
They grow up in Petit Martinique.
And you see
Petit Martinique is one family.

Because if anything wrong in Petit
Martinique,
You go there you get dead,
because...
And if you get dead there
No one would not say
"Well, me kill this man"
Because they all is one;
You stranger have to keep off.

You see?

That is why, you see,
If you have a daughter she going to
confirm
And she conceive
She can never go to the Bishop to
confirm,
Because she conceive with baby.

Not so you know,
But in the way going
She was a candidate
In the way going to confirm
She get the baby.
And then, she remain there.

Is thanks of she that make
Petit Martinique green
up today.
Krik! Krak!

Source: Daniel Aikens, singer and story teller, recorded in La Resource, Carriacou, by Alan Lomax (August 2, 1962), transcription by Ron Kephart (Patois and English Creole) and Donald Hill (English Creole), in *Saraca: Funerary Music of Carriacou*, Rounder Records, CD 1726 (2000).

Commentary

Daniel Aikens relates this tale in Carriacou English Creole, as he moves between the mesolect form of the language that retains some features of standard West Indian English (acrolect), and the basilect form, which is completely informal and is close to a different language. His short song is sung in basilect, French Creole.

This was a live performance recorded by folklorist and ethnomusicologist Alan Lomax, in Carriacou, Grenada, in 1962. It is told from a Carriacouan perspective and is about the mythical origins of the people from Petit Martinique, a dead volcanic cone that is a half-mile round and sits a mile off the northeast shore of Carriacou. In the early 1970s, the population of the island was about 500 people. Most adults owned boats and fished or hauled cargo in local, interisland trade. The people of the island were depicted by some Carriacouans as incestuous, since their marriage customs allowed for marriage between family branches that would not be tolerated in Carriacou. Petit Martiniqueans also had a reputation for solving disputes among themselves and not through legal authorities. Taken together, these supposed customs are reflected in this origin myth, where incest is hinted at and where Petit Martiniqueans, as "one family," are leery of strangers.

The Chosen People

Maroon is de people who God have blessed to do certain miracles that they feel should spread round and round, throughout de whole globe, or throughout de whole constituency, in other words. Remember, you should hear about when de Maroon fight and fight and fight so till when dem go right at Stony River. Right. Is there they had signed de last treaty, which is their pledge.

Source: *Robert Dennis, interviewed by Kenneth Bilby (May 17, 1978), quoted in Kenneth Bilby,* True-Born Maroons *(Gainesville: U of Florida P, 2005), 248.*

Commentary

This time, the brief comment by Robert Dennis is told to anthropologist Kenneth Bilby in mesolect Jamaican English Creole. These chosen people are Jamaican maroons, originally either slaves freed by the Spanish to fight the British when they took the island or runaway slaves. Maroons fought slavery and British rule for decades until 1739, when the first of a series of treaties ensured their rights, sometimes in exchange for returning newly runaway slaves from their midst. The notion that an ethnic group is "chosen" by God is extremely common among the peoples of the world. Some groups even go so far as to call themselves "the People," implying that if you are not one of the People, you are not human.

Ọba's Ear, a Yoruba Sacred Myth

In Havana in 1947, Berta, my wife, first heard the Yoruba myth of how Ọba cut off her own ear.... Ọba was cooking yam porridge (*amalá*), the favorite food of her husband, Shango. She was stirring and stirring it, when Ọshun came to her house. Ọshun asked, "What are you cooking?" "Yam porridge for Shango." Ọshun said, "It will please him more if it has one of your ears." So Ọba cut off her ear and cooked it in the porridge. When Shango ate it, he got his real strength. Ọba took off her kerchief and showed him that she had cut off her ear because she loved him so much. Shango got mad and left her. He went to live with Ọshun, which is what Ọshun wanted. This is why Ọba covers her left ear with her hand when she dances.

Shango is a Yoruba God of Thunder, and the two women are goddesses of the River Ọshun, which flows past Oshogbo, Nigeria, and the River Ọba, which is a tributary of the River Ọshun that flows past Ogbomoosho. Ọya, who appears in other versions of this myth, is goddess of the River Ọya, which is the River Niger. In Yoruba belief, all three goddesses were wives of Shango.

In 1948 when we went together to Cuba, half a dozen informants told us this myth in fragmentary form. A composite of these accounts would go as follows. Shango was the lover of Ọshun, but the husband of Ọba, and Ọya was trying to take him away from Ọba. Shango did not like Ọba's cooking, but Ọya was a very good cook. She told Ọba to cut off an ear and cook it with okra stew (*quimbombo*) for Shango. Ọba did so in order to keep Shango at home, and she covered the wound so that Shango would not see that her ear was missing. But Shango saw the ear in his stew and was angry, and never wanted Ọba again. She left in shame, and he took Ọya as his wife.

Source: *William Bascom, "Ọba's Ear: A Yoruba Myth in Cuba and Brazil," in* African Folklore in the New World, *ed. Daniel J. Crowley, 3–4 (Austin: U of Texas P, 1977).*

Commentary

Ọba, Ọshun, and Shango are three deities in the Yoruban pantheon. The Yoruba are a very large ethnic group, centered in Southwestern Nigeria. Their mythical home is the city of Oyo, and Shango, reputedly an early king of Oyo, is the God (orisha) of thunder and lightning and has many devotees. Two of his wives are Ọshun, who became a powerful river goddess, and Ọba, also a river goddess with the same name as the deity (and river). Ọya was his third and last wife.

In another version of the myth, Shango favored Ọshun, since she was such a good cook. Ọba thought she could entice him by adding her ear to his food, but he was repulsed and she was cast out. The River Ọshun meets the River Ọba in a series of rapids. The moral of the story is that appearance is not everything and what seems to be satisfying may not be.

Folktale

Slowpoke Slaughtered Four

Once and twice makes thrice upon a time there was a king, and the king had a daughter who solved every riddle that was put to her. No riddle was too difficult.

The time came for the daughter to marry. The king sent out criers to spread the word that whoever brought a riddle the princess couldn't solve would become her husband and inherit the kingdom; but let her solve it and the suitor would be hanged by the neck until dead.

Since the princess was beautiful and the kingdom enormous, princes, marquises, sages, and professors from all over came courting, and all were strung up at the gallows as the princess guessed their riddles, one after another.

There was a widow living in this kingdom who had a son that had not been spoiled by the ways of the world. People were unkind and called him Juan Bobo. Juan, having heard tell of the king's proclamation, decided that he, too, would go to the palace with a riddle for the princess. His cautious mother tried to stop him. But Juan Bobo had made up his mind. At last, with a heavy heart, the mother gave her permission.

While he saddled his mare, his mother made cassava cakes for Juan to take with him. Thinking it would be better for her good-hearted son to die peaceably on the road than on the gallows in the great city, she put a dose of poison into the cakes.

Juan Bobo set out. After traveling awhile he got off his mare and lay down to nap under a mango tree. While he slept, the mare found the cassava cakes and ate them all in one gulp. The cakes killed the mare instantly. Then four crows arrived to peck at the corpse, and the crows too, were killed.

Juan woke up, saw what had happened, and continued his journey on foot after plucking the crows and stringing them around his neck. As he passed through some woods, seven thieves waylaid him and stole the plucked crows. When the thieves ate the crows, they fell over dead.

Juan took one of the thieves' rifles and continued on, keeping an eye out for something to eat. He saw a squirrel, took aim, but missed. Instead, his shot found a rabbit that happened to be pregnant. He skinned the rabbit, then built a fire to roast it, using some newspapers that were lying nearby.

He went on. He came to a river, and as he crossed the river he looked down from the bridge and saw a dead horse with three crows on it, floating in the water.

At last he reached the palace gates and asked permission to present a riddle to the princess. When they saw him at court, they laughed, and some were stricken with pain, knowing the poor man was about to die. But Juan Bobo, unconcerned, went up to the princess and said to her with great seriousness.

I started out on Slowpoke, and
Slowpoke slaughtered four; when
These had murdered seven more, I
Shot at what I thought I saw and
Killed what I couldn't see;
The flesh I ate was not yet born,
Though fully cooked with words;
And when I crossed from there to
Here, a corpse was carrying three.

The princess began to think. She had three days to solve the riddle. The first two nights she tried to get the answer by having one of her maids, and then another, go to the room where Juan was staying. The third night the princess herself slipped into Juan's bedroom. "Let me have your nightgown," he said, "and also your ring. When morning comes I'll tell you what you need to know."

The princess did as she was asked, and when morning came, Juan whispered the answer in her ear.

So the princess explained the riddle before the court and the king sentenced Juan to the gallows. The poor man asked permission to speak. "She didn't know the answer," he cried, "until I told her what to say." The king asked for proof. Juan held up the nightgown and the ring. "Enough!" cried the king, and he gave orders for the wedding to proceed immediately.

The two were married and lived happily from that time on, for Juan Bobo turned out to be cleverer than all the great princes who had passed through the king's court.

Source: *John Bierhorst, ed.,* Latin American Folktales: Stories from Hispanic and Indian Traditions *(New York: Pantheon Books, 2002), 219–21.*

Commentary

The Juan Bobo stories were once common in rural Puerto Rico and consist of funny or ironic accounts of the adventures of the hero. Juan Bobo may seem slow-witted but he is not; he often outsmarts his adversaries. Beyond the sense that "Everyman" can win out in the end, the nuances of Juan Bobo's character express the spirit of the "jibaro," or rural Puerto Rican. Like Juan Bobo, the jibaro may seem naïve in his ways but he is persistent and loveable, perhaps the spirit of Puerto Rico itself.

Language

What's in a Name?

African languages come alive in the sea islands in names and naming practices. Most Gullah-speaking people have two kinds of given name; one used in school and with strangers is English, the other is the basket name or nickname, "nearly always a word of African origin.... In many instances both the given-name and surname are African words" (quote from Turner 1973 (1949), 40). To the African, the power to name is the power to control. Even when the Gullah name is English it follows African naming practices, like those of the Twi, Dahomeans, Mandingo, Yoruba, Ibo, tribes of northern Nigeria, and the Ovimbundu of Angola (Pollitzer 2005, 109).

To read the Gullah personal names listed by Turner is a fascinating entrée into the secret life of the sea-island black people as well as a convincing argument for African affinity. Opposite them are "West African words that are phonetically identical with or strikingly similar to them [with] several meanings the words have in a number of West African languages (Turner 1973 (1949), 42). Examples from nineteen African languages in a dozen categories illustrate the colorful and creative usage of words in naming children.

Time, date, or season is expressed in many of these Gullah names in the twentieth century as it was in the eighteenth. *Aba* (Fante) indicates a girl born on Thursday, *ajowa* (Ewe) one born on Monday. *Bimbi* (Fula) means early morning, *marece* (Hausa) the late afternoon, and *klema* (Mandingo) the hot season.

Ali (Mandingo) is a name given the fifth male child, and *ata* (Twi is the male of twins. *Olugbodi* (Yoruba) is bestowed on a child born with extra digits.

Appearance is reflected in many of these basket names. In Yoruba, *adu* refers to one who is very black, *arupe* to a dwarf, and *pele* to tribal marks on the face. *Dafa* for fat latterly means mouth full in Vai.

The body is a common source of names along the coast. *Juso* (Mandinka) is similar to the world for liver; *sisi* (Twi), the lower part of the back; *kowa* (Mende), a large stomach; and *ebeni* (Kongo), the breast.

Sex is reflected here as well. In Kongo, *lonzo* means inordinate sexual desire; *yonga,* to copulate; and *wilama,* to be pregnant.

Various diseases are represented in this lexicon. *Kurang* (Mandinka) means to be ill, *kungo* (Bambara) hysteria, *pitsi* (Ewe) leprosy, and *bombo* (Mende) smallpox. Perhaps such illnesses could be cured by *ingkishi* (Kongo), a charm or medicine, or by *wanga* (Umbundu), witchcraft.

As in Africa, animals and plants are represented. *Esa* (Umbundu) is corn and jaba (Bambara) onion; *begbe* (Mende) means a frog and *beyi* (Wolof) a goat.

Many names reflect actions or feelings; *buri* (Mandinka) means to run; *keniya* (Kongo) to grin; *kambalala* (Kongo) to pass a hill along its base in order to avoid climbing. Emotion shines through the word *ayoka* (Yoruba), one who causes joy everywhere; a bond of affection appears in *fabere* (Mandingo), a generous father; and *sabinya* (Bobangi) is to forgive.

Most impressive are personal names that show an African connection through some place or thing unique to that continent. *Asante* (or Ashanti) in Twi means the country, people, and language of the Gold Coast, and *Ga* refers to a tribe of that region. Several cities of Africa are remembered as well: *Loanda* in Angola and *Wida* (Whydah) in Dahomey. *Nago* is the Fon name for the Yoruba language of southern Nigeria.

Kings of Dahomey during the slave trade are recalled: *Akaba* ruled from 1680 to 1708, and *Agbaja* from 1708 to 1729. *Uzebu* (Bini) refers to the quarters of the chief in Benin City; *Totela* is the title of the kings of Kongo; and *Muzumbu* is a foreign minister in Angola.

Islamic influence is present in several words: *Aluwa* (Wolof) is a tablet in wood on which one writes verses of the Koran; *Hadijata* (Mandingo) is the first wife of Mohammed. Various African legends enrich Gullah names; *Akiti* is a famous hunter in Mandinka folklore who, by conquering the elephant, became king of the bush. The secret societies characteristic of Sierra Leone link the two worlds: *Poro* for boys and *Sande* for girls (Mende).

Equally impressive bridges are the names of species of plants and animals found only in Africa. *Afo* (Yoruba) is the baobab tree; *akodu* (Ewe) is the banana. *Bambo* or crocodile is the totem of a Mandinka clan; *dile* (Mende) is a boa constrictor. *Boma* is a black python, and *pongi* (both Kongo), for chimpanzee, gave rise to the scientific name of another great ape, the orang.

In some cases a master recorded an African name as he understood it from his own European heritage; thus, *Keta,* a common name in Yoruba, Hausa, and Bambara, became *Cato;* the Mandingo name *Haga* became Hagar.

As slave families grew and blacks chose their own names, the concept of kinship, so central to the African way of life, was reflected in their practices. Frequently, a child was named for a grandparent. In Africa, while the relationship of a parent to a child might be a harsh one of superordinate to subordinate, their authority was checked by a gentle grandparent who maintained a more friendly familiarity.

That African names and naming practices still live on is shown by ninety-eight nicknames on Johns Island. Some thirty-one are related to a name found in Turner's list with an African equivalent, but a few are newly found Africanisms.

Do-um, suggesting "do it," was earned for assiduous application to an endeavor and audacity in sexual adventures. *Cunjie* with very broad cheek bones may have come from the Hausa word for cheek. *Yaa* for a girl and *Yao* for a boy, meaning Thursday, keeps alive the Ewe practice for naming a baby for the day of the week on which it was born. Even an English-appearing name like *Joe* may be an abbreviation of *Cudjo,* a male born on Monday. Similarly, *Phoebe* may really be *Fiba,* a girl born on Friday. Gussie may not be from Augustus but from the Bambara *gasi,* meaning misfortune; and *Pompey* is not necessarily the famed Roman general but the Mende name *kpambi,* meaning a line, course, or red handkerchief.

A derogatory term, such as *Boogah,* meaning something frightful in Vai, or *Nuttin,* for nothing, seems strange until one recalls the African practice of giving an uncomplimentary name to the newborn so that the ancestors might not be jealous and take the child back.

Even an English nickname follows the African practice of noting appearance, personality, or relationship. Thus *Blue* or *Shadda* (Shadow) are assigned to those quite dark in skin color. One named *Licky-too* defeated an antagonist both in verbal and physical combat; *Butcher* is a big, aggressive man ready to slaughter one who offends him; and *Prosper* was conferred on a distinguished and successful member of the community.

Kinship is cherished through nicknames today. *Bubba* is the equivalent of the English brother; *Betsy Ben* indicates that Ben is the son of Betsy; and *Minna Bill* is the nickname for Minna's grandson Bill. Yes, there is even *Do-um Bubba,* the younger brother of *Do-um.*

Source: *William S. Pollitzer,* The Gullah People and Their African Heritage *(Athens: U of Georgia P, 2005), 112–14.*

Commentary

Naming—both formal and informal—presents a key to family and kinship systems. In addition to their historical origins, names tell a lot about social relationships. Nicknames—called "home names" in some parts of the English-speaking Caribbean—are as important as family and individual names. Each implies a system. Family names are clues to how people reckon descent, such as taking the father's family name, the mother's family name, or both. This in turn tells us who may be considered as a family member and who is not. Individual names and home names may indicate personal qualities or may define friendship ties as opposed to family ties. Changes in naming systems mirror changes in how families are constituted.

Proverbs

Lawyer house buil'[t] [u]'pon fool head—Jamaican (70)

What de good a [of] education if him got no sense?—Jamaican (48)

Annancy [the spider-man of myth] rope tie him massa [master]. [to overreach oneself] (45)

What you lose in the fire, you will find in the ashes—Martinique (141)

When a liar tells the truth, no one believes him—Haitian (161)

Fool di talk but no fool dis listen—Creole (Belize) The fool talks but it's no fool that listens. (70)

When fowl merry, hawk ketch [catch] him chicken—Jamaican (18)

Two dogs after a bone are never in agreement—Haitian (166)

Source: *Patrick Ibekwe,* Wit and Wisdom of Africa: Proverbs from Africa and the Caribbean *(Oxford: New Internationalist Publications, 1998).*

Commentary

Proverbs play an important role in Afro-Creole life. Used to punctuate one's conversational points in everyday conversation, they show up in more formal settings as well. In Trinidad and Tobago, lines from calypso songs that contain proverbs are sometimes used in parliamentary debates. Traditionally, they were used in the same way in moot courts in West Africa.

CUSTOMS

Everyday Life

"Houdini's Picnic" in Harlem

In Harlem there are two good hot West Indian bands, the Caribbean Serenaders and the Krazy Kats, and musicians selected from these bands are hired to supply the music at picnics. The Committee sends out folders bearing this proclamation: "Let us Dine and Dance! People talk about Dance? Mister, look Dance! Madam, look Dance!"

One night I went to one of the Committee's picnics with Mr. Ralph Perez, a Puerto Rican of Spanish descent who works in the export department of Decca Records, Inc....

The picnic Mr. Perez took me to was held in a long, narrow hall on the third floor of a seedy building on Lenox Avenue, just below 116th Street. When we arrived, at ten o'clock, only about fifty people were there. "Picnics are apt to start late and wind up at the break of day," Mr. Perez said. Against one wall there was a row of slat-backed chairs. A number of stout, middle-aged women were sitting on these chairs, smoking cigarettes and gossiping. A space had been roped off for the band. Beyond this space, in the far corner of the room, there was a short bar and five tables covered with white oilcloth. At these tables sat young

Negro and Creole women in evening dresses, drinking. I saw one take a pint of whiskey out of her handbag. She poured some of the whiskey in a paper cup, drank it straight, and put the bottle back in her handbag. "They're waiting for their menfolks to arrive," Mr. Perez said. "The men in this neighborhood work late, most of them. The men you'll see here tonight will be elevator operators, barbers, hotel workers, musicians, and a few professional people." We went over and stood at the bar, which was tended by a buxom, smiling woman. Mr. Perez said she was Mrs. Lynch, a Committee member and manager of Isabel's Salon, a Harlem beauty parlor. Assisted by two solemn, pretty children, her daughters, Mrs. Lynch was transferring bottles of beer and pop to a washtub which was half full of cracked ice. Back of the bar was a sign: "PATTIES AND PAYLOU SERVED FREE AT THE BAR AT INTERMISSION, DRINKS WILL BE SOLD AT MODERATE PRICES." Mr. Perez said the favorite drink at a picnic is rye mixed with orange pop. "Most people bring their own whiskey," he said. When Mrs. Lynch finished putting the bottles in ice, she said, "I told Houdini to run out and get the whiskey we going to sell there tonight, and he's sure taking his time." Mrs. Lynch had white strings hanging from the lobes of her ears, and I asked her what they signified. "Just dental floss," she said. "I had my ears pierced for earrings and the doc told me to keep pierces open with floss. It may look unusual, but it don't hurt." I heard some noise on the stairs, and then the band arrived. It was made up of Gregory Felix and three members of his Krazy Kat band—a drummer, a violinist, and a piano-player. The piano-player was a girl named Wilhelmina Gale. "I'm the clarinet," said Mr. Felix, "and Houdini's going to play the shakers and the gin bottle. Consequently, we got a five-piece band." Miss Gale went to the upright piano and removed its front and top boards. Then, with no preliminaries at all, she and the others took their places and began playing a rumba. Almost immediately, as if by signal, people started coming up the stairs in droves. Soon there were more than two hundred Negroes in the little hall.

Source: *Joseph Mitchell, "Houdini's Picnic," in* McSorley's Wonderful Saloon (New York: *Pantheon Books*, 1992), *254–56.*

Commentary

Mitchell's article, originally published in the *New Yorker* in 1939, concerns his visit to Harlem at the close of the Great Depression. It is one of the greatest pieces ever written on calypso by a non–West Indian. Primarily through his columns in the *New Yorker* magazine, Mitchell was one of the creators of social realism in journalism in the United States. While other writers concentrated exclusively on the doings of the elite, Mitchell took the reader, in plain English, into the world of everyday people leading everyday lives. Furthermore, there was no pretension nor racism in his accounts, which unfortunately were common attributes in the best of white, American journalism of the era, such as *Time* magazine, *The Baltimore Sun,* or the *New York Times.* In this brief extract we glimpse a West Indian variation on the Harlem "house rent party," when poor people would gather to pay rent or to stir up some quick income. Mitchell's accurate portrayal of this event gives the scholar a small indication of the West Indian contribution to the "Harlem Renaissance," which by then was largely played out. It also chronicles an important period in the history of Trinidadian music, as it pushed out of its island home and into North America and new audiences.

Tea Meeting in Nevis

The Nevis tea meeting is a remarkable combination of pageant, mock fertility ritual, variety show, and organized mayhem. The proceedings, which probably developed most immediately out of fund-raising church events introduced in the nineteenth century, are still found on a number of other islands in the West Indies, but in many different forms (DeCamp 1968). Until recently, tea meetings were often held on Nevis on summer evenings during the full moon. A hall was engaged, and a *King* and *Queen* and their *court* chosen. Costumes were carefully prepared for the royalty and for the other performers. One the night of the performance, the King and Queen were called for by a fife and drum (*Big Drum*) band. They went to the place of the meeting, where the rest of the community had gathered. They sat on the stage while members of the audience came up and performed some prepared routine—a song, poem, dialogue, speech, or dance, done by one or two performers, or a team song and dance such as Japanese Fan Drill or Baby Drill. The participants wore costumes appropriate to whatever role they played. In the middle of the evening tea (cocoa or some other hot drink) was served, and some ceremonial cakes, fruit hanging from a *harbor* [*sic*], and kisses from the King and Queen were ceremoniously auctioned. Then the King, the Queen, and members of the court made elaborate and ironic speeches. The speeches were followed by other acts from the audience, which continued until dawn if the meeting was a good one. In the back sat the scoffers, who made loud and often obscene comments about the performers and their routines.

Organizing, or attempting to organize, the proceedings were two *chairmen*. They were supposed to give a sense of continuity and order to the show and to determine who should perform at what time and when the tea should be served. One of them usually called the meeting to order by making a plea for decorum; this speech announced the tone for the night.

> Ladies and gentlemen, this afternoon we stand here to accompany this company here, ladies and gentlemen, and I want to hear, this afternoon, have decorum. Decorum. Remember the alphabet, ladies and gentlemen: A is for attention, B is for behavior, C is for conduct, and D is for DECORUM. And ladies and gentlemen, as we march on further, we go to J is for justice and P is for peace that is Heaven for the flocks. I ask you to remember those few letters in the alphabet: A, B, C, D, P, and J. Ladies and gentlemen, I won't procrastinate much more of the valuable time while I ask ______ to provide me with a piece.

As the chairmen continued to make their introductions and to comment on each act, it became clear that they are the premier performers. They not only had to make these interpolated speeches but also had to attempt to outshine the other performers, and most important, each chairman had to prove himself the best speaker there. As they put it, each wanted to be regarded as "the cock with the brightest comb." They preened their feathers by making long, inflated, macaronic speeches (16–17).

Source: *Roger D. Abrahams,* The Man-of-Words in the West Indies: Performance and the Emergence of Creole Culture *(Baltimore: Johns Hopkins UP, 1983).*

Commentary

The tea meeting is one of many folk plays, traditional speeches, and other leisure time or seasonal activities that were widespread in the eastern Caribbean before the era of the radio, television, and other electronic media. Verbal dexterity is always part of such performances, and sometimes sight gags are, too. Often outlandish performance was attached to Christmas or Carnival season and involved music and dance routines.

Roger Abrahams practically invented the study of folk performance in the eastern Caribbean. The reader is advised to explore his many publications on Caribbean folklore.

The Calypsonian Defeats Alcoholism and Becomes an Agent of Egalitarian Values in Trinidad

Fortunately, Pretender, after listening to a lecture in which the lecturer called alcoholism a disease, decided to seek help at the St. Ann's Mental hospital in 1964. "I never thought I could-a stop drinking...I never wanted to stop drinking...I felt that drinking was a part-a life. Is better you drink and dead than aint drink." How Pretender was cured of his habit makes good reading in my opinion for any would be alcoholics. His story too, provides, for psychologists and other interested social science thinkers, information on how the mind of an alcoholic works. He attributed his recovery to Dr. Beaubrun and calypsonian Unknown who both spoke to him about his health. Noting that he saw many persons who went for treatment were coming back "more drunk," he refused all treatment at first. However, the persons who went for treatment were coming back "more fat and rosy." Being a very thin man he made a resolution.

> Ah say ah go go up dey, rejuvenate the body and (still) beat the liquor. So ah went up weighing about 86 pounds...But God send me a day to hear whey dem people AAA saying...cause I so vex ah want to blind all-a dem...The chairman was saying that the alcoholic is not a bad man or worthless man, he is a sick man...and ah start to bawl: 'not guilty.' I thought it was me, so ah say: 'arrest him. I'm going to sentence alcohol to death, not no six months, not even lifetime, to death.' And I came out dey the 3rd of May, and from since that day, ah never even eat fruit cake, Ferrol, nutten. Man put dat in a kaiso [calypso] nah man! I is de happiest man to know ah sick. I was happy to know ah sick;

> it aint me. I use to wonder what it is get in me. Dr William have he big party down Charlotte street. I go in and take up hi big chicken leg and start eating oui! And the more dey tell me.... Chalkie you never wrong you know! You never wrong!

Preedie's talk confirmed what Andrew Carr once told me. Carr felt very much ashamed for calypsonians following the behaviour of Preedie who walked into Kimling restaurant and told Eric Williams, then campaigning for national elections, that if he wanted to run Trinidad and Tobago he must first "learn to share." "With that," said Carr, "Preedie picked up the chicken leg from Eric's plate and start to bite and eat it." Carr felt that were it not for Preedie, the police would have been summoned. Moreover, Eric Williams, according to Carr, "Must have had a soft spot for calypso," for he dismissed the whole affair with a smile. Years after in the comforts of the Regal Calypso tent, Eric confided to me about the importance of the artform and of the great contributing that guys like Pretender had made to the development of the people of Trinidad and Tobago. Though silent on many cultural issues involving calypso, Eric understood it all along.... After surrendering himself to the various medicines and prescriptions, Preedie never again up to his death in 2002, touched alcohol. "Ah don't eat fruit cake and ah don't even take cough syrup, since those things have in alcohol." Pretender, it can be said, like Spoiler, Caruso, Jaguar and Unknown, were well-known street alcoholics who were characteristic of many mid twentieth-century artistes who faulted the society for neither recognizing nor understanding the talent they possessed, while adoring foreigners and lesser able European knights; these calypsonians demonstrated their hatred of the elite and those in authority by becoming what upper-class society perceived them to be, drunkards (114–15).

Source: *Hollis ("Chalkdust") Liverpool,* From the Horse's Mouth: Stories of the History and Development of the Calypso *(Diego Martin, Trinidad: Juba, 2003).*

Commentary

Hollis Liverpool is a historian from Trinidad whose calypso name is the Mighty Chalkdust, or "Chalkie." More than other scholars, he knows calypso from the inside out, having won calypso competitions both at home and abroad. He also has counted as friends many of the important calypsonians of the last century, including Aldric Farrell, the Lord Pretender. Although there is wide variation in the lifestyles of people who are (or were) professional calypso singers, heavy drinking was a habit of some of the calypso greats and none was known as an alcoholic more than Pretender. This true story of Pretender's encounter with the former prime minister of Trinidad and Tobago, Eric Williams, himself a historian, is instructive. In the tradition of the West African praise singer or, for that matter, the medieval European court jester, allowance was given to calypsonians, behavior that would not be tolerated by ordinary people was almost expected of them. Ordinary middle-class Trinidadians, in the late colonial period in which this incident is set, "looked down" on calypsonians while at the same time admired them for their wit and their ability to criticize or praise the elite.

Outsider Art

Canute Caliste was born in L'Esterre Carriacou, Grenada, on July 15, 1914. As with most Carriacou people of his generation, "Papa C. C." is "African." Mr. Canute is Ibo, an African heritage of many people from his part of the island and one of the four most important groups on the island. The others are Cromanti (the "first nation"), Manding, and Temne. This identification with Africa predates the 1960s and was shared by only a few societies in the Americas (the others are the Haitians and various maroon groups).

When Canute was nine years of age and was walking near the local oyster bed between his home village of L'Esterre and Harveyvale, he had his first encounter with a mermaid. As he crossed a bridge that jumped a tongue of the lagoon, he heard the waves crashing against the rocks. With great surprise, he saw a mermaid sitting on a rock, combing her hair. "So when I peak, you see, I think it's a spirit and then I screech out and when I screech out she just like so, pum-joomp, she go down in the water... So I'm running and I see she was coming behind me...". About a week later, Mr. Canute saw the mermaid in a vision; she told him that she was "Queen of the Sea," "God's Sister," and that he should not be afraid. She placed The Book, the Bible, against her chest and said, "You will live by this until you die." The mermaid had given him the confidence to engage in any pursuit he chose in life.

Canute dropped out of school to help his parents grow subsistence crops. It is possible that he learned how to read and write a little before dropping out of school. Through the course of his life he became a sailor, took up carpentry, boat building, seafaring, music, and painting. He also had many children; twenty-two to be exact (three with his wife and nineteen others with eight girl friends).

From childhood, Canute painted scenes on interior house partitions, on boards, and on any likely surface. Sometime after 1961, the Canada-based Madonna House Lay Catholic Order started a branch in Carriacou. While on a visit to Mr. Canute's house in L'Esterre in the late 1960s, one of the sisters noticed that he painted figures on wood and on scrap board. Sister Trudy thought that there was something to his painting but she knew very little about it. The sisters suggested that Mr. Canute paint on pressboard so that his paintings could be sold to tourists. Then, they sent one of his paintings to a curator at the Royal Museum in Saskatchewan. They wanted to find out if his painting was "childlike" or was "good." The curator wrote them back saying that his painting was an excellent example of "primitive" art and not childlike at all. It was the work of a master painter who is unschooled. He suggested that they should not interfere with his painting style in any way.

The sisters began to sell his paintings at the Madonna House in Carriacou.... [His paintings went on to attract tourists locally and he achieved a following in Europe and North America.]

Although Papa C. C. continued to paint subjects upon request, the body of his work strongly suggests his world, not that imposed by the others. He has painted the mermaid (his favorite theme), tourist beach houses, whaling, planting cotton, "African" houses (a local term for "grass" or wattle and daub houses), boats of all kinds, the Empire State building (seen on his first visit to the United States), the Grenada war, the Big Drum Dance, Quadrille dances, government buildings and churches, kites, islands, the "jackular" (the devil), boat building, the "bush" (trees, plants), "beasts" (animals), Jesus, the Last Supper (with 14 disciples!), jet planes, pierrots, graveyards, and many other topics. His folk art paintings are now sought in many parts of the world and hang in galleries in the Caribbean, Europe, and the United States.

Mermaids in Carriacou

Carriacou has many examples of the presence of a water spirits or mermaids. Carriacou's mermaids seem related to Mami Water, the ubiquitous water goddess in West Africa. When we look at Carriacou's mermaid—her under-ocean travels, her ability to control weather, her arbitration of luck or fate—we see attributes identical with those possessed by Mami Water. The main difference is that in Carriacou only the "Shango Baptists" that [sic] have organized rituals directed to her. Mr. Canute and the others who are not "Shango" Baptists know of her through personal experience and not involvement in a religious organization.

Mermaid in Lagoon, painted by Canute Caliste, Carriacou, 2000. Credit: Clemencia Alexander.

Canute Caliste's mermaid is a "light skinned woman" with a finned tail, which sometimes has a zipper. He told me once that he saw her unzip her fin to reveal two normal feet. It was in the middle 1970s, when he was on his first visit to New York City, to perform for the Carriacouan community in Brooklyn and at the American Museum of Natural History, where I was a curator. He was watching television in his hotel room and the mermaid appeared on the TV screen.

In Carriacou, the mermaid is usually in the lagoon where he first spotted her. Her hands may be either in a waving position, at her side, or carrying a cross. In one painting there are three mermaids. In the middle 1970s, he began writing captions at the bottom of the painting, which reveal his ideas about the mermaid's attributes: "the Queen of Peace," "The Maide going out for a view," "The Maid having fun in the lake," "The Mermaid resting in her gardain," "Framed Mermaid cry out for peace and joy to the world," "Studying the days in the year—peace and love to the whold," "The Mermaid said on earth peace bee on to the siner on earth," and "the Mermaid in the lake restin praying for sinner on euth."

Source: *Donald R. Hill, "A Carriacouan View of the African Diaspora: 'African' Themes in the Paintings of Canute Caliste."* Calabash, a Journal of Caribbean Arts and Letters *3, no. 2 (Fall/Winter 2005). (Published only on the internet at http://www.nyu.edu/calabash/vol3no2/0302148.pdf)*

Commentary

Tourist art, once dismissed by folklorists and art critics alike for not having "authenticity" (that is, for not being created for the people and culture of which the artist is a part), has taken on a legitimate status in the postcolonial world. Scholars now feel that the art sold primarily to tourists by artists who have not been formally trained (in the Western sense of the term) may represent a true interpretation of their culture for foreigners. That is, the artist gives the tourist what he thinks the tourist wants. Since that artist can only "see" the world in the light of his culture, tourist art reflects one vision of that traditional culture.

Caribbean Foodways

In food patterns of eating... as well, Indians were to show their capacity for adaptation. Those caste distinctions that made impossible commensality in India were, in the conditions of migration, broken down, and vegetarianism was to have little appeal among Indo-Trinidadians. Tandoori cooking remains unknown among Indians in Trinidad and the Caribbean, and curry is made with a curry powder, rather than by mixing a curry paste. But it is the prevalence of "curry" in Trinidadian food that impresses, and in most respects Indo-Trinidadian food bears an astonishing similarity to certain varieties of Indian food. As one author of a cookbook on Caribbean food was to note in 1974, "the Indians have had a deep effect upon the Caribbean Cuisine primarily through their enthusiasm for curry, which is becoming as much a part of Caribbean as of Indian cooking." Trinidadian fast food, usually eaten with chutney, is mainly of Indian origin: their *saheena* is like *pakoras,* "doubles" is a variation on the *channa* batura, though more in the form of a chick-peas sandwich, and their *kachowrie* has a marked similarity to its namesake in India. Though many Afro-Trinidadians will not admit it, even their own main meals are now predominantly Indian in origin, for alongside *callooloo* there is curried goat, and roti is easily the most popular food in Trinidad. Indeed, to understood [*sic*] just how far roti has come to be a marker of "Indianness," and the resentment felt by some Afro-Trinidadians, consider that in the 1961 election, the black party took up the slogan: "We don't want no roti government." Roti shops proliferate, and though in India the middle-classes have adopted a Western-style breakfast, complete with poor white bread and corn flakes, in Trinidad roti with *dhal* and *subzi* or *tarkari* constitutes the bread and butter of most people at breakfast and dinner and often at lunch as well. The prevalence of Indian food is reflected in calypso, and many songs sing, often with mockery, scorn, and disturbing caricature, of 'roti' and 'chutney.'

Source: *Anonymous, http://www.sscnet.ucla.edu/southasia/Diaspora/athome.html.*

Commentary

Caribbean foodways, from source crops to preparation and consumption, reflect influences from many parts of the world. Foods developed by Native Americans, Mediterranean peoples, Middle Easterners, and West Africans mix comfortably with cuisine from India, Indonesia, and China to create some of the most cosmopolitan meals to be found anywhere in the world. In Creole cooking, East Indian food is especially important and in some places—especially the southeastern Caribbean and the countries of South America that face the Atlantic Ocean—Indian food is the fast food of choice regardless of ethnic group.

Divination with 16 Cowries

In Cuba, cowrie shell divination (*dilogún*) not only came to realize highly sophisticated interpretations based upon two throws of sixteen shells and their permutations, as opposed to simple combinations, but also "borrowed" Ifá's highly codified format of prayers, proverbs, taboos and advice, stories, and sacrifices. It is worth hypothesizing that the theory and practice of the modern Lucumí religion, including the shape of the pantheon, the religion's ritual means and ends, and the status and reach of the *oriaté,* would be much impoverished and more dependent upon Orunmila's *babalawos* were it not for innovations in the *dilogún* system. Obadimelli was apparently at the forefront of *dilogún* innovation.

Since the early twentieth century, the Afro-Cuban cowrie system (*dilogún*), in most cases, has required that the diviner cast sixteen shells to the mat twice, consecutively, such that two figures or signs (*odu/letra*) "come out," depending upon whether the shells fall "mouth up" or "mouth down."...

...The *dilogún* system of *odu,* like that of Ifá, is a system for classifying, conserving, and interpreting knowledge, as well as transforming the human situation through the application of sacrificial formulas based in the nature's *ache.* Like Ifá, it is a generative, metaorganizing grid, which groups, relates, and ranks the *orichas,* as well as worldly phenomena, within its signs and stories. It sets up protocols for which *orichas* one needs to "receive" and enunciates the proscriptions and prescriptions that initiates must follow in serving their stable of *orichas.* It comes as no surprise that the seniority protocols of the *orichas* in the pantheon are shaped by the positions they occupy within the ranked *odu* of the *dilogún* and Ifá systems. For example, the most senior *odu Ellionle*..., is the principal oracular domain of the Owner of All Heads, Obatalá, and claims as its defining proverb, "The head rules the body and only one king governs a town."...

Source: *David H. Brown,* Santería Enthroned: Art, Ritual, and Innovation in an Afro-Cuban Religion (*Chicago: U of Chicago P, 2003), 132–33.*

Commentary

Ifá is a system of Yoruba divination presided over by male babalawos. Oriaté is the person who presides over ocha ceremonies, which use a different system of Yoruba divination. Dilogún is the name of the Lucumí oracle expressed through the sixteen cowries, which utilizes its own odu or classification system of sacred knowledge, separate from the Ifá odu. Orishas are gods in the Yoruban-Lucumí religion. Aché is God's "life force" and is found in nature. Obatalá heads the orisha pantheon, Orunmila are orishas, and Obadimelli was a Lucumí priest.

Yoruba religious practice in Cuba has a complex history involving many African religious ideas dynamically integrated with Roman Catholicism and other religious ideas in Cuba.

The Haitian Combite (Cooperative Labor)

Though strenuous physical labor is involved in the work of the *combite,* for the Haitian it symbolizes recreation and enjoyment—the stimulus of working with one's fellows, the pleasure of gossiping with friends, and the partaking of the feast which marks the climax of the day. All this makes the occasion one to be anticipated and enjoyed, and no one witnessing ten or fifteen men on horseback, each with a hoe over his shoulder, shouting and laughing as they clatter by at full gallop, can fail to sense their eager desire to arrive at their destination, a near-by *combite.*

When a man or a woman needs help in preparing a field...a request is made of key-men in the district informally called *chefs d'esquade.* They have the reputation of being those to whose call a number of men, perhaps a dozen, perhaps two or three times that many, will respond and come to give the aid that is desired. Such a person is given a "bouquet"—a bottle of *clairin*—which insures the appearance of himself and his group on the date set. A *combite* may be held at any time during the week except Sundays...and Tuesdays...There is no requirement in either law or custom to respond to the call for communal work, and the larger landowners, who usually reside in the towns, rarely participate in a *combite.* So great is the pleasure derived from work of this sort, however, and so living is the realization among the peasantry of its potential part in a *combite* to which he has been summoned. Sometimes a man who has been faithful in his attendance at *combites* and has worked well at them falls ill during the time for planting or for clearing his ground of underbrush or for hoeing. In such case a *combite* is summoned, and even though this man is unable to offer the usual feast, his services are remembered and the men work with a will to insure the proper preparation of his ground.

The scene in a field where a large *combite* is at work is an arresting one. The men form a line, with a drummer in front of their hoes. The *simidor,* who leads the singing as he works with the others, adds the rhythm of his song to the regular beats of the drum, thus setting the time for the strokes of the implements wielded by the workers. This drum, slung about the neck of the drummer, is of the European form, never the hollowed-out African type that figures in religious rites. Its sound can carry far, however, and thus it not only beats the time for the hoes, but notifies all concerned that the *combite* is under way. The size of the *combite* is judged by the number of drums and *lambi,* or conch-shell horns used, for where two or three of either are required, an especially large group of workers is usually assembled. It may be observed in passing that it is undoubtedly that sound of this *combite* drum, heard in the mountains or through the brush by travelers, that has so often been mistaken for the "mysterious booming" of the *vodun* drums.

The preparation of the food is the work of the women of the household giving the *combite,* aided by the female relations and the wives of friends and neighbors. This is no small task, for goats and even a bullock may be killed to feed a large *combite,* while in addition other dishes to go with the meat must be cooked. Each woman is given charge of a great pot and does her best to see to it that an appetizing dish is ready for the men when their work is done. While the food is being cooked, the real object of the *combite,* clearing of the field, is being pursued. A *chef d'esquade,* usually with a small group, begins the afternoon's labor, and, being a fast worker, he himself sets the pace. As more men arrive, he walks about, encouraging the constantly increasing number of men in their efforts, seeing to it that the tempo originally set is continued, and when necessary picking up a hoe to restore a lagging rhythm. Occasionally the *chef d'esquade* will stand in front of the men to make sure that all keep together, and if the lazy cannot be roused to work by direct order or through ridicule, he will drive them away.

The work progresses with incredible speed as the line moves down the field. In one case a *combite* of between fifty and seventy-five men completely cleared a field of several acres in a single afternoon, and this without undue effort or what appeared to be the expenditure of much energy. The flashing of the hoes in the brilliant sunlight accentuates the color of the scene; each implement is raised high about the head of the one who wields it, to be brought down at the proper instant and in almost perfect accord with the hoes of all the other men in line. Pauses are frequent, and men often drop out of the line for a longer period of rest. . . .

Source: *Melville J. Herskovits,* Life in a Haitian Valley (*Garden City, N.Y.: Doubleday, 1971), 70–73.*

Commentary

Melville Herskovits conducted fieldwork in the community of Mirebalais (in Artibonite valley) in Haiti in 1934, toward the end of the U.S. military occupation of the island that began in 1915. The combite, or communal work group, was not characteristic of all of Haiti at the time but it was found elsewhere in the country and, in various forms, on other islands. In Carriacou, for example, it was called a helping or a community maroon (not to be confused with the people also called maroons who escaped slavery by establishing their own communities in remote parts of the region). The work of taking down and moving a building described in the next section is a kind of community work that once took place in Carriacou.

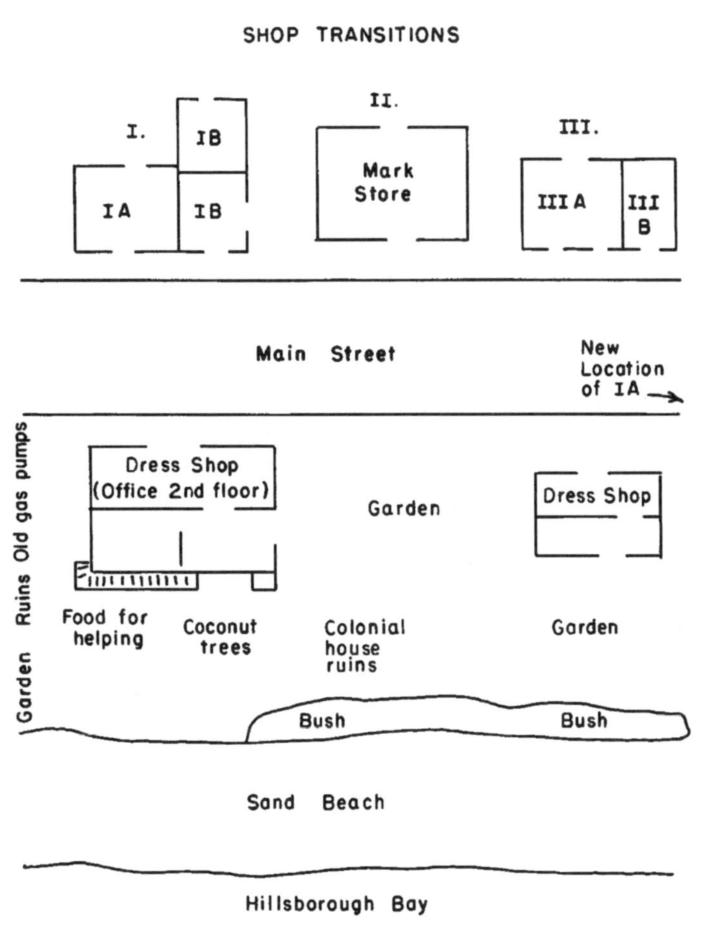

Diagram of shop transitions in Carriacou, 1971.

Folk Architecture: Moving a Building from Here to There using Cooperative Labor

Shops come and go at a rapid rate in Carriacou. Across Main Street from the dress shop are three buildings, the one in the middle being the Mark Store.... From the second floor of the dress shop, which I rented as an office, I was able to watch the changes that took place in these buildings...

[Mr.] John owned the building [next to] the Mark store but not the land. In March, 1970 the largest room of this building was empty, having formerly been a coffin shop. The other rooms housed Johnny Jessup's rum shop in front, facing Main Street, and his house in the rear. Jessup, a cobbler by trade, was born in St. George's and had settled in Carriacou. He married a Carriacouan and raised a family. His shop was frequented by a few villagers when they came to town and by Grenadians and Vincentians who had immigrated to Carriacou and married. Occasionally one of his brothers from Grenada would come to stay for a week or two. For the most part, the men who drank in Johnny Jessup's were road workers or minor government employees (guards, the steam roller driver). Jessup's gardens were on property owned by John. He would often assist one or more members of the John family in cutting coconuts from the grove behind the dress shop and in various other odd jobs. His pig was kept in the grove.

In the first days of June 1970 Jessup and several others began to paint the old coffin shop, at the direction of John. By June 8 most of this work was completed and some shelving had been built. Ensen, a "Vincee" [a person from St. Vincent] who had been

Morgan Langdon (Johnny Jessup in the story), in the newly constructed rum shop made from Building 1A, 1971. (All names in the story are pseudonyms.) Photo credit: Don Hill.

raised by a Carriacouan, had returned from London, where he had lived for 10 1/2 years, and opened a shop. In England he was a door-to-door salesman and it is said that he owned some apartment buildings there. He seemed to have a good deal of money for when he returned he purchased a small car, traded it for another, and then purchased a third. He bought a small sloop and nets....

Over the next nine months his shop underwent a series of changes. At first it was a general foods store, offering a small range of tinned foods and produce. At the same time Ensen engaged Hillsborough fishermen to make seine nets and to fish [on] his small sloop. He hired a girl to tend the store and when the fishermen brought in a catch, either from the sloop or with the seine, the fishermen and Ensen sold them in front of his shop....

While Ensen was able to generate prestige for his various activities he was not able to make much money in any of his endeavors. Nonetheless, as of November 1971 he still had enough savings and was full of ideas to continue. Perhaps those qualities that made him a successful salesman in England were not suited for Carriacou.

In May 1971 the Ensen shop had been closed for some time. Johnny Jessup continued living and working in his side of the building. At this time John received word from England that the owner of the property was intending to return to Carriacou to develop his property. These plans were not carried out immediately and may not ever be. Yet these intentions set off certain reactions in Carriacou: a "house break" was held and the building was removed from the site on which it had stood for more than 20 years.

On May 14, a Friday, the John family began preparations for the house break on the following day. Typically, a house break is a helping and all labor is given in exchange for food. To this end Mrs. John directed several women and her assistant—a young man who works for the John family—to clear the coconut grove behind the dress shop and to gather rocks for the fire bed on which the food would be cooked.

On the morning of the fifteenth women began cooking. The Johns sacrificed several chickens, saying "peace and prosperity," and scattering rum and water about the ground. Then Mrs. John directed one of the helpers, a man from Grenada who was not familiar with the ritual, to sacrifice several more "fowls" across the street at the site of John's building. Several people noted how each chicken died but I could not get the reading. John directed the moving of the building. On this day only Ensen's shop was to be moved. The helpers, with hammer, crowbar, and little else, began first to remove the shelving. Some of the helpers became overzealous and ripped out boards mercilessly. John had to tell the joiner to supervise them more closely. Meanwhile, the Jessups continued their daily activities in the other side of the building. Johnny Jessup tended shop as he aided in the house break. A gaping hole opened in the side of Jessup's shop as planks were pulled from the interior wall separating it from Ensen's. After the shelves were removed, the sides of the building were taken out in complete sections and carried up the street by 10 or 12 men. At the new site a cement floor had been laid so that a carpenter was able to direct the resetting of the structure immediately.

By early afternoon Ensen's section of the building had been moved and partially set on the new site. Jessup's part, except for the large hole in one wall, remained. Looking at the hole, Johnny Jessup grabbed a piece of "galvanize" [metal] and plugged it. The heavy work of the day done, the men crossed the street to eat the meal prepared by Mrs. John and the women. The eating lasted for several hours as most of the work had been completed.

On the morning of May 23, Johnny Jessup and his family moved from their house and shop, which still stood, to Ensen's old shop (and before that the coffin shop), at its new site across the street. There was no rush to tear down Jessup's old place. John hadn't decided what to do with it. Some of the lumber, however, was soon used to patch up the new house and shop across the street...and the rest was eventually taken to the John family home in Brunswick village where it was stored. This was the last change in shops on either side of the Mark Store, which along with the dress shop across the street, did not change throughout the year and a half.

Source: *Donald R. Hill,* The Impact of Migration on the Metropolitan and Folk Society of Carriacou, Grenada, *vol. 54, part 2, Anthropological Papers of the American Museum of Natural History (New York: American Museum of Natural History, 1977), 259–62.*

Commentary

This piece shows how, in the era when most houses on Carriacou were made of wood (mid-twentieth century), such "board houses," as they were called, were relocated from place to place. Since most of the forest on Carriacou had long been cut down for boat building and housing, wood was imported from Guyana and Canada and was very expensive. Hence, moving planks or even a side of a building intact, was both wise and thrifty. The custom has all but disappeared today, since most people now build out of cement. Note that I substituted pseudonyms in this account.

Use of Space

(Harold Courlander, writing in 1970, recounts in translation Eugène Aubin's description of a Vodou hounfour in Haiti. Bracketed sections below are Courlander's.)

A Hounfor Seen at the Turn of the Century

In 1906 the French writer Eugène Aubin saw and described a hounfor in the Cul-de-Sac Plain, a few miles from Port-au-Prince. His description suggests that the physical characteristics and concept of the hounfor have changed little in the intervening years.

[The] hounfor is fronted by a peristyle, which is used for the Vodoun dances and services; it is a large area, with a floor of beaten earth, covered with a straw roof. On three sides the walls rise to support the roof; on the fourth there is the inscription:

Société la Fleur de Guinée
Roi d'Engole
[Flower of Africa Society
King of Angola]

indicating the name of the patron of the society [the loa Roi Angole, or Wangol], over which the houngan presides. The hounfor is an ordinary house, a little larger than average. The sanctuary contains a principal pé [altar], running the whole length of the room on one side, and another altar, a little smaller, in one of the corners. These pés are altars largely made of brick, in which the underpart is decorated with hearts and stars in relief; above, draperies hand from the ceiling. The lateral pé is divided into three compartments. There are, therefore, four sections in all, consecrated to each of the loa served in the hounfor: Aguay Aoyo [Agwé Woyo], Damballa, Ogoun Badagry, and Loco [Loko], Nago King, Maître Aguay is represented by the customary little boat; a medallion is consecrated to Monsieur Damballa, shown holding two snakes in his hand; a figure on horseback represents Ogoun Badagry, with a woman at one side holding a flag; Papa Loco is pictured in full uniform, smoking a pipe and fanning himself. The walls are covered with religious paintings [Catholic lithographs]. The back of the altar is occupied by numerous carafes in baked clay, called canaries, which contain the... mystères [spirits taken from the heads of the dead] gathered in the hounfor; in front are bottles of wine, liqueurs and vermouth presented to them in homage; then the plates, the cups for the mangers-marassas [feasts for the twin spirit], crucifixes, hand bells, assons for directing the dance or calling the loa; plates filled with polished stones [celts] inherited from the Indians—"thunder stones," symbols of Damballa, which Saugo [Sobo] the god of lightning hurls from the sky into the enclosure of his favorite papaloi [houngan]. Beside these miraculous stones are many coins of copper or silver [property of the loa]. The loa... possess coins of Joseph Bonaparte, King of Spain, minted in 1811, of Frederick VII of Denmark, 1859; of Charles IV of Spain, 1783, and of President Boyer, dated year 27 and year 30 of Haitian Independence. On the ground there is placed a coconut-oil lamp; in the corner, the flags of the hounfor and the saber of [the] laplace, the man who acts as master of ceremonies in the services. In the court, the bases of four sacred trees... are surrounded by circles of masonry [low brick walls]. These reposoirs are inhabited by the loa Legba, Ogoun, Loco and Saugo [Sobo or Sogbo] (31–32).

Source: *Eugène Aubin, from* En Haiti *(Paris, 1910), translated and quoted by Harold Courlander,* A Treasury of Afro-American Folklore *(New York: Smithmark, 1996).*

Commentary

The Vodoun religion of Haiti comes mostly from Dahomey (now the country of Benin). Elsewhere in the Caribbean it is called Rada and is the belief system of the Fon people. The Fon are related to the Yoruba and Vodou shares loa (gods, or Orishas, in Yoruba) with the Yoruba, including Ogun, and Shango. The hounfor is a ceremonial house where Vodou rites take place.

MUSIC, DANCE, AND SONG

Jamaican Dancehall

What is "Dancehall"?

Originally, the term "dancehall" was used to describe a place or "hall" used for the staging of dances and similar events. There is no general consensus on how the term became identified with this form of Jamaican popular culture. One can speculate that the proliferation of stage shows and other staged events backed by the sound systems resulted in dancehall's identification as a music that is tied to a space and place. However dancehall music can be defined as that genre of Jamaican popular music that originated in the early 1980s....

...Dancehall culture is a space for the cultural creation and dissemination of symbols and ideologies that reflect and legitimize the lived realities of its adherents, particularly those from the inner cities of Jamaica...

Categories or Typologies of Affectors and Affectees

I use the two broad terms "affectors" and "affectees" to outline the heterogeneous nature of the actors within dancehall culture....

Affectors are primarily creators of dancehall culture and affectees are primarily consumers of dancehall culture...

The Affectors: Creators of Dancehall Culture...

Song creators engage in the creation of the lyrics and the rhythms that form the foundation of dancehall music....

Sound system operators own and/or operate the mobile sound systems that travel locally, regionally and internationally to provide music and hype for dancehall events....

Promoters/producers provide the economic backing and support for the staging and promotion of dancehall events, the promotion of dancehall artistes and the dissemination of dancehall music locally, regionally and internationally.

Dynamic hype creators are the male and female models, dancers and slang creators in dancehall culture....

Visual creators engage in activities that result in the creation and dissemination of visual images of the dancehall culture....

Deejays/DJs are engaged in the oral performance of dancehall music. One should note that many deejays also function as song creators and promoters/producers. Deejays include several subcategories, a few of which are as follows:

1. *Girls dem deejay:* This subcategory is defined as the male deejay who chiefly engages in the performance of songs that focus on women and their sexuality....
2. *Slackness deejay:* This subcategory is defined as the deejay who chiefly engages in the performance and dissemination of songs that are perceived and labeled as sexually explicit, lewd and vulgar. This subcategory may often, but not always, cut across the above category of the girls dem deejay....
3. *Bad-man deejay:* This subcategory is defined as the deejay who engages chiefly in the dissemination of songs containing graphic descriptions of perceived violent and criminal acts, including illegal gun- and drug-related activity. The ideological orientation of this deejay is usually evidenced by his style of dress as well as his facial contortions and menacing body language during onstage performances....
4. *Rastafari deejay:* A Rastafari deejay overtly subscribes to the religious ideology and world view of Rastafari....

5. *All-rounder deejay:* This subcategory is defined as the deejay who engages in the performance and dissemination of songs that cut across all the foregoing categories without focusing on any one category. . . .

The Affectees: Consumers of Dancehall Culture

The composite categories or typologies of dancehall affectees that I have identified are separated into gendered groups as follows: the female categories are Miss Hotty Hotty, Miss Vogue, Miss Thing and independent ooman/big ooman. The male categories are don/shotta, don youth/yute, freaky hype type and big man/dads/faada/heavy man.

Source: *Donna P. Hope,* Inna di Dancehall: Popular Culture and the Politics of Identity in Jamaica *(Kingston, Jamaica: U of West Indies P, 2006), 26–32.*

Commentary

Dancehall is the evolved form of sound systems that Jamaicans created in the 1950s, to bring recorded music and patter to large groups of people in town squares or in community centers. The description above, updated from the point of view of a performer from Stolzoff's pioneering work (2000), amply demonstrates the high-tech nature of dancehall music. This contemporary "wired" culture has not impeded the spread of folkways; for Jamaicans who participate in dancehall culture, modern technology is in integral part of both the medium and the message of popularized folklore.

A Shanto from Guyana

1. One day I met an old woman selling
And I wanted something to eat
I say I was going to put a bit in she way
But I turn back when I meet
I thought she had bananas, orange or pear
But was nothing that I need
For when I ask the old woman what she was selling
She said she was selling weed
2. She had she coat tie up over she waist
And was stepping along with grace
She had on a pair of old clogs on her feet
And was wriggling down the street
Just then she started to name the different weeds
And I really was more than glad
But I can't remember all that she call
But these were a few she had
3. Man Piaba, Woman Piaba
Tantan Fall Back and Lemon Grass
Minnie Root, Gullie Root, Grannie-Back-Bone, Bitter
Tally, Lime Leaf and Toro
Coolie Bitters, Karile Bush, Flat o' the Earth and Iron Weed
Sweet Broom, Fowl Tongue, Wild Daisy, Sweet Sage, and even Toyo
4. She had Cassava Mumma, Coocoo Piaba, Jacob's Ladder
and Piti Guano
Fingle Bush, Job's Tear, Piti Payi, a Jumbie Bottle
And White Cleary

Bile Bush, Wild Cane, Duck Weed, Aniseed, Wara Bitters
and Wild Gray Root
She even had down to a certain bush Barbajans does call
"Puss in Boot"
5. When I hear how much bush she had
I left dumb till I couldn't even talk
She started to call from Camp Street corner
Never stop til she reach Orange Walk
The woman had me so surprise that I didn't know what to do
That a girl come and gimme a cuff in me eye
And I didn't even know was who
6. Sweet Broom, Sweet Sage, and Lemon Grass
I hear them good for making tea
Oh well, I hear Zèb Grass and Wild Daisy
Is good to cool the body
The woman tongue was even listed [lisped]
And she was calling out all the time
She even had a little kanwa eye [cast eye]
And the other that left was blind
7. She had Bitter Guma, Portogee Bumboh, Congo
Lana and Twelve o'clock Broom
Sarsaparilla, Wild Tomato, Soursop Leaf and Hafabit Weed
Yoruba Leaf, Sweet Pinpota Bush, White Fleary and Christmas Bush
Scotch and Sandies and even Monkey Ladder and
All the rest you may need
8. She had Fat Bush, Elder Bush, Black Pepper Bush
French Toyo, Qupera, and Capadulla
Tamarind Leaf, Money Bush, Soldier Fork Leaf, Pumpkin
Blossom and even Devil Dua
Leeman, Congo Pom, Pingalor, Physic Nut and
Lily Root
In fact the only bush that she didn't got
Was bush in he everyday suit

Source: "West Indian Weed Woman," Bill Rogers, Bluebird B-4938, NY Friday, November 19, 1934.

Commentary

This song was composed by Bill Rogers (Augustus Hinds), a Guyanese entertainer who performed in theaters in the Eastern Caribbean. He dubbed his type of song "shanto," a Guyanese version of Trinidadian calypso. Some of the verses and the general sense of the song are found in folk versions elsewhere in the Caribbean, some of which were influenced by Rogers' several recordings of the song.

The "West Indian Weed Woman" is an herbal merchant who roamed the streets of Georgetown, Guyana, selling her leaves, spices, roots, and other natural, traditional medicines. Some herbs cured the body while others cured the mind (Gaskin 2006).

Dance

The Calinda

In Louisiana... [the Calinda] ... was always a grossly personal satirical ballad, and it was the favorite dance all the way from there to Trinidad. To dance it publicly is not allowed this side the West Indies. All this Congo Square business was suppressed at one time; 1843, says tradition.

The Calinda was a dance of multitude, a sort of vehement cotillion. The contortions of the encircling crowd were strange and terrible, the din was hideous. One Calinda is still familiar to all Creole ears; it has long been a vehicle for the white Creole's satire; for generations the man of municipal politics was fortunate who escaped entirely a lampooning set to its air.

In my childhood I used, at one time, to hear, every morning, a certain black *marchande des calas*—peddler woman selling rice croquettes—chanting the song as she moved from street to street at the sunrise hour with her broad, shallow, laden basket balanced on her head...

"It was in a stable that they had this gala night," says the song; "the horses here were greatly astonished. Preval was captain; his coachman, Louis, was master of ceremonies. There were Negresses made prettier than their mistresses by adornments stolen from the ladies' wardrobes (*armoires*). But the jailer found it all so funny that he proposed to himself to take an unexpected part; the watchmen came down—"

No official exaltation bought immunity from the jeer of the Calinda. Preval was a magistrate. Stephen Mazureau, in is attorney general's office, the song likened to a bullfrog in a bucket of water. A page might be covered by the roll of victims. The masters winked at these gross but harmless liberties and, as often as any others, added stanzas of their own invention.

The Calinda ended these dissipations of the summer Sabbath afternoons. They could not run far into the night, for all the fascinations of all the dances could not excuse the slave's tarrying in public places after a certain other *bou-djoum!* (that was not of the Calinda, but of the regular nine-o'clock evening gun) had rolled down Orleans Street from the Place d'Armes; and the black man or woman who wanted to keep a whole skin on the back had to keep out of the Calaboose. Times have changed, and there is nothing to be regretted in the change that has come over Congo Square. Still a glamour hangs over its dark past. There is the pathos of slavery, the poetry of the weak oppressed by the strong, and of limbs that danced after toil, and barbaric love-making. The rags and seminakedness, the bamboula drum, the dance, and almost the banjo, are gone; but the *bizarre* melodies and dark lovers' apostrophes live on. (Cable 1959, 388–90)

Source: *George W. Cable,* Creoles and Cajuns: Stories of Old Louisiana, *ed. Arlin Turner (Garden City, N.Y.: Doubleday Anchor, 1959).*

Commentary

Cable's not-always-accurate and racist account of the nature of the Calinda song and dance is instructive. It shows that Calinda lyrics capture the sense of topical, even critical, songs existed in slavery times. Such songs continue to be extremely widespread throughout the area and are found in many different genres. Describing carnival songs in Martinique, Henry Edward Krehbiel wrote: "These satirical songs spring up like poisonous fungi" (quoted in Hill 1993, 1).

***The Lajabeless* (The Devil Woman)**

For a night and a day Nabadeen was lost
Mountain and rivers, he had to cross
For a night and a day, Nabadeen was lost
Mountain and rivers he had to cross

Ladjablès chayé li alé.
[The Devil Woman took him away]
This is the story of Nabadeen
Of St. James village he was highly esteem
With his book in hand, he went by a stream

Ladjablès chayé li alé.
On a log of wood he sat by the ground
When suddenly darkness came around
Strange whispering came to his ear

Ladjablès chayé li alé.
She led him over mountain, valleys and plain
If he would slide, he surely would break his brain
She led him over many precipice and rocks

Ladjablès chayé li alé.
She hypnotize him with her magic spell

The Indian laddie had such a fright
He was led away by a woman in white
This is the rumor they heard next day:

And unfortunately he began to dream
He, being a student of human nature
He went to study his literature
This is the rumor they heard next day

Saying, "Go back home, young man, be aware!"
But the awful voice of the woman in white
That gave him such a serious fright
That is the rumor they heard next day

That his body should feel some electric shock
There must have been some angel by his side
Or otherwise he would have died
That is the rumor they heard next day

As though she were a devil from the gates of hell
Her eyes were large like goblets of fire

And she said, "Let us climb up
higher!"
She led him to a room that was like
a tomb
There Nabadeen nearly met his
doom
That is the rumor they heard next
day
Ladjablès chayé li alé.

Source: from "The Lajebeless Woman–Calypso" (Philip Garcia), Decca 78rpm record, BCD 16623–2/5, Lord Executor: acc. Harmony Kings' Orchestra, recorded in Trinidad on March 1, 1938.

Commentary

The lajabeless is a beautiful woman with one human and one cloven foot, which she hides with a long, white dress. She chases after young men at night, hoping to lure one to a cliff and scare him into falling off. If he escapes she yells at him as he runs off, "You lucky! You lucky I didn't catch you!"

SEASONAL FESTIVALS AND OTHER EVENTS

1. Day of the Kings

Up until the law of abolition of slavery, that is, until 1880, there was one day, January 6 of each year, when both the free and the slave Afro-Cuban negroes celebrated their festival; in the Catholic Church it was epiphany, the Adoration of the Three Magi, commonly called Día de Reyes, "Day of the Kings."

The "Day of the Kings" was a free day for the Africans in Cuba, and the creole negroes were equally enthusiastic in joining the clamor of celebrations....

That day, black Africa, its people, its costumes, its music, its tongues, its song and dance, its ceremonies, its religions and political institutions, were brought across the Atlantic to Cuba, especially Havana. The tyranny and might of slavery that coldly separated parents and children, husbands and wives, brothers and sisters, compatriots, was for one day mitigated as the negroes came together in the streets, with their own, with those of their tribe, their caravels, proud in the ceremonial attire of their land, venting their rousing monotonous African chant, charging the air with the noise of their drums and their bells and other primitive instruments, enjoying above all an illusion of freedom, in an orgy of ritual, dance, music, song and cane spirit....

Cuban scholar Ramón Meza has left us this full description of the "Day of the Kings."

> From daybreak, all over can be heard the monotonous beat of those big drums made out of hollowed tree trunk and covered on one end by a patch of ox-hide tempered by fire. The house servants would leave very early in the morning. The plantation slaves would come in from the nearby estates: some jammed into rear railroad wagons, others crammed onto carts that carried the enormous

barrels of sugar, and not a few came on foot. All were hurrying to join their respective *cabildos* whose chief was generally the elder of the tribe or *nation* to which they belonged.

All around, circles would be formed. The enormous drums would be placed to one side as the battery; astraddle, the drummers, tirelessly beating the taut ox-hide with their callused hands, to which were attached hollow metal or wooden spheres, filled with small stones and decorated with feathers, shaking their shoulders, grinding their teeth, their eyes half-closed, as if possessed with ineffable fulfillment. Two or three couples would dance in the middle, going into the most extravagant contortions, jumping and whirling, their steps in tune to the wild drum beat. The joy and agitation bordered on frenzy. The captain, that poor broken-down bundle of flesh, bone and nerves, surely relived the days of his youth; for he not only shouted till he was hoarse but often delighted in joining the group of dancers. The one bearing the banderole would blaze it over the group. The profusion of peacock feathers on the heads of dancers, quivering from their agile movements, shone with metallic iridescence in the glaring sunlight that bore heavily down on that motley crew. The tiny mirrors on the hats, the sequins and the lamé of the costumes, the large earrings of polished gold dangling from ebony ears, the collection boxes passed around for the *aguinaldo,* the cutlasses, they all glinted, as dazzling to the sight as the noise was deafening to the ear. Looks sparkled on those faces of pure African race; red mouths and pointed white teeth opened to let out wild shouts and laughs. Bells, drums, horns *rayos,* triangles and huge gourd rattles accompanied the voices to a deafening pitch.

At midday, the merriment was at its height. On Mercaderes, Obispo and O'Reilly Streets, there was a continuous procession of *diablitos,* all making their way to the Plaza de Armas. The place was soon crowded and it was hardly possible to pass by Government Palace. Onlookers packed the balconies and the sidewalks and climbed the bases of columns, windows and stone balconies surrounding the square. The rows of laurel trees with their spreading dark-green foliage, the variegated and flowering shrubs of the square, the slender palms cutting an elegant panache silhouette against the purest blue sky, the sailors of all nations coming down in groups to watch half-bewildered such an exotic sight, the soldiers guarding the nearby buildings, the many flags flying in the wind and the thousand and one colors adorning the negroes' attire, in all truth, painted a picturesque spectacle. In turn, *cabildos* would come into the Palace courtyard. There the vaults resounded for many hours with the thunderous drumbeat, wild chant and enthusiastic cheers of the Africans. And while below the dancers demonstrated the best of their skills, the captain of each *cabildos,* pointed hat tucked under his arm, sack across his chest; the standard-bearer, his standard resting against his shoulder; and the teller with his tin box all went up the Palace stairs in the most orderly fashion and, vociferously professing their loyalty, received at least half an ounce in gold for the collection. That day the

Palace was demonstrably generous. From the windows rained cigars and coin pieces of varying value, onto which hundreds of hands avidly hurled themselves in dispute. The old negro women, the most expressive or the most nervous, were the ones who most shook on high their hollow gourd rattles covered in netting, delirious almost in asking god to watch over and preserve for many years the health of His Excellency the Governor General.

Then they would leave the Palace to make room for the others to file in, in perfect order: the *Congo* and *Lucumí,* with their great feathered hats, blue-striped shirts and red percale pants; the *Arará,* with their cheeks lacerated from cuts and branding iron, covered in shells, crocodile and dog teeth, threaded bone and glass beads, the dancers from the waist down in a voluminous vegetable-fiber hooped skirt; the *Mandingo,* very fancy in their wide pants, short jackets and blue or pink silk turbans, embroidered with marabou; and the many others with the difficult names and whimsical costumes that were not entirely in the style of those of Africa but changed and modified by civilized industry.

But not all the negroes joined the *cabildos,* which the creoles and certain of those belonging to the nation thought the less of. Rather than attire themselves in the outlandish dress that made up the costumes of their countrymen, they would dress as Paris dandies. Elegance consisted in the exaggeration of fashion, which is why the weaker sex showed a preference for ribbons, baubles, tassles [*sic*], large earrings, fancy shawls, a profusion of rings, bracelets, and contrasting bright colors. In the stronger sex this preference found marked form in wide collars, frilled shirtfronts, large cravats and a choice of the most brightly colored jacket and pantaloons. Others would be dressed as sailors, carrying a small, constantly moving boat on a piece of crumpled canvas, painted green and white, representing the sea spray and waves, asking for their *aguinaldo* at more or less acceptable intervals. Others were on their own, dressed as minstrels, getting their money through clowning. A good many carried glass-cased Virgins of Regla or Brown Virgins of El Cobre, replete with ribbons and offerings, using them to personally profit on the candid devotion of others.

In the more distant parts of the city and on the less crowded streets, *ñáñigos* did as they pleased, their rough cloaks somewhat reminiscent of the gown of Holy Office, but so big and bulky that arms and legs were like simple side appendages. All the gross and barbaric imagination of the African tribes was carried to an extreme with the *ñáñingo* [*sic*]. The institutions, the symbols and dress were all highly repugnant. It was a sight to see the wild mass following from among the lowest class of people, regardless of age, sex and race, for that ridiculous feathered symbolic figurehead to each of those fierce groupings gorged on cane spirit and cock's blood, who, according to public hearsay, could swear a mortal wound on any human breast. The other tribes drew attention for their picturesque, exotic song, costume and dance: everything about the *ñáñigos* was wild, somber, and nauseous. Replete with daggers and knives, they marched slowly, not in formation but grouped behind the dancers, who were incessant in their offensive convulsions, shaking the many bells tied around their waists. And when two, on the whole enemy groupings of this nature met, for they would always be declaring war on one another, the war would be on and in the fighting there would ensue ferociously cruel wounds and killings.

Source: *Fernando Ortiz, introducing Ramón Meza's description of the "Day of the Kings," ann. and trans. Jean Stubbs in 1993. 2001. "The Afro-Cuban Festival 'Day of the Kings,'" in Judith Bettelheim, ed.,* Cuban Festivals: A Century of Afro-Cuban Culture, *1–5. (Princeton, N.J.: Markus Wiener).*

Commentary

Among other things, the "Day of the Kings" was a way for enslaved and freed Africans to perform for their community, to lay claim to their specific African or Creole identities, and to generally have a good time (and even to settle scores). Cabildos are clubs of African slaves in Cuba whose membership is determined by African ethnicity or groups of people who were enslaved in Africa and shipped to Cuba from the same port. The ñáñigos are members of the Abakuá secret society, a male order that originated in the Calabar region of southeastern Nigeria.

Muḥarram and Hosay

Each year during the first ten days of Muḥarram *(al-muharram),* the first month of the Islamic lunar calendar, Shi'i Muslims throughout the world join in a common observance to commemorate the martyrdom of the Prophet Muhammad's grandson, the *imām* Husayn. Husayn died in the seventh century on the plains of Karbala, in what is now contemporary Iraq. The dramatic commemoration, known variously as *ta'zīyeh* in Iran, Muḥarram in India, and *Hosay* in Trinidad, is the focal point in the religious life of the Shi'i mourning community. Because Imam Husayn's suffering and death is seen as the most important tragedy in history, the annual reactualization of the event is the central Shi'i ritual observance of the year. Muḥarram is a metahistorical phenomenon because the observance related to it makes possible individual identification with, and direct experience of, Imam Husayn's vicarious suffering. During the observance, subjective apprehension is not spatially and temporally bound, for the historical battle that occurred in 61 A.H./680 C.E. is made present through the pious actions of Shi'i Muslims the world over. . . . (1)

3. *Hosay* in Trinidad

The Trinidadian style of commemorating Husayn's martyrdom seems very different from the Iranian and Indian forms at first glance, and much of the scarce literature on the rite makes ample mention of its purported creole nature. A closer look at the complex event reveals continuities with its older counterparts, constantly reminding us of its north Indian sources of origin. *Hosay,* as it is expressed today, is a direct by-product of earlier

Early twentieth-century postcard of Hosay Tadjahs in Trinidad.

muharram observances that were brought to Trinidad by indentured East Indians who came to work on plantations as early as May 30, 1845. However, although the Indian origins of the rite can be observed clearly in Trinidad, there is no question that the ritual performance has gone through a fairly lengthy process of indigenization. . . .

While Trinidadian Shi'i Muslims ideally show emotion for Husayn through public displays of drumming to signify the incidents pertaining to Husayn's death and through the painstaking construction of the model tombs known as *tadjahs,* we also find that the observance becomes marked by gaiety and celebration for the revelers who participate in the public processions as audience members. . . .

The craftsmen and others associated with the forty-day preparation of *Hosay* do not condone the merrymaking on the streets during the public processions. Nonetheless, the historical transformation of *muharram* from a predominantly solemn observance to a public celebration is a distinctive process on the island. It marks the event as a characteristic form of Trinidadian performance. Through it, East Indians participate in Creole culture, but they also reassert their own Indian ethnic identity by performing a tradition that is perceived to have come to Trinidad from India in an unaltered state. The various uses and understandings of tradition as something unchanging and frozen in time are a vehicle for the ongoing negotiation of ethnicity in a relatively new and multicultural nation-state. (6–7)

Source: *Frank J. Korom,* Hosay Trinidad: Muharram Performances in an Indo-Caribbean Diaspora *(Philadelphia: U of Pennsylvania P, 2003).*

Commentary

Indians came to Trinidad from British India beginning in 1845 and worked as indentured laborers following the abolition of slavery, when a new agricultural population was needed to replace enslaved people of African descent. In recent years Trinidad, with a population that identifies itself as approximately 40 percent of Indian descent and 40 percent of African descent, the rise of Indo-Trinidadians to political equity with Afro-Trinidadians has resulted in a rivalry that has been largely peaceful but emotionally charged. By whatever name one calls it, the Indian-based cultural traditions are undergoing "transculturalization" with the Creole traditions and are in the process of, perhaps, forming for the first time on the island a national culture that is more than Creole culture. This can be seen in the cross-pollination of Creole Carnival with chutney calypso and with the participation of Afro-Trinidadians in Hosay.

Rara in Haiti

One Rara band that I often followed in downtown Port-au-Prince started the evening with a religious ritual that activated the spirits and asked them to work on behalf of the band. The band members gathered around a small bonfire outside the Vodou temple that was their base. They knelt over a rope and a rock, using techniques of travay maji (magical work) to "tie up" the other neighborhood Rara bands who were their competitors. As they sang songs to the spirits, the band members one by one bathed their torsos and heads in a special infusion of medicinal leaves. This instructed the spirits to afford them protection against spirits working for other bands, as well as against any physical violence.

After the ceremony, we danced into the streets as the band played a song for Ogou, the lwa (spirit) of militarism and discipline. The song was a common one, straight out of the Port-au-Prince Vodou repertoire and easily recognizable. We were having a good time, moving quickly, and I felt the exhilaration of taking over the streets of the capital with sound and bodies in motion. Dancing a lively two-step down the middle of the street, I felt that we owned the air itself. The bamboo horns electrified the black night of the unlit city with sparks of sound. The band was moving through one of the most central, most crowded areas of the city, an area that was a stronghold of support for President Aristide, who had been ousted in the coup d'état. "Ogou Badagri, what are you doing?" roared the crowds song.

Then several things happened at once. The tune changed abruptly: "Marie, where did you go? I have nowhere to put my big dick." All of a sudden the Rara band was singing a betiz song, a vulgar ditty out of last month's Carnival. Phenel, my field assistant, yelled to me, "Liza, Babylon is here," using the term that the downtown street culture had picked up from the Rastafari movement to signify the military or their atache agents. Sure enough, a military atache stepped from behind a pillar to confront the reveler. As Phenel grabbed me by the shoulders and took us both down to the pavement, the atache open-fired on the entire Rara band with a semiautomatic rifle. Either the protective baths were working, or the atache intended simply to frighten us, because nobody was hit. After a brief panic, the band was up and streaming down a side street away from "Babylon."

Moments later, everyone paused to rest and drink kleren (cane liquor). "What was that?" I panted to Phenel as we swigged liberally from the liquor bottle that passed our way. The cold heat of the raw, fermented cane helped calm our nerves. As he lit a cigarette, Phenel's eyes met mine in the brief glow of match-light. "That militaire didn't like us singing for Ogou," he replied in a low voice. "Ogou stands for the army, you know, so to them, any song for Ogou could be talking bad about the military. The songleader tried to switch to betiz, but it was too late." My mind raced with questions, but the music started up again. Despite having a close call with a spray of bullets, the band set off down the narrow streets of Port-au-Prince, merrily singing the vulgar songs of Carnival.

Source: *Elizabeth McAlister,* Rara! Vodou, Power, and Performance in Haiti and Its Diaspora *(Berkeley: U of California P, 2002), 8–9.*

Commentary

Collecting folklore is not always a parlor activity of collecting old tales or songs; here Elizabeth McAlister and her Haitian friend risk their lives by following a rara Carnival band at a time of political turmoil. This is the one major Caribbean Carnival that takes place *during* Lent, not immediately before Lent. Blessed by Vodou gods, rara bands are filled with bamboo trumpets and other instruments and costumed performers. They sing risqué, politically charged, or other topical songs while large groups of ordinary revelers press against the rara bands as they move down the street, stopping for a while at favored places, such as in front of a church or a town square.

WORKS CITED

Abrahams, Roger D. 1983. *The Man-of-Words in the West Indies: Performance and the Emergence of Creole Culture*. Baltimore: Johns Hopkins UP.

Anonymous. n.d. "III. Indian Culture and Its Transformations in Trinidad," http://www.sscnet.ucla.edu/southasia/Diaspora/athome.html.

Bascom, William. 1977. "Ọba's Ear: A Yoruba Myth in Cuba and Brazil." In *African Folklore in the New World*, ed. Daniel J. Crowley. Austin: U of Texas P.

Bierhorst, John, ed. 2002. *Latin American Folktales: Stories from Hispanic and Indian Traditions*. New York: Pantheon.

Brown, David H. 2003. *Santería Enthroned: Art, Ritual, and Innovation in an Afro-Cuban Religion*. Chicago: U of Chicago P.

Cable, George W. 1959. "The Dance in Place Congo." In *Creoles and Cajuns: Stories of Old Louisiana,* ed. Arlin Turner. Garden City, N.Y.: Doubleday Anchor Books. (Orig. pub. in *Century Magazine*, February and April 1886.)

Courlander, Harold. 1996. *A Treasury of Afro-American Folklore: The Oral Literature, Traditions, Recollections, Legends, Tales, Songs, Religious Beliefs, Customs, Sayings, and Humor of Peoples of African Descent in the Americas.* New York: Smithmark.

DeCamp, David. 1968. "Mock Bidding in Jamaica." In *Tire Shrinker to Dragster,* ed. Wilson J. Hudson. Austin: Encino Press.

Gaskin, Molly R. 2006. *Medicinal Plants of Trinidad and Tobago and the Caribbean.* Trinidad: Pointe-a-Pierre Wild Fowl Trust.

Herskovits, Melville. 1971. *Life in a Haitian Valley.* Garden City, N.Y.: Doubleday. (Orig. pub. 1937.)

Hill, Donald R. 2005. "A Carriacouan View of the African Diaspora: 'African' Themes in the Paintings of Canute Caliste." *Calabash: A Journal of Caribbean Arts and Letters* 3, no. 2 (Fall/Winter).

Hope, Donna P. 2006. *Inna di Dancehall: Popular Culture and the Politics of Identity in Jamaica.* Kingston, Jamaica: U of the West Indies P.

Ibekwe, Patrick. 1998. *Wit and Wisdom of Africa: Proverbs from Africa and the Caribbean.* Oxford: New Internationalist Publications.

Korom, Frank J. 2003. *Hosay Trinidad: Muharram Performances in an Indo-Caribbean Diaspora.* Philadelphia: U of Pennsylvania P.

Liverpool, Hollis "Chalkdust." 2003. *From the Horse's Mouth: Stories of the History and Development of the Calypso.* Diego Martin, Trinidad: Juba.

Mitchell, Joseph. 2001. "Houdini's Picnic." In *McSorley's Wonderful Saloon,* New York: Pantheon Books, 1992 253–266. (Orig. pub. in the *New Yorker*, May 6, 1939, 61–71.)

Ortiz, Fernando. 2001. "The Afro-Cuban Festival 'Day of the Kings.'" In *Cuban Festivals: A Century of Afro-Cuban Culture*, ed. Judith Bettelheim. Princeton, N.J.: Markus Wiener. (Article orig. pub. 1960.)

Pollitzer, William S. 2005. *The Gullah People and Their African Heritage.* Athens: U of Georgia P. (Orig. pub. 1999.)

Stolzoff, Norman C. 2000. *Wake the Town and Tell the People: Dancehall Culture in Jamaica.* Durham, N.C.: Duke UP.

Turner, Lorenzo Dow. 1973. *Africanisms in the Gullah Dialect.* Ann Arbor: UP of Michigan. (Orig. pub. 1949.)

Four

Scholarship and Approaches

Relatively few Caribbeanists are formally trained folklorists, anthropologists, or ethnomusicologists. More often, aficionados of Caribbean folklore have come from other fields. Therefore, some devotees use broad humanistic theories. The methods and theories concerning folklore have been ethnographic/descriptive, historical, performance oriented, everyday-life studies, Creolist, and interpretive (postmodern). Often, several methods and theoretical approaches are used together to examine a genre of Caribbean folklore.

Examination of the approaches to Caribbean folklore reveals a pattern. Anecdotal or purely descriptive uses of folklore may seem to lack a theoretical basis, and highly theoretical studies may have very little actual folklore content. Therefore, descriptive or ethnographic studies that accurately express a folklore genre tend to hold up well over time and are not susceptible to theoretical fads. Furthermore, theoretical insights may be so abstract and speculative that they say little about actual beliefs and behavior and may not attend to a broader range of data that a descriptive account of a folklore genre is able to cover. On the other hand, bits and pieces of Caribbean folklore that have not been well documented, or extremely detailed studies, may tell us little about the larger picture, something that theory can do well. Theoretical studies may be insightful and make a major contribution to understanding Caribbean culture.

Each approach to the folklore of the Caribbean is a product of a historical moment in the study of Caribbean people. That is, folklore theory is culture bound by the time and place in which it developed. The ethnographic and historical studies of the Caribbean, carried out by students of Franz Boas, were dominant in the first half of the twentieth century and were especially important at universities on both coasts of the United States. In the late 1960s, historical approaches

Striking the drum at the Fortress, Puerto Plata, Dominican Republic. This postcard from the early 1900s shows Creolized Dominicans playing European band instruments.

were supplemented by performance-oriented ethnography of periodic festivals and individual rites of passage (such as baptism, confirmation, marriage, funerary practices). Folklorists at the University of Texas at Austin and at the University of Pennsylvania continue to be especially strong in performance-centered folklore studies. By the 1980s, scholars and critics influenced by Clifford Geertz's interpretative theory and by Stuart Hall's postcolonial theory utilized folklore to achieve wide yet subjective understandings of the postcolonial world. Two Caribbean writers won the Nobel Prize in Literature: Derek Walcott in 1992 and V. S. Naipaul in 2001. Both have used Caribbean folklore to great effect, although in the case of Naipaul mainly early in his long career.

More recently, especially in Great Britain, Creole theories focusing on adaptive Creole culture rather than African origins have gained influence in Atlantic studies programs. In a parallel development, orthographies of Creole languages have added to the debate concerning the conditions that led to their development and about whether such languages owe much to African or Western European languages or whether they should simply be studied as unique situational communication.

BRONISLAW MALINOWSKI, FRANZ BOAS, AND EARLY ETHNOGRAPHIC APPROACHES TO FOLKLORE

Ethnography is the study of the way of life, or some part thereof, of a group of people. It consists of conducting fieldwork by living with those people and noting what they say and what they do. At the end of the nineteenth century and the beginning of the twentieth century, ethnographic methods developed in England and the United States at about the same time. Polish-born British social anthropologist, Bronislaw Malinowski lived in the Trobriand Islands, off the east coast of New Guinea, for several years in the 1910s. He practiced a kind of fieldwork called participant observation, and his theory of society is called functionalism. This approach was to live among the people he studied—relatively cut off from his Western roots—and annotate the lives of Trobriand Islanders as he participated, to a limited degree, in their daily activities. In his field notes and in his many publications over the years, he documented their basic institutions: economic, trade, political, social, and religious systems that he believed made up a society (he did not use the term *culture*, although his notion of what constituted society was close to how American anthropologists used *culture*). He thought that these social institutions "hang together" in a totality—that is, society—and that as any one institution changed, the other institutions of society changed.

A couple of decades earlier, in the United States, German immigrant Franz Boas studied the culture of the Inuit (Eskimos). Later, and for most of the remainder of his life, he studied the indigenous people of the northwest coast of North America. Boas spent months at a time with the Kwakiutl Indians, not the continuous years that Malinowski lived in the Trobriands. Even more than Malinowski, however, the message he conveyed to his students was to go out into the preindustrial world and document as much as you can, before all is lost to industrialization.

Boas founded modern anthropology in the United States by combining the study of language, archaeology, human biology, and culture into a single discipline. He was also a founder of the American Folklore Society. Today, scholars no longer attempt to study all these fields, although many schools still require some work in each discipline (except folklore!) as part of a PhD in anthropology.

Boas's idea was to document everything he could about a group of people. He felt it did not matter what you studied first; it would all come together in a cultural "whole." His fieldwork was especially strong in the documentation of folktales and other oral traditions, architecture, craft, ritual, and dance. The Boasian tradition of scholarship is alive today in the research of postmodern scholars in many fields, including cultural anthropology, ethnomusicology, and folklore.

Boas felt that as Europeans and North Americans spread around the world, establishing colonies in many countries and encouraging diverse peoples to take up Europeanized culture and religion, many valued local traditions were being lost. He did not trust the colonizers or missionaries to document reliably how so-called Third World people lived. There was a need for well-trained fieldworkers to write accurate, objective ethnographies or studies of peoples' lifeways, paying special attention to the local people's views of their own culture. This technique is called relativism, and it is an essential method in cultural anthropology today, just as Malinowski's "participant observation" has continued to be an important field technique.

Boas went so far as to suggest that most accounts of a people before the professional ethnographer arrived were useless, since they were likely to be highly biased. This was a faulty judgment on Boas's part; not only were anthropologists also biased to some degree but historical documents written before anthropology turned out to be very useful, if one knows the perspective from which they are written.

Nevertheless, the rules that Boas and Malinowski set down for objective study of the people of the world were good ones, even if they could not be completely maintained in practice. Today, however, postmodern scholars claim that objectivity is not possible, since one's biases always intervene. However, these same scholars owe a debt to Boas on other grounds, especially in carrying out the method of relativism to its logical conclusion: that every culture should be studied by its own lights and every culture is as worthy of study as every other culture. Others, including this author, believe that there is still a place for objective folklore studies, even with a relativist method.

Like most anthropologists and folklorists today, Boas was an egalitarian; he thought that people had essentially similar capabilities. What made them different—and cultures could differ greatly—was their separate histories. The job of the ethnographer was to document those histories accurately. The practice of ethnography would lead to a series of objective studies that would show historical links between peoples. Through these links, Boas hoped to replace the speculative cultural evolution model of the nineteenth century, which assumed that cultures evolved through a series of stages, somewhat independent of other cultures.

HISTORICAL APPROACHES TO CARIBBEAN FOLKLORE

It is only natural that a historical approach would dominate Caribbean folklore theory, since folklore is tradition and tradition only exists when culture is passed on through time. The first great scholar of note concerning the folklore of the Caribbean was Fernando Ortiz. Trained as a lawyer, his intellectual bent turned to documenting Cuban culture, from the point of view of criminology (Stubbs, translator's preface to Ortiz's "The Afro-Cuban Festival 'Day of the Kings,'" in Bettelheim 2001). His first major book on Afro-Cuban culture was *Los Negros Brujos* (Black Magicians, 1995b). First published in 1906, *Los Negros Brujos* was a critique of Afro-Cuban magic, which he condemned (Moore 1997, 34). The book also was one of the first studies in the Caribbean of the African origins of Afro-Caribbean people. Even though his studies may be considered paternalistic toward Afro-Cubans by today's standards, Ortiz eventually became a champion of Afro-Cuban culture and a leader in the movement to recognize its importance in Cuban life. Most of his books and essays consisted of historical studies and contemporary descriptions of Black Cuban culture. His research anticipated that of Melville Herskovits in that he was the first scholar to trace the parts of Africa that contributed to Afro-Caribbean customs. His works are the most detailed studies that have been made of Afro-Cuban culture. Because of his extensive publications, knowledge of many folkloric customs that no longer exist has been preserved. *Los Negros Esclavos* (Black Slaves) was published in 1916. This book covers the period of black slavery in Cuba and points to the negative effects of slavery. *Un Catauro de Cubanismos* (Cuban Slang, 1923) was his first important work on the Afro-Cuban contributions to Cuban Spanish. His most famous book is *Contrapunteo Cubano del Tabaco y el Azúcar* (1940; translated into English as *Cuban Counterpoint: Tobacco and Sugar*, 1995a). It predates the structuralism of the French anthropologist Claude Lévi-Strauss in that Ortiz metaphorically contrasts the impact of the cultivation of sugar cane and tobacco on Cuban culture. It also explains Ortiz's most complete analysis of transculturalization. *La Africanía de la Música Folklórica de Cuba* (Africanisms in Folkloric Cuban Music, 1950), *Los Bailes y el Teatro de los Negros en el Folklore de Cuba* (Dances and Theater of the Blacks in Cuban Folklore, 1951), and *Los Instrumentos de la Música Afrocubana* (Afrocuban Instruments, 1952–1955), taken together, are the most complete studies ever attempted of the music, dance, instruments, and folk theater of a Caribbean people. Recently, Ortiz's "The Afro-Cuban Festival 'Day of Kings'" (in Bettelheim 2001, 1–40) was been published in English, augmented by David H. Brown's "The Afro-Cuban Festival 'Day of the Kings': An Annotated Glossary" (Bettelheim 2001, 41–93). The article and a glossary document a festival in which slaves participated annually on January 6, one that mixed Christianity with African religions. Ortiz's detailed ethnography of the festival, based on a historical document, is rich in folkloric content.

In addition to his scholarly studies, Ortiz became a guiding light of the Afro-Cubismo cultural movement among Cuban artists and intellectuals that began in the 1920s. In the 1940s, he coined the term *transculturalization*. He also rejected the concept of acculturation, as used by Herskovits and others, since the latter term implied that change was unidirectional, from the dominant culture to the dominated culture. *Transculturalization* instead refers to an exchange of cultural traditions, as has occurred in Cuban between African and Hispanic culture in Cuba (see Moore 1997, 167).

Although W.E.B. Du Bois pioneered the study of black culture in the United States a generation earlier, the formal study of the African connection to Afro-American cultures throughout the hemisphere at the university level began in the United States in the 1920s with the work of Melville Herskovits. Herskovits was a student of Boas and, like his mentor, focused on historical studies. He was interested in the formal study of African societies (his Ph.D. dissertation was on the "East African Cattle Complex") and in African influences on the cultures of the Americas, not in Native Americans or so-called tribal peoples from other parts of the world. In 1927, Herskovits took a job at Northwestern University in the sociology department, as that department's only anthropologist (Anonymous, http://www.library.northwestern.edu/africana/herskovits.html). He became the school's first chair of the newly created Department of Anthropology in 1928, and in 1948, Northwestern established the first program in African studies at a major university in the United States. Herskovits became the first chair of the Department of African Studies in 1961, two years before his death. At the time, it was felt that there was very little retention of African culture in the Americas. In any event, retention of African culture would be counterproductive to African Americans, since, it was thought, African culture was inferior to European culture and its extension, white American culture.

In the notes to their brief visit to the Saramaka (a maroon group that lived in the then colony of Dutch Guiana, now the country of Surinam), Melville sketches his approach to the African-influenced cultures of the Americas (Price and Price 2003). His historical approach was broadly similar to theories expressed by Alfred Kroeber, one of Boas's first students, and later by Herskovits's comrades Ralph Linton and Robert Redfield, members of the first full generation of university-trained anthropologists in the United States. What these Boasian scholars[1] maintained was that any culture was made up of minimal characteristics, or traits, which could spread more or less independently or in clusters from one group of people to another. The idea was to examine and list those traits and group them into culture areas, or groups of related cultures. Cultures were historically related to each other when they shared certain traits. Such "culture areas" tended to exist in ecologically similar zones so that people who lived in grasslands, for example, tended to share characteristics relating to the exploitation of their environment, while people who lived on a seacoast tended to share traits that were useful in fishing. However, they could not be considered ecological anthropologists—save for one of their ranks, Julian Steward, who developed ecological ideas—since the overriding factor in determining what traits made up a particular culture within a culture area was based on their shared history, not their local environment.

Herskovits applied the concept of the culture area to Africa, which he divided into regions of similar culture. But he spent most of his career establishing a theory that would explain under what conditions African cultural traits could be

1. Although Boas's ideas engendered many theories among his students, he did not subscribe to this version of historical anthropology that Herskovits and others developed, thinking always that the time for theory would come later, after solid ethnographies of the world's peoples had been written.

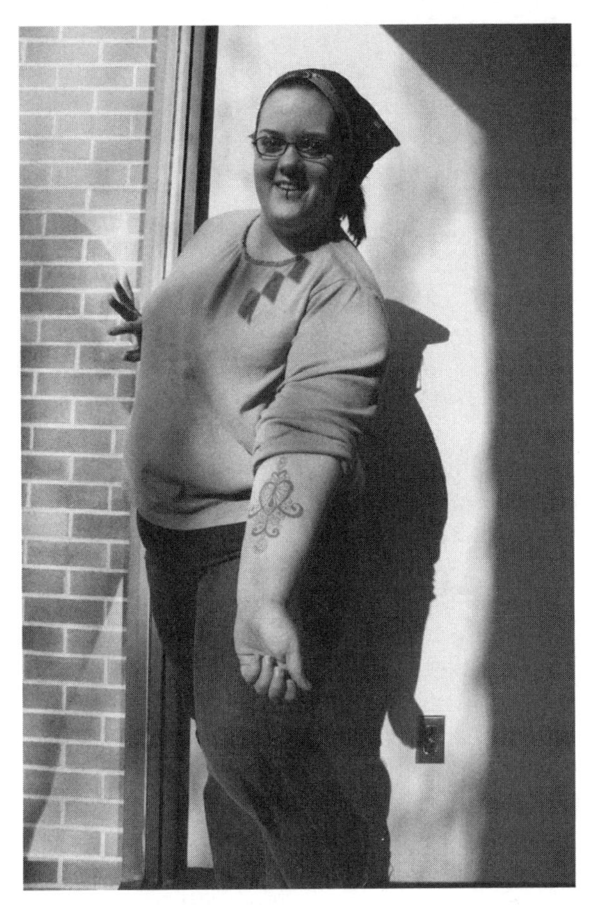

New York college student Shelly Olmstead has a stylized Vodou Veve symbol tattooed on her arm for the goddess Erzulie, Oneonta, New York, 2007. This illustrates the spread of West African symbols in the Americas. Photo credit: Don Hill.

retained in the Americas, what conditions would lead to a loss of African culture, and what conditions would lead to a mix of African and European (as well as, perhaps, Native American) cultures in the Americas. He thought most African retentions would occur in those areas of culture that were least affected by slavery, such as folklore (including some aspects of religion, magic, belief, and music). Most changed—that is, elements of European culture in the Americas that were adopted by people of African descent in the Caribbean—would be agricultural practices, political and legal systems, and trade; that is, the parts of culture most important to the slave owner's needs. Somewhere in the middle would be family systems and social relationships. In this theory, Herskovits used many of the terms developed together with other anthropologists, including *diffusion, culture change, acculturation, retention,* and *syncretism*. Diffusion refers to the spread of culture traits from one culture to another. Culture change refers to any change in a culture that takes place when exposed to another. Acculturation refers to the acceptance of culture traits into a culture when it is undergoing constant contact with another. Retention refers to a particular cultural trait from a culture that otherwise has been greatly modified or lost. For example, a particular West African vocal technique of singing with a raspy voice might be considered an African retention in a Caribbean song that otherwise is based on a European tune. Syncretism, Herskovits's own term, refers to the combination of cultural traits into a new custom that exhibits characteristics borrowed or modified from two distinct, historically unrelated cultures.

Syncretism was perhaps the most controversial of Herskovits's theoretical terms. In a classic example, Herskovits points to Afro-Caribbean religions. For example, in the Afro-Cuban religion called Santería, a particular Roman Catholic saint, such as Santa Barbara, might take on the characteristics of the Yoruba god Shango. Because of syncretism, culture traits that superficially seem to be of European origin might also contain an African retention. For this reason, the role of African culture in the Americas could be more pronounced than earlier scholars thought.

In his classic work, *The Myth of the Negro Past,* Herskovits set down what was then the characteristic "take" on African culture. According to the myth, only the deficient "Negroes" were enslaved; they were though to be childlike and easily manipulated. Since they came from everywhere in Africa, none of their natal culture could possibly survive. If such culture did survive, it was inferior to white culture, which the Negroes wanted to emulate. Therefore, it was claimed, the Negro, unlike supposedly civilized immigrants to the Americas from Europe (especially northwestern Europe), had no past.

His argument against the stereotype was as follows. Negro cultures were various, and some of them were technologically on par with European culture 500 years ago, before the European expansion, which is a relatively recent phenomenon. Also, there was no evidence that the weakest Negroes were enslaved. Herskovits suggested that people taken to the Caribbean and the Americas in chains originated mostly from the western side of Africa, where similar cultures could be grouped into three culture areas (the western Sudan, West Africa, and the Congo basin). Therefore, Africans had as much a past as the European immigrants to the Americas had. That past was rich and varied, yet it had common elements and it was clearly not to be dismissed.

After Fernando Ortiz and Elsie Clews Parsons, Melville Herskovits was one of the first scholars of significance to document traditional Caribbean life, written in a series of ethnographies with his wife, Frances. According to Richard and Sally Price (2003), Frances was the better fieldworker and, in an era that downplayed women's contribution to scholarship, it is noteworthy that she is listed as coauthor of three of their Caribbean and South American ethnographies, *Rebel Destiny, among the Bush Negroes of Dutch Guiana* (1934), *Suriname Folklore* (1936), and *Village Trinidad Village* (1947). Melville Herskovits's other Caribbean book is *Life in a Haitian Valley* (1937). Collectively, these village studies describe the folklife of rural Afro-Caribbean people.

Melville Herskovits was the first major anthropologist to make detailed community studies of people of African descent in the Americas. Moreover, he was one of the first scholars to live in the Afro-Caribbean villages he studied, although for relatively short periods by the standards established by Malinowski in the Trobriand Islands. Although he wanted to document the African heritage in the communities he studied, he was careful to weigh the evidence for such cultural retentions and in no way attempted to minimize the influence of European American cultures on rural Afro-Caribbean customs. Nevertheless, today some scholars consider him to have been an early champion of Afrocentrism, a theory that I will now examine.

AFROCENTRISM

Afrocentrism in the broadest sense is simply recognition of an African heritage, among other cultural strands, in the Americas. In a more dogmatic version, it is a radical diffusionist theory holding that most culturally important traits in the Americas have an African origin. While many scholars accept Afrocentricism in the former sense, only controversial radicals are Afrocentric in its radical interpretation.[2]

As a theory that notes the influence of African culture on Caribbean cultures, an Afrocentric position borrows from Melville Herskovits's ideas concerning the presence of African traits in Caribbean culture. For example, Leonard Barrett's short, first-person account entitled *The Sun and the Drum: African Roots in Jamaican Folk Tradition* (1976) owes a debt to Herskovits. Afrocentric scholars were among the first to recognize a positive emotional bond to Africa, one that should be respected and nurtured, not held in disdain. The latter often had been the case during the colonial era in the Caribbean, when Caribbean peoples were more likely to identify with England, France, or Spain than Africa.

---

2. Of course, all scholars recognize the African origins of all humans. As I understand radical Afrocentrism, however, that fact is not their major argument. They maintain that relatively recent prehistoric and historic cultures in the Americas, from the time of the ancient Egyptians on, had significant African input.

Some Afrocentric scholars, however, take an extreme diffusionist position, well beyond the charge of disciplined scholarship. The concept of diffusionism first developed in Europe in the late nineteenth and early twentieth century. Franz Boas's theories could be considered diffusionist in that he showed great interest in the historical spread of a culture from one area to another or of a culture's influence on a geographically contiguous culture through time. For Boas, meticulous historical research showing the connections between related cultures was a reaction against nineteenth-century cultural evolution. In its most extreme formulation, the theory of unilineal cultural evolution held that cultures evolved independently of one another and that certain cultures, having evolved either for a greater length of time or faster, were superior to other cultures.

A diffusionist theory that has made a mark on radical Afrocentrism is the heliocentric theory of Grafton Elliot Smith. Early in the twentieth century, Australian scholar Smith argued that the most important elements in European culture came from ancient Egypt. For Smith, Egyptians were fundamentally different from sub-Saharan Africans and were a Mediterranean, "white" people. Afrocentric scholars, on the other hand, argue that ancient Egyptians were essentially African, both culturally and racially, but like Smith they argue that European culture was based on an African, Egyptian culture.

John Henrik Clarke was a leading Afrocentric scholar who developed broad theories concerning Africa, Europe, and the African content of the cultures of the Americas. In his article entitled "African Culture as the Basis of World Culture" (in Conyers and Thompson 2004, 243–52) Clarke argues, somewhat like Herskovits before him, that people of African descent in the Americas have been robbed of a sense of history and dignity by being left out or misrepresented in white history. He turns to West African civilizations and to Caribbean slave revolts, especially in Haiti and Jamaica, as points of pride. He also notes the need for black (Africana) studies departments in colleges, primarily for young black students, so they can know and understand their culture history and the depth of white oppression. Clarke's zealous pride in African culture and in African descent are more akin to political activism than scholarship.

Clarence E. Walker, a critic of the Afrocentric approach, quotes Molefi K. Asante, as giving a succinct definition of the field:

> The Afro-centrist seeks to uncover and use codes, paradigms, symbols, motifs, myths, and circles of discussion that reinforce the centrality of African ideas and values as a valid frame of reference for acquiring and examining data. Such a method appears to go beyond western history in order to revalorize the African place in the interpretation of Africans, continental and diasporan. (in Walker 2001, xviii)

One of the major premises of Afrocentrism is a sense of pan-African nationality. But Walker and others argue that this is a created concept and that in Africa, as elsewhere in the world, there were many different peoples speaking different languages who at times are at odds with one another. Even in the Caribbean setting, enslaved Africans tended to form groups based on their "national" origin (69–73) or on bonding established during the slave experience. In addition, escaped slaves, such as the maroons of Jamaica, sometimes fought the colonialists but sometimes worked with them against the African and Creole people who were still enslaved. Walker claims that rather than a sense of African unity, there was at times antipathy between enslaved and liberated Africans in Jamaica. Furthermore, the slave experience was so disruptive that new identities needed to be forged in the Americas that were not simply an extension of "Africanness." Those new identities were in part the creation of enslaved people themselves and in part a response to the demands of plantation life. Walker's approach concerning the achievements of people of African descent in the Caribbean seems close to that of the Prices, who describe themselves as " 'creation theorists.' " This approach "argue[s] for a scenario of more rapid creolization" rather than strict African cultural retention (2003, 79–80). Yet as the Prices admit, "... when the Herskovitses emerged from the 'deep interior' [of Surinam], they bore the seeds of a garden that many of us are still harvesting" (80).

OTHER HISTORICAL APPROACHES

Today, many scholars of Caribbean folklore use historical documents, regardless of their theoretical approach. A good source of folklore from historic sources is found in Abrahams and Szwed, *After Africa* (1983), which brings together extracts from seventeenth- through nineteenth-century British travel documents. Similar sources of folklore in primary documents are slave narratives, some of which refer to Caribbean experiences. One compendium entitled *The Classic Slave Narratives* was edited and introduced by Henry Louis Gates, Jr. (1987). The first great slave narrative was written by Olaudah Equiano (Gustavus Vassa) in the eighteenth century. Also in the Gates edition is the narrative by Mary Prince, written in the early nineteenth century. While neither narrative contains much folklore, and both are sensationalist accounts of the horrors of slavery, they do give gripping evidence of the trials through which enslaved people went as a part of their "everyday" lives.[3] *The Autobiography of a Runaway Slave* (Barnet 1968) holds more interest for folklorists. This work chronicles the life of Esteban Montejo, a runaway slave at the close of the slave era in Cuba. It covers Montejo's life both as a slave and in his early years in freedom. Interviewed by Miguel Barnet

3. Studies of everyday life are closely related to folklore; see de Certeau 1984 and de Certeau, Giard, and Mayol 1998.

when Montejo was a very old man, his story is full of details of slaves' lives, including music and rituals.

A sense of history, together with ethnography, is found in the research conducted by Andrew Pearse in Trinidad in the 1950s. Pearse, whose British training had a Marxist bent, attended a seminar taught by Melville Herskovits at Northwestern University. He worked with folklorists Daniel Crowley and Jacob D. Elder, and together they documented the customs of the island. Pearse wrote an important article on nineteenth-century Carnival in Trinidad and illustrated how the social and political climate of the British colony influenced their folkloric Carnival (1956).

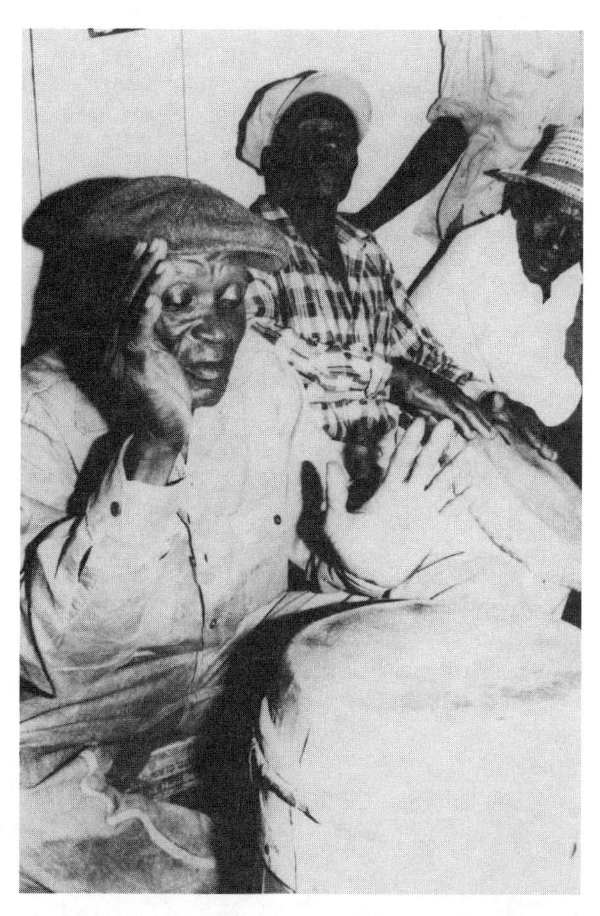

The Big Drum of Carriacou. Famed drummer Sugar Adam, at right, looks on. Photo credit: Don Hill.

Big Drum Dance scholar Lorna McDaniel (1998) used Pearse's original descriptions of the drum dances of Carriacou, Grenada, as a foundation for her own extensive research. Beginning with Pearse's work and historical sources, she dated various songs in the Big Drum Dance repertoire and thereby created a history of the ritual. Finally, British historian John Cowley (1996) has continued Pearse's historiography in his use of newspaper accounts of Trinidad's nineteenth-century Carnival. Cowley gives the reader a moment-by-moment account of the development of the folk tradition, including the masquerading and the music, throughout the century.

Pearse's work influenced my own ethnohistorical approach, as did the work of Sidney Mintz, who wrote: "Nearly all Caribbean societies show a dual or bipolar distribution of cultural forms, probably often stemming from (or paralleling) the traditional spheres of the masters and the slaves" (in Hill 1977, 204). In a study of the culture of Carriacou, Grenada, I claimed that their culture consisted of both "metropolitan" (colonial) and folk institutions that had parallel functions:

> The metropolitan part of Carriacouan society has been directly controlled or influenced by the colonial power. Once a British colony, Carriacou has the civil and religious institutions typical of any colony. Yet Carriacouans maintain a traditional social organization which parallels, in many ways, the functions of their metropolitan institutions. Sometimes these two aspects of the social organization are clearly separable and Carriacouans choose between alternate institutions in solving specific problems (subsistence gardening or purchased food, moot settlements or civil courts, bush or western medicine, folk religion or Christian churches). At other times there is a fusion between metropolitan and folk aspects within these institutions (for example, in the elaborate marriage customs). (1977, 196)

With respect to religion, the islanders were mostly Anglican or Catholic (the metropolitan religions) as well as believers in the Old Parents (ancestors) and the ceremonial Big Drum Dance, the heart of their folk religion. They were part of Grenada politically, with a parliamentary system, police, and courts, but their folk society also had mechanisms of social control within families and moot courts. They bought food in shops but also raised their own corn and beans and raised cattle and yard animals using folk techniques that seemed to be an amalgam of African, Native American, and European folk-farming practices.

The most influential work on African and Afro-American art, including Caribbean folk art, is Robert Farris Thompson's *Flash of the Spirit* (1984). After over two decades, it remains the standard book for researchers who seek to discover historic connections between traditional African arts (including sculpture, architecture, graphic design, and iconic writing) and cognates in the Americas. Much of the book demonstrates how both African techniques in the creation of art and the symbolic content of art objects are transformed in settings in the Americas. Thompson seeks to create a study of art that parallels the work done by

Waterman and other ethnomusicologists in identifying African elements in the music of the Americas. He maintains that techniques, designs, and philosophical ideas embedded within objects survived the Middle Passage into the Caribbean and the Americas. As a historian of African art, Thompson begins with the art in selected regions of West and west-central Africa and shows how their arts are manifested in the Americas. The art and philosophy of selected African ethnic groups (the Yoruba, the Kongo, the Fon, the Mande, and the Ejagham) are shown to have their counterparts in the arts of the Americas. Thompson does not examine the art of any specific region in the Americas; rather, he jumps from place to place, finding cognates with the art of the African ethnic group under consideration. Many of the examples of African art in the Americas come from the greater Caribbean region. For example, he finds that the Ejagham people of southeastern Nigeria and southwestern Cameroon (such as the Ibibio) developed a system of ideographic writing whose symbols have been widely adopted in the Caribbean, especially in the Abakuá male secret society of urban Cuba.

George Brandon's *The Dead Sell Memories: Santeria from Africa to the New World* (1997) is a study that traces the roots of this Afro-Cuban religion from the Yoruba of Nigeria to Cuba, over the span of five centuries. Using a wide range of scholarly studies, Brandon demonstrates how various village-level religious practices in Nigeria coalesced into widespread beliefs during the rise and fall of Yoruba states. Versions of this pan-Yoruba religion were brought to the Americas both during the slavery era and after the end of slavery. In Cuba, where the religion was alternately banned or tolerated by the Spanish, the faith was called "Lucumí." Sometimes Cuban Lucumí represented a mixture of West African religious notions, combined with Roman Catholicism in clubs (cabildos) where new versions of the faith emerged as Santería. Today, in Cuba and in other parts of the Americas where Cubans have gone, there are versions of the religion that range from being more African (Lucumí) to more Afro-Catholic (Santería).

David H. Brown's *Santería Enthroned* (2003) adds to Brandon's work by detailing the history of Santería in Cuba and by describing the ritual art. The book combines several approaches, including historic accounts of the religion, documentation of Creole innovations in the Santería iconography, and analysis of Yoruba cosmology.

The idea of collecting and presenting oral remembrances from the maroons and their legends, myth fragments, and myths in a coherent fashion is the core of Kenneth Bilby's *True-Born Maroons* (2005). The Jamaican maroons are the descendants of slaves who fought with and were freed by the Spanish when the British took the island in the seventeenth century. Many more runaway slaves who escaped from the plantations established by the newly arrived British joined the maroons. Groups of Maroons fought wars against the British for decades; most won treaties from the British, who allowed them to establish their own nations in remote corners of the island.

A student of Richard and Sally Price, Bilby presents Jamaican Maroon history as it is related in conversations that he has recorded with their leaders for nearly 30 years. He has supplemented these oral accounts with various written colonialist sources that he has located in libraries in the Caribbean and Europe. Bilby's is the most complete study every attempted of the maroon's own story. It contrasts their versions of African origins, enslavement, obtaining freedom, wars with the British, treaties and, later, British treachery against one of the groups with colonial versions of the same events. Bilby clearly shows how maroon oral tradition lives on and finds its identity in contemporary Jamaican society. He demonstrates that truth or falsity of oral tradition, including myth, is not the real yardstick by which verbal folklore should be measured. Rather, the use to which such stories are put and the power of their retelling is a guideline for living out life as a maroon in all generations since they established their identity centuries ago.

Caribbean Festival Arts (Nunley and Bettelheim 1988) accompanied an exhibit that originated at the Saint Louis Art Museum. Each chapter in the book traces the history of costumes associated with a type of annual Caribbean festival, although dance, music, and other folk arts are also considered. Christmas masquerades (including Jonkonnu), Trinidad's Carnival and Hosay festival, and festivals in Cuba, Haiti, and New Orleans are all covered. The book is the single best source for Caribbean folk costume associated with annual celebrations.

Some of the many studies of vernacular Caribbean music have a historical bent. Walter Jekyll's collection of edited Jamaican songs and dances (1907) is one of the earliest scholarly studies of both the British and African influences on the music of Jamaica. Fernando Ortiz's extensive research on Afro-Cuban music has already been noted. Richard Waterman's analysis of the African antecedents of Caribbean music formed the basis of later studies of musical connections between the two areas. Waterman was a student of Melville Herskovits, and his Ph.D. dissertation (1943) was an examination of the 252 recordings Melville and Frances had made in their field trip to Toco and Port of Spain, Trinidad. (Some of these important recordings are available on two CDs: Hill et al. 1998; Hill et al. 2003.) His classification of the major elements in West African music that influenced music in the Americas has become the standard and is still occasionally referenced in publication today (for example, see Alberts 1998). Waterman's list of African musical elements that may be found in music of the Americas include dominance of percussion, multiple meter (use of two or more meters at one time—common in West Africa but rare in the Americas), offbeat phrasing of melodic accents (e.g., syncopation), and overlapping call-and-response patterns (perhaps the main feature of African melodic forms). Gerhard Kubik, in his book on *Africa and the Blues* (1999), has referred to, and revised, some of Waterman's ideas, especially the notion of the dominance of percussion, which was the case in coastal West Africa but not in the Western Sudan, where stringed instruments were more prevalent.

A recent historical study of Cuban folklore is *Cuban Festivals: A Century of Afro-Cuban Culture* (Bettelheim 2001). The editor, Judith Bettelheim, was a student of Robert Farris Thompson. The lead chapter is the first English translation of Fernando Ortiz's classic "The Afro-Cuban Festival 'Day of the Kings'" as Ortiz had edited the article in 1960. The article, with Ortiz's lengthy quote from Ramón Meza, describes Kings Day, a holiday celebrated by people of African descent in Cuba before the end of slavery in 1886 (see chapter 3 for an extract). Meza mentions the cabildos to which some African groups belonged, as well as the festive behavior of the ñáñigos, the male secret societies that originated in the Calabar region of southeastern Nigeria. The piece is full of illustrations of people in costume, contains descriptions of the activities of Kings Day, and compares these customs with those found on other islands. David H. Brown's annotated glossary of special terms used by Ortiz and Meza follows the article. The remainder of the book describes the vicissitudes of the Carnival in Santiago de Cuba, as described by Bettelheim.

Perhaps the northernmost extension of indigenous Caribbean culture is that of the Gullah, the people of African descent who live in the coastal islands of Georgia and South Carolina. Gullah culture developed when enslaved people from Sierra Leone and other parts of West Africa were settled in the area as rice farmers. For part of each year many of the free white population of the area left the islands for inland locations, and so a special culture developed that was rich in African retentions. A good historical account of these people is *The Gullah People and Their African Heritage* by William S. Pollitzer (2005).

PERFORMANCE-CENTERED APPROACHES

According to Richard Bauman, performance is "a mode of communicative behavior and a type of communicative event" (Bauman 1992, 41). Performance may communicate "an aesthetically marked and heightened mode of communication, framed in a special way and put on display for an audience." Bauman notes that an analysis of performance "highlights the social, cultural, and aesthetic dimensions of the communicative process." A performance-centered approach to folklore contrasts with a "text-centered" approach, which abstracts a folklore genre from its natural setting (42). Like a language in use, each folklore performance is unique to the culture within which it is performed and to the moment of performance.

Béhague, an ethnomusicologist who has worked extensively in Afro-Brazilian communities and is in agreement with what Bauman states above about folklore in general, notes that emphasis on "the search for historical authenticity of sound production" has "limited the desirable broader conceptualization of performance" (Béhague in Bauman 1992, 174). The ethnomusicologist should be more concerned with "the actual musical and extramusical behavior" of the musicians and their audience, the way the community defines the performance, and the performance context. A musical performance is an "event" and a "process" and is "integrated into the field of musical action as nonverbal communication."

The folklorist should note the following (emic or performer and culturally derived) categories of performance:

> (1) special codes, reserved for and diagnostic of performance; (2) special formulae that signal performance; (3) figurative language such as metaphor; (4) formal stylistic devices; (5) special prosodic patterns of tempo, stress, pitch; (6) special paralinguistic patterns of voice quality and vocalization; (7) appeal to tradition; and (8) disclaimer of performance. (Bauman, quoted in Béhague 1984, 5)

One of the most important scholars of West Indian folklore and the leading exponent of performance-centered approaches to Caribbean folklore is Roger D. Abrahams (1983). He rejects historical approaches to folklore that mechanically treated pieces of folklore, such as tales, as traits that can be best studied comparatively when wrenched from their cultural setting. He favors a functionalist approach that deals with aspects of folk culture in their appropriate performance settings. Abrahams (in Bauman 1978, xxvii–xxviii) is interested in the "expressive system within which creative interactions are generated," the relationships between audience and performers, how folklore genres are introduced into "the regular flow of a group life," and in "techniques of composition."

> This branch of folkloristics, then, illustrates the range of ways in which expressive individuals, and especially performers, inherit devices of value, power, and meaning in the traditional repertoire. In line with other ethnographic enterprises, the profile is carried out to discover whatever systems (the poetics of the community) underlie the interactions of the group.

In his many articles and books concerning Caribbean and African American culture, Abrahams has consistently championed functional, structural, and performance-centered studies that tease out certain principals of West Indian culture. His Caribbean work has focused on folk plays, speechifying, joking, gossip, music, folktales, and other aspects of folk culture.

Abrahams wrote in essay:

> The functionalist perspective has made us sensitive to the elements of social control that underlie so much of what people say to and perform for one another. Most public performances call for some highlighted display of the ideals of the group. Theoretically, performances discuss how to act and how not to act under set conditions, expressive acts that provide patterns of emulation and avoidance. (1983, 77)

Critics of the functionalist approach to gossip have noted that there may be individual uses of the rhetorical devices of performance, but Abrahams notes that folk typologies of speech acts and events exhibit "continuities between gossip and the more public modes of performance" (78).

FOLKLORE OF EVERYDAY LIFE

The study of everyday life overlaps with the Boasian, performance-centered, and interpretative approaches to folklore. The American idea of "everyday life" tends to be descriptive and takes in "this and that" about any activity that may be broadly conceived as folklore (Schoemaker 1990). For example, when I make a recording of Caribbean music, in a hotel in Cuba or on a small island in the eastern Caribbean, I also record before, during, and after the musical performance. Sometimes, most of what I have recorded is not music at all but small talk before or during the performance. Furthermore, I do not try to get optimal recording conditions in the way "musical" ethnomusicologists might—quiet people down, control the starting and stopping times of the song, and the like—but I place the recorder in the best possible location to pick up both the music and any audience response to it and then let the tape run. As Roger Abrahams might say, the trick is to record "events," not music. Sometimes the context is more interesting, more telling, than the music alone. Although any tape recording or video documents a limited set of behaviors that good participant observation could pick up, a recording of an event may be considered analogous to DNA evidence; the recording may contain the stuff of the total event, if not the total event itself.

Captive Passage: The Transatlantic Slave Trade and the Making of the Americas (Anonymous 2002) contains a series of papers that rely heavily on objects, photographs, and documents to trace the history of the slave trade from African homelands, through the Middle Passage, to the Americas. The volume depicts many of the "accoutrements" of slavery, including illustrations of chains, paintings of slaves being whipped, and other scenes that show a slave's life. In a sense, the theoretical orientation of the book is toward everyday life during the era of slavery in the Americas, except that in this case that life is grim indeed. Through the text, which serves mostly to describe the graphics, there emerges a vision of enslavement in which traditions continuously evolve as a means of coping with the harsh treatment. Photographs may also grasp the essence of a person in a setting with a sympathetic, harsh, or otherwise revealing lens. (For example, a detailed photograph of a room, a house, or a yard may suggest not just a cultural setting but relationships between people and things.)

Although it was written well before everyday-life studies and postmodern theory developed, "Houdini's Picnic," a classic essay written by Joseph Mitchell for the *New Yorker* magazine in 1939, describes a party held in Harlem at which the calypso singer Wilmoth Houdini performed. In his detailed account, Mitchell captures the flavor of a people as they celebrate their lives at the close of the Great Depression.

The European approach to everyday-life studies is theoretical, subjective, and deductively applied to ordinary activities, clarified by the example rather than the empirical approach in which examples inform theory. This approach is loosely tied to documentary filmmaking, neorealism in literature, and a socialist sense of the glorification of common people. Note, for example, how Michel de Certeau dedicates his *The Practice of Everyday Life*:

> To the ordinary man.
>
> To a common hero, an ubiquitous character, walking in countless thousands on the streets. (1984, vi)

In studying a neighborhood, Pierre Mayol ("Living," in de Certeau, Giard, and Mayol 1998, 7–8) feels that the scholar of everyday life must balance noting the setting where activities take place and the "socioethnographic analysis of everyday life" that unfolds within that space. Relationships that link a person's private world to a public arena are the key to the study of daily life in an urban setting. One must examine both behaviors, interpret "expected symbolic benefits" gained through these behaviors, and thereby create a "discourse of meaning" whereby an urban dweller moves through his or her ordinary activities. De Certeau notes that common people are subversives; they take what is provided and, through bricolage and other means, create regular lives and habits from the dehumanizing attacks on people by the culture of consumption (1984, xiii).

One of the notions that ties the study of everyday life to postmodern theory is that of ennobling people as they go through their normal routines. Whereas performance-oriented and postmodernist Caribbeanists tend to focus on extraordinary occasions such as Carnival or other festive events as a means of empowerment, scholars of everyday life examine normal routines carried out by economically and politically powerless people, who turn common occasions, through webs of meaning, into the unique. Maybe this is what the Prices mean when they label their (and Sidney Mintz's) approach to the culture of people of African descent in the Americans as "creationist" theory (2003, 79–80), focusing on the endless creativity of African American populations in a variety of settings rather than on a static African cultural heritage.

INTERPRETATIVE (POSTMODERN) THEORY

For over 30 years, a loose set of literary approaches to the study of culture and society has dominated ethnography and folklore. Under the rubric of postmodernism, the following terms have also been used to describe this movement, including *postcolonial, textual analysis, narrative, deconstruction,* and *interpretation*. Not all postmodern scholars agree as to what postmodernism is. Here, I try to sort out some of the contentious issues with respect to Caribbean folklore.

To define *postmodernism,* we must first define *modern.* The modern era is bracketed by the rise of organized science, the industrial revolution, the dominance of capitalism, and, on the other end, by a diffuse loss of faith in science, industry, and rationality. The period dates roughly from the last third of the eighteenth century until the mid-1970s. Modern literary theory was a critique of the social upheavals brought on by the modern age and captured a sense of loss. The communist and socialist theoretical critique of capitalism may also be considered modern in the sense used here. Modern literature used parody, irony, metaphor, and other literary devices to illustrate the loss and alienation of modern life.

Postmodern literature and social criticism has greatly influenced folklore theory and virtually everything else in the humanities. The theory even moved some anthropologists from the social sciences toward the humanities in their thinking. Postmodern ethnography came to prominence in folklore in the 1970s, with text-based and literary-based analyses of folk genres gradually supplementing and sometimes replacing earlier folklore theories, such as viewing folklore as the distribution of traditional cultural traits or folklore as performance. In recent years, some postmodern theorists have moved away from "text" in the classical sense of a "body of words" or a "set content" toward a dynamic approach that examines events as they unfold in the moment, rather than the "deconstruction" of text.

Postmodern theory moves beyond modernist theory; some postmodern thinkers do not lament the limits they place on the value of science and objectivity; on technology, industry, and capitalism; and for a few scholars, even on the importance of history. Postmodernism is the ultimate extension of Boasian relativism in that folklore may be best understood in context or "in the moment." Whether text-based or situation-based, postmodernism examines folkloric events from the "inside out," not as a dispassionate outside observer. Folklore-as-text is deconstructed, or picked apart, to reveal its meaning. However, as I understand postmodernism, meanings may be spun out of a particular text like sausages flying from a meat grinder: the meaning is in the eye of the beholder. The folklorist translates (deconstructs and interprets) the meaning from the culture in question to the reading public through a process called "intersubjectivity."

Most postmodern scholars are critics of colonialism. Perhaps the most prominent scholar from the English-speaking Caribbean is Stuart Hall, a British social critic (anonymous, n.d.). Of mixed race and Jamaican origin, Hall is very much concerned with the issue of identity. He says that one's identity does not so much change as grow as one moves through various social and cultural environments.

In the colonial era, Caribbean peoples tended to identify with the mother countries. Today, the issue is very complex. There are "ethnic" identities, such as "black" or "Indian" (meaning of East Indian descent), or "white," to mention the three most prominent. There are also are country-based identities (e.g., Trinidadian, Cuban, Crucian). Many folkloric activities—such as stories about one's origins, Carnival masquerading, and vernacular music—are concerned with stating, formulating, or redefining one's identity and the boundaries of one's group identity.

The most interesting and important folklore ethnography to come out of the greater Caribbean area (including Guyana, Suriname, and French Guiana) in the last generation is the work of Richard and Sally Price and their student Ken Bilby. Although they cannot be pigeonholed as "postmodern," especially in their treatment of "history," they share some characteristics with some postmodern thinkers. All three have focused on maroon groups for much of their lengthy careers, the Prices primarily in Suriname and Bilby primarily in Jamaica. Much of their work centers on explaining the maroon sense of history and self-identity to a nonmaroon reading public.

The best statement of well-considered contemporary ethnography, including postmodern touches, is Richard Price's preface to the second edition of *First-Time: The Historical Vision of an African American People* (2002). The book threads its way through maroon and Dutch accounts of how the Saramakan maroons came to be a nation within the Dutch colony of Suriname. It represents a major break from the older objective ethnography, which was grounded in social science and economic primacy, toward engaging individual Saramakans to tell their story, as elegantly interpreted by Price, of their origins in the First-Time, when they coalesced into their self-assured identity of an African people who had escaped and remained free from enslavement between 1685 and 1762. It is not a history in the conventional sense, however, but a living document for the Saramakans today and for those of us who seek to understand. It is not subjective in the sense of other postmodern works but objectively (i.e., accurately) engages Saramakan people and the historical record to set down different "voices" of past events, either from the past or in the present.

First-Time is the first leg in Price's journey toward being one of the major creators of a revised and careful postmodern ethnography. He again took up the Saramakans' story in *Alabi's World* (1990), in which he presents four "voices" in their story; the Saramaka themselves, Moravian missionaries, Dutch bureaucrats, and his own interpretations. Each voice is set in a different typeface. Then, he and Sally Price move to fiction in order to further examine deeper truths of anthropological research:

> ... takes the form of a field diary of a museum-collecting expedition and, on the versos, that of a collection of ethnographic memorabilia (a miscellany of literary citations and line

drawings), and *Enigma Variations: A Novel*, which is a fictionalized account of adventures in art forgery and ethnography where questions of "authenticity" predominate. My most recent foray into Afro-Caribbean historical consciousness, *The Convict and the Colonel*, plays perhaps most radically with voice, time, and other aspects of narrative to explore the changing shape of historical thought among postcolonial Martiniquans, but the questions raised by *First-Time* about discourse and event, history and memory, continue to fuel the endeavor. (2002, xiii)

Philip W. Scher's *Carnival and the Formation of a Caribbean Transnation* (2003) discusses the notion of "transnation" in a study of Carnival in Trinidad and Brooklyn. He sees Carnival as expressing the nationality of Trinidadianness in whatever setting the Trinidadians "play mas" in Carnival. There are as many versions of this identity as there are Trinidadians who masquerade.

Advertisement for Martiniqueans playing beguines at a Paris club, early twentieth-century postcard.

Some recent interpretative studies move away from the careful literary innovations of the Prices and set objectivity adrift by questioning such concepts as history, Creole, colonialism, and textual analysis, and they zero in on power as expressed in the moment. That is, a current trend is to see folkloric expression, in the very instant of performance, as empowering the powerless. There is great value to this academic insight, as long as it does not exclude, as some intellectuals do, other, valuable approaches to folklore.

CREOLIST APPROACHES

As noted in chapter 2, the term *Creole* may be defined as a people, a culture, or a language. A lot of folklore theory revolves around this concept, especially Creole culture and language.

Creole Culture

In his introduction to *Afro-Creole: Power, Opposition, and Play in the Caribbean* (1997, 1–12) Richard D. E. Burton bundles Caribbeanist theories into three types. The first is essentially the approach best exemplified by Melville Herskovits, which notes the reformulation of African culture in Afro-Caribbean culture.[4] The second position is that there is little African content in Caribbean culture. The third approach is that Afro-Caribbean culture is a mixture of European and African culture. Burton holds that Caribbean culture must be understood both over the centuries that it developed and at specific times in the past. In thus combining both diachronic and synchronic approaches, he demonstrates that Afro-Caribbean culture is always dynamic and that some mixture of these approaches may represent Caribbean culture, or some aspect thereof, depending on the time slice one takes and what aspect of culture one examine:

> *Afro-Creole* is best seen, therefore, as a mosaic of themes, images, and ideas, but like creole culture itself it is an "unstable mosaic," and I have not tried to impose order and pattern where they do not appear to exist, or to fit every piece of the argument into a single all-embracing conclusion. (12)

Perhaps the most influential book taking the Creolist perspective is Paul Gilroy's *The Black Atlantic: Modernity and Double Consciousness* (1993). He is a harsh

---

4. Burton somewhat misrepresents the Herskovits position. While Herskovits was the first major North American scholar to fully appreciate the African content in the culture of the Americas, he was well aware that in some aspects of culture, very little if any African content remained. Please refer to the section in this chapter that reviews the Herskovits approach.

critic of cultural exclusivity, the idea of "cultural nationalism," as expressed in the extreme Afrocentric approach, for example. He goes on to state the following:

> This book addresses one small area in the grand consequence of this historical conjunction—the stereophonic, bilingual, or bifocal cultural forms originated by, but no longer the exclusive property of, blacks dispersed within the structures of feeling, producing, communicating, and remembering that I have heuristically called the black Atlantic world. (2–3)

Creole Languages

A Creole language is a language created out of two or more relatively unrelated languages. Most Creole languages spoken today were formed during the last 500 years through contact between Western Europeans and Africans. Creole languages are currently spoken in pockets along the West African coast, on the islands of the Caribbean, and on islands in the Indian Ocean. All experts in Creole languages agree that among the major Creoles are those that combine English, Dutch, or French and various West African languages. There is disagreement as to whether Portuguese and Spanish Creoles exist, but many linguists say these languages also have been Creolized.

Perhaps the most widely spread folklore genre is the informal language nearly everyone speaks in the Caribbean at home or among friends or peers. Until recent decades, most Creole languages were not written, and if they were, they had no consistent spelling. These were vernacular languages, learned as a first language in the home and continued throughout life as a parallel form of communication to the formal language of school, business, government, and other public forums. Therefore, by definition, Creole languages are folkloric, since their grammar, syntax, and vocabulary are traditional and are passed from person to person in informal settings, through word of mouth. Creole languages comprise an extensive texture of words, proverbs, stories, and beyond that, meanings and visions that form the basis of everyday Caribbean life. No genre of Caribbean folklore is free of Creole language, since the names for folklore genres are usually expressed in Creole.

It is assumed that Creole languages were derived from pidgin languages—that is, limited sets of vocabulary and linguistic rules—which developed in various parts of the world and were used as communication between people who spoke different languages. Pidgins were used in commerce, but eventually a group of people emerged, most likely descendants from the original groups that spoke different languages. These people learned the pidgin as a first language, and it contained fuller vocabularies and augmented grammars or rules. Linguists today agree that Creole languages are full and complete languages and are capable of communicating any thought that any language may communicate. That is, they are not, like pidgins, limited forms of communication. Because they vary from place to place and from speaker to speaker, they form a very deep well of folkloric resources that is tapped by native speakers as well as scholars and writers to express all manner of notions that seem suited for their pithy form of expression. What Shakespeare was to English through his drawing in regional variants of vernacular English into his plays, contemporary Caribbean writers and performance artists are to Creole languages, sometimes even writing or performing entire short stories, novellas, or routines in a Caribbean Creole language.

Some scholars believe that French Creoles began during a "homesteading" phase of settlement in the Caribbean when mostly European peoples mixed in Nevis and over several generations developed the base language that became French Creole. Other scholars believe that Africanized Creole languages began in West Africa when enslaved Africans from different cultures who spoke different languages were brought together as slaves on their trek to the coast and during their sometimes several months' incarceration in slave forts and castles that dotted the coast. It was in these circumstances that different Africans were brought together for the first time and that they simultaneously had their first prolonged contact with one or more European languages, whether Portuguese, Spanish, Dutch, French, or English.

Furthermore, Creolists do not agree as to whether Creole languages are primarily modified versions of European tongues that contain varying amounts of African words or whether they are languages with a large European vocabulary grounded in major syntactical and grammatical features modified from African languages. What seems clear, however, is that Creole languages are not fixed, they are fluid. They change through time, from place to place, and perhaps most important, they change according to the setting. That is, typically a Caribbean person will speak a standard language, a Creole language that is related to that standard but not intelligible to someone who speaks the standard alone, and various gradients between the two. Here we introduce the concept of deep language, the basilect. In Caribbean communities as in all communities, the idea of a language—as in "I speak English, which is different from French"—is an oversimplification. Actually, there is just communication and an infinite way that communication may take place. Languages are flexible, and it is only with the rise of written-out and formalized "standard" languages in recent centuries that "separateness" of languages seems to exist.

In former times, linguistic communities varied extensively: if one was not literate and wandered, say, 100 miles from one's home, one would find people speaking differently, with different accents and different vocabularies, and maybe even different grammatical rules, even though the language from point A changes only gradually until one arrives at point B. So it is with Creole languages.

Some Creoles may contain more African-based grammar and syntax, some less. Some may contain more African-based vocabulary, some less. As one moves from speaking the standard European language to speaking the deepest Creole, one gradually introduces changes in grammar, syntax, and vocabulary. Moreover, moving from standard to Creole is a social and cultural move, from a metropolitan sense of Caribbean culture that connects one to the mother country, the home of the standard language, to a local, even familial, culture that immerses one in the uniqueness of being a Caribbean person.

WORKS CITED

Abrahams, Roger D. 1983. *The Man-of-Words in the West Indies: Performance and the Emergence of Creole Culture*. Baltimore: Johns Hopkins UP.

Abrahams, Roger D., and John F. Szwed. 1983. *After Africa*. New Haven: Yale UP.

Anonymous. 2002. *Captive Passage: The Transatlantic Slave Trade and the Making of the Americas*. Washington, D.C.: Smithsonian.

Alberts, Arthur S. 1998. *More Tribal, Folk and Café Music of W. Africa*. Rykodisc CD, B00000DGYB.

Barrett, Leonard. 1976. *The Sun and the Drum: African Roots in Jamaican Folk Tradition*. Kingston, Jamaica: Heinemann.

Bauman, Richard. 1978. *Verbal Art as Performance*. Rowley, Mass.: Newbury House.

Bauman, Richard, ed. 1992. *Folklore, Cultural Performances, and Popular Entertainments: A Communications-Centered Handbook*. New York: Oxford UP.

Béhague, Gerald, ed. 1984. *Performance Practice: Ethnomusicological Perspectives*. Westport, Conn.: Greenwood Press.

———. 1992. "Music Performance." In Bauman, *Folklore, Cultural Performances, and Popular Entertainments*.

Bettelheim, Judith, ed. 2001. *Cuban Festivals: A Century of Afro-Cuban Culture*. Princeton, N.J.: Markus Wiener.

Bilby, Kenneth M. 2005. *True-Born Maroons*. Gainesville: U of Florida P.

Brandon, George. 1983. *The Dead Sell Memories: Santeria from Africa to the New World*. Bloomington: Indiana UP.

Brown, David H. 2003. *Santería Enthroned: Art, Ritual, and Innovation in an Afro-Cuban Religion*. Chicago: U of Chicago P.

Burton, Richard D. E. 1997. *Afro-Creole: Power, Opposition, and Play in the Caribbean*. Ithaca, N.Y.: Cornell UP.

Conyers, James L., Jr., and Julius E. Thompson, eds. 2004. *Pan African Nationalism in the Americas: The Life and Times of John Henrik Clarke*. Trenton, N.J.: Africa World Press.

Cowley, John. 1996. *Carnival Canboulay and Calypso: Traditions in the Making*. New York: Cambridge UP.

de Certeau, Michel. 1984. *The Practice of Everyday Life*. Berkeley: U of California P.

———, Luce Giard, and Pierre Mayol. 1998. *Living & Cooking.* Vol. 2 of *The Practice of Everyday Life.* Minneapolis: U of Minnesota P.
Equiano, Olaudah. 1789. *The Life of Olaudah Equiano or Gustavus Vassa, the African.* 2 vols., with a new intro. by Paul Edwards. London: Dawsons of Pall Mall, 1969.
Gates, Henry Louis, Jr., ed. 1987. *The Classic Slave Narratives.* London: Mentor.
Gilroy, Paul. 1993. *The Black Atlantic: Modernity and Double Consciousness.* Cambridge, Mass.: Harvard UP.
Herskovits, Melville. 1971. *Life in a Haitian Valley.* Garden City, N.Y.: Doubleday. (Orig. pub. 1937.)
Herskovits, Frances and Melville. 1934. *Rebel Destiny,* New York: McGraw-Hill Book Co.
Herskovits, Melville. 1941. *The Myth of the Negro Past.* Boston: Beacon Press.
———, and Frances Herskovits. 1936. *Suriname Folklore.* Columbia University Contributions to Anthropology, Vol. 28. New York: Columbia UP.
———, and Frances Herskovits. 1947. *Trinidad Village.* New York: Knopf.
Herskovits Library of African Studies. Web site about Melville Herskovits. http://www.library.northwestern.edu/africana/herskovits.html.
Hill, Donald R. 1977. *The Impact of Migration on the Metropolitan and Folk Society of Carriacou, Grenada.* Vol. 34, part 2, of the Anthropological Papers of the American Museum of Natural History. New York: Museum of Natural History, 193–391. New York: American Museum of Natural History.
———, Maureen Warner-Lewis, John Cowley, Lise Winer, eds. 1998. "Peter Was a Fisherman: The 1939 Trinidad Field Recordings of Melville and Frances Herskovits, Vol. 1." Rounder Records, CD 1114.
———, and Lise Winer, eds. 2003. "'Rastlin' Jacob—The Music of the Spiritual Baptists of Trinidad: The 1939 Trinidad Field Recordings of Melville and Frances Herskovits." Rounder Records, CD 1115.
Jekyll, Walter, comp. and ed. 1907. *Jamaican Song and Story: Annancy Stories, Digging Sings, Ring Tunes, and Dancing Tunes.* London: David Nutt for the Folk-Lore Society.
The Journal of the International Institute. "A Conversation with Stuart Hall," Ann Arbor, Michigan. http://www.umich.edu/~iinet/journal/vol7no1/Hall.htm.
Kubik, Gerhard. 1999. *Africa and the Blues.* Jackson: U of Mississippi P.
McDaniel, Lorna. 1998. *The Big Drum Ritual of Carriacou: Praisesongs in Rememory of Flight.* Gainesville: U of Florida P.
Montejo, Esteban. 1968. *The Autobiography of a Runaway Slave.* Ed. Miguel Barnet and trans. Jocasta Innes. New York: Pantheon.
Moore, Robin D. 1997. *Nationalizing Blackness: Afrocubanismo and Artistic Revolution in Havana, 1920–1940.* Pittsburgh: U of Pittsburgh P.
Nunley, John W., and Judith Bettelheim, eds. 1988. *Caribbean Festival Arts.* Seattle: U of Washington P.
Ortiz, Fernando. 1916. *Los Negros Esclavos, Estudio Sociologico Y de Derecho Publico.* Havana, Cuba: Revista Bimestere Cubana.

———. 1923. *Un Catauro de Cubanismos* [Cuban Slang]. Havana, Cuba: Apuntes Lexicográficos.

———. 1950. *La Africanía de la Música Folklórica de Cuba* [Africanisms in Folkloric Cuban Music]. Havana, Cuba: Dirección de Cultura de Ministerio de Educación. (Orig. pub. in 5 vols.)

———. 1951. *Los Bailes y el Teatro de los Negros en el Folklore de Cuba* [Dances and Theater of the Blacks in Cuban Folklore], Havana, Cuba: Dirección de Cultura del Ministerio de Educación.

———. 1952–1955. *Los Instrumentos de la Música Afrocubana* [Afrocuban Instruments]. Havana, Cuba: Los Instrumentos de la Ministerio de Educación. 5 vols.

———. 1995a. *Cuban Counterpoint: Tobacco and* Sugar. Durham, N.C.: Duke UP. (Orig. pub. as *Contrapunteo Cubano del Tabaco y el Azúcar,* 1940.)

———. 1995b. *Los Negros Brujos*. Havana: Editorial de Ciencias Sociales. (Orig. pub. 1906.)

Pearse, Andrew. 1956. "Carnival in Nineteenth Century Trinidad." *Caribbean Quarterly* 4, no. 3/4: 175–93.

Pollitzer, William S. 2005. *The Gullah People and Their African Heritage.* Athens: U of Georgia P.

Price Richard. 1990. *Alabi's World.* Baltimore: Johns Hopkins UP.

———. 2002. *First-Time: The Historical Vision of an African American People.* Chicago: U of Chicago P. (Orig. pub. 1983.)

Price, Richard, and Sally Price. 2003. *The Root of Roots: Or, How Afro-American Anthropology Got Its Start.* Chicago: Prickly Paradigm Press / U of Chicago P.

Scher, Philip W. *Carnival and the Formation of a Caribbean Transnation.* Gainesville: U of Florida P, 2003.

Schoemaker, George H. 1990. *The Emergence of Folklore in Everyday Life.* Bloomington, Ind.: Trickster Press.

Thompson, Robert Farris. 1984. *Flash of the Spirit: African and Afro-American Art and Philosophy.* New York: Vintage.

Walker, Clarence E. 2001. *We Can't Go Home Again: An Argument about Afrocentrism.* New York: Oxford UP.

Waterman, Richard. 1943. "African Patterns in Trinidad Negro Music." Ph.D. diss., Northwestern U.

Five

Contexts

Caribbean folklore has been widely used in literature and in popular music and dance. To a lesser extent, island folklore has been woven into film, the tourism industry, art, and fashion and design.

FOLKLORE IN CARIBBEAN LITERATURE

Pick up almost any novel written by a Caribbean author or about the Caribbean and one encounters folklore. As Georges and Jones state, "Folklore is often the principal means a writer uses to convey, illustrate, or reinforce a major theme in a literary work" (1995: 3). Magic, myth, and folktale-like recollections, or references to music, dance, or some other folkloric element are present in stories set in the islands. The very contrasting cultural roots—African, European, and touches of Asian and Native American—are what give the islands an appearance of exoticism, to which folklore contributes. However, I find this perception of the exotic strange, since the Caribbean has been within the Western sphere for over 500 years. If the Caribbean is exotic, so are we all.

A good start in the use of folklore themes in Caribbean literature is found in the *Encyclopedia of Caribbean Literature* (Figueredo 2006). Short biographies of most of the authors mentioned in the text that follows are found in the encyclopedia, as are biographies of many others, as well as essays on Anancy stories (about the trickster spider), dub poetry (a performance style of poetry that comes out of a Jamaican vernacular lyrical style of music), Santería (an Afro-Cuban religion), and so forth.

Well before contemporary authors utilized the subject, folklore was found in slave narratives. Furthermore, folklore is present in nonfiction travel books and very literate ethnographies, in the way the tourist industry alludes to the Caribbean in the images of the islands that they depict, and even how advertisers in the United States incorporate Caribbean themes into their pitch.

The Slave Narratives and Travel Accounts

Slave Narratives, written in the eighteenth and nineteenth centuries, provide a rich but grim look at the everyday life of an enslaved Caribbean population, although the image of that life is often incomplete and designed to further the just aims of the emancipation movement. Two of the most famous slave narratives historically bracket the history of the narratives and deal with Caribbean settings. Olaudah Equiano (Gustavus Vassa) wrote an account that helped encourage the fight against slavery (1789; see also Gates, ed., 1987). Although recent research has questioned whether Equiano was African born, he had been a slave. His narrative included an account of his experience in Caribbean waters. Esteban Montejo (Barnet 1968) was born into slavery in Cuba in 1860 and spent his early life as a sugarcane worker and, occasionally, as a cimmaron (a maroon, or runaway slave). After abolition, he became a free worker. His story is filled with descriptions of the split between field hands and house slaves, and he describes traditional African religions as they were modified in Cuba. He also describes the various ethnic groups that make up the rural peasantry in Cuba, especially after abolition.

Roger Abrahams and John Szwed, a folklorist and a cultural anthropologist, respectively, have done more than any other scholars have since the 1970s to document Caribbean folklore, especially in the English-speaking Caribbean. In *After Africa* (1983) they not only extract slave narratives, but they also trace historic writings in English that are rich in folkloric practices. Compiled in an era before digital documents were available, this volume gave scholars and general readers alike their first accurate look at what contemporaries wrote about Afro-Caribbean populations from the seventeenth through the nineteenth centuries. This remains the single best volume on historic folklore in the West Indies, and simply listing the table of contents tells why: "Slave Accounts...," "Ways of Speaking," "Anancy Tales," "Religion and Magic," "Festivals, Carnival, Holidays, and JonKanoo," "Music, Dance, and Games," and "Miscellaneous" customs, including "Domestic Life, Work Conditions, Dress, Housing, Body Modifications, Weddings, Medicine, Rebellions, and Discipline." The book also includes biographical notes on the authors, both well-known and obscure.

"Literate" Studies

By literate studies, I refer to nonfiction works. There are a few nonfiction books of relevant folklore about the Caribbean that reach a very high level of emotional intensity and subjective clarity that is more often found in fiction than in nonfiction. Those books are also included here.

The political critique of colonialism by Franz Fanon, *Black Skin, White Masks* (1967), alludes to the song depicted on a 100-year-old postcard. Fanon writes this about a typical Martiniquean visiting metropolitan France for the first time:

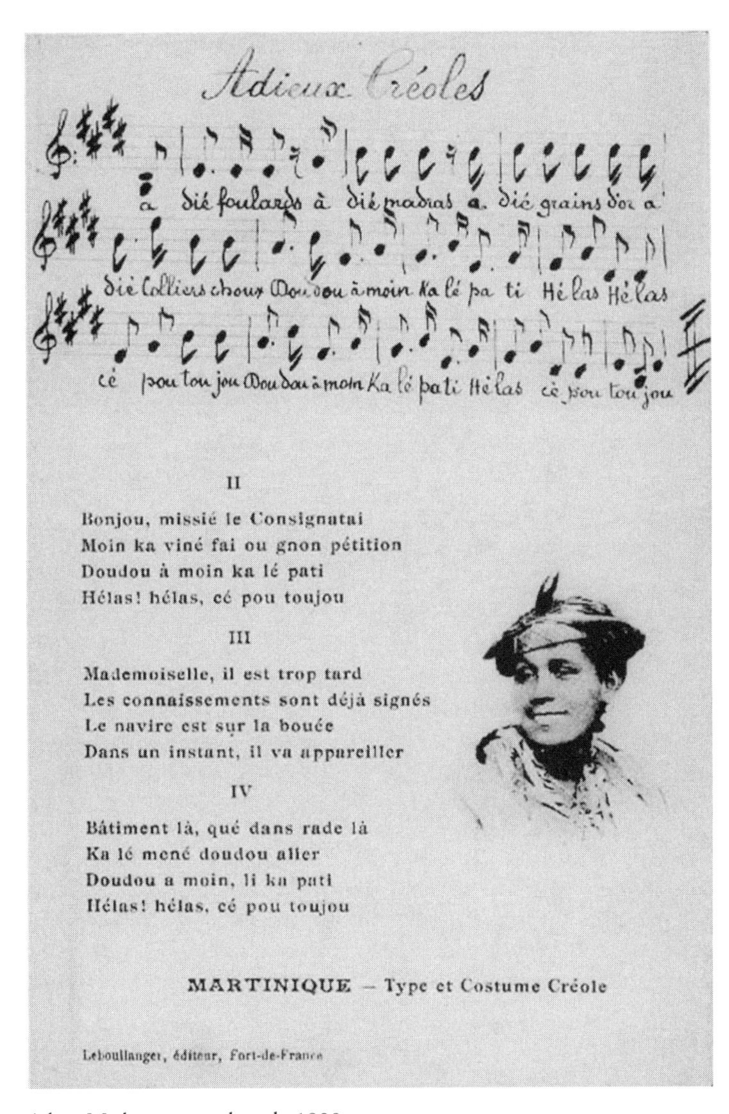

Adieu Madras postcard, early 1900s.

"La doudou," Martiniquean Creole woman, postcard from the early 1900s.

The black man who arrives in France changes because to him the country represents the tabernacle; he changes not only because it is from France that he received his knowledge of Montesquieu, Rousseau, and Voltaire, but also because France gave him his physicians, his department heads, his innumerable little functionaries—from the sergeant-major "fifteen years in the service" to the policeman who was born in Panissières. There is a kind of magic vault of distance, and the man who is leaving next week for France creates round himself a magic circle in which the words *Paris, Marseille, Sorbonne, Pigalle* become the keys to the vault. He leaves for the pier, and the amputation of his being diminishes as the silhouette of his ship grows clearer. In the eyes of those who have come to see him off he can read the evidence of his own mutation of his power. "Good-by bandanna, good-by straw hat..."

Now that we have got him to the dock, let him sail; we shall see him again. For the moment, let us go to welcome one of those who are coming home. The "newcomer" reveals himself at once; he answers only in French, and often he no longer understands

> Creole. There is a relevant illustration in folklore. After several months of living in France, a country boy returns to his family. Noticing a farm implement, he asks his father, an old don't-pull-that-kind-of-thing-on-me peasant, "Tell me, what does one call that apparatus?" His father replies by dropping the tool on the boy's feet, and the amnesia vanishes. Remarkable therapy. (23–24)

There are two folkloric references in this passage from Fanon's classic work. The first concerns the song, from which we get a crude English translation of its title, "Adieu Foulards, Adieu Madras" ("Good-by bandanna, good-by straw hat..."). The foulard is the nineteenth-century French Creole silk handkerchief. The madras is a scarf made up as a head tie that is stereotypically worn by a mixed-race, attractive woman. The full outfit is called a douiette, which also includes a long skirt over many petticoats and plenty of jewelry. Today, this traditional Creole dress signifies many things, from an innocent nostalgia for simpler times to a symbol of miscegenation and the race-based cruelties of the slavery era. The douiette, complete with foulard and madras, stands for the French Caribbean itself, much like the image of Cecilia Valdés, the illegitimate child of a white slaver and a mulata, or mixed-race woman, has come to represent Cuba. As Richard D. E. Burton (1993, 81) puts the issue:

> Another important mythological representation of the colonial relationship that came to prominence under the Third Republic revolved around the figure of *la doudou,* the smiling, sexually available black or colored woman (usually the latter) who gives herself heart, mind, and body to a visiting Frenchman (usually a soldier or colonial official) and is left desolate when her lover abandons her to return to France, having, of course, refused to marry her though often leaving her with a child who will at least "lighten the race." The stereotype of *la doudou* goes back to the eighteenth century and received its classic formulation in what is without doubt the best-known song in the French West Indies, "Adieu foulards, adieu madras," believed to have been written by the governor of Guadeloupe, de Boullée, in 1769. This song, Régis Antoine has written, soon became a "kind of official hymn" in French colonialist discourse...

Eventually, the image became a multilayered and complex symbol of the unique Caribbean experience. It pops up repeatedly in quests for regional identity, in hammering out a just relationship between black and white, in defining what it is to be Creole, and in how to incorporate (or not incorporate) into the Creole complex non-Creole populations, such as the East Indians of Trinidad and Guyana.

Fernando Ortiz's *Cuban Counterpoint: Tobacco and Sugar* (1995), which contrasts the social and cultural settings of growing tobacco or sugarcane, is perhaps the single best volume of literary merit concerning this cultural mix of black and white that is Caribbean culture. Ortiz's most famous work, the study includes elements of Cuban folklore along the way as the author contrasts the lifestyles of growing tobacco as opposed to growing sugar. Its subjectivity was a harbinger of contemporary interpretive ethnography. He creates opposing cultural worlds of the free, "white" tobacco farmers and the Afro-Cuban slaves of the latifundia (massive sugar plantations). He notes transculturalization in the form of the spread and blending of Hispanic and Afro-Cuban cultures. Ortiz contrasts the process of transculturalization with the more static notion of acculturation, developed by Melville Herskovits and other North American anthropologists, which seems to suggest a one-way process of culture change from a subjected people to the dominant people.

Perhaps the most famous study of Cuban music is Alejo Carpentier's literary classic, *La Música en Cuba* (1989). Carpentier was a Cuban intellectual, radical, writer, musician, and musicologist, perhaps Cuba's greatest intellectual of the twentieth century. His study may be considered a precursor to modern examinations of social class and race with respect to music—in this case the interplay between the European classical tradition in Cuba and traditional Afro-Cuban music—and interpretative ethnography. With Ortiz and others, he championed both vernacular Cuban music and its integration into Cuban popular and classical music. *La Música en Cuba* is now available in an English translation with an excellent introduction by Timothy Brennan, as *Music in Cuba* (2001). This work is mentioned in this section rather than in the section on music because of its literary merit.

In *First-Time: The Historical Vision of an African American People* (2002 [1983]), Richard Price traces the history of the Saramakas, or the maroons of Suriname, one of the mainland South American countries that is often regarded as being at least partly Caribbean in culture. The book opens with the following: "In a sacred grove beside the village of Dángogó, shaded by equatorial trees, stands a weathered shrine to the Old-Time People (Awónêngè), those ancestors who 'heard the guns of war' "(5). A story then unfolds, based on Saramakan folktales and myth fragments, sometimes expressed through shreds and patches of culture rather than traditional storytelling (see chapter 4). Price also quotes extensively from colonial documents. This multilayered history tells of how this maroon people escaped from slavery, fled to the backwaters of the rainforest, and established their own society by fighting off the colonial Dutch.

At the northern end of our area, New Orleans spawned a folk-tinged literature in the nineteenth century, the most important example of which is Cable's *Creoles and Cajuns: Stories of Old Louisiana* (1959), which includes "The Dance in Place Congo" (366–93) and "Creole Slave Songs" (394–432). Congo Square was a locale where slaves and free blacks congregated for drum dances in the early 1800s. Cable's story is not exactly accurate, but it does give a glimpse of one of the few places in what is now part of the United States where slaves were allowed such activities. *Blues for New Orleans: Mardi Gras and America's Creole Soul* (2006), was written by Roger Abrahams, with Nick Spitzer, whose longtime public radio program *American Routes* framed the folk roots of Gulf Coast culture; John Szwed, Abrahams's frequent collaborator and an authority on jazz; and Robert Farris Thompson, whose *Flash of the Spirit* (1984) is covered in chapters 3 and 4 of this book. While not a literary work, *Blues for New Orleans* is included here because it is an impassioned plea, in the wake of Hurricane Katrina, for saving New Orleans's Mardi Gras. It is the academic's equivalent to Derek Walcott's *Omeros* (1990). On the theoretical level, Abrahams and his fellow authors build the strongest argument to date for understanding the essentially Creole nature

George Lewis, New Orleans Creole clarinetist, who played archaic jazz, 1961. Photo credit: Don Hill.

of American culture, even beyond New Orleans. Abrahams makes the case that American culture itself is constantly being Creolized from various sources, especially from people emigrating from the islands to the south.

Fiction

Sometimes I think all Caribbean literature utilizes folklore; certainly, what makes Caribbean writers distinctive is their use of local, often folkloric, themes, to illustrate universal dilemmas. Just browse the *Encyclopedia of Caribbean Literature* (Figueredo 2006) at random or read *The Caribbean Novel in English: An Introduction* (Booker and Juraga 2001). Almost every Caribbean author writes about grassroots life in colonial or postcolonial Caribbean, about issues of identity and anomie, or draws on rich Creole language and Caribbean settings to create texture. Therefore, it is not possible to trace the use of folklore in all Caribbean literature; rather, I will sketch a review of some of the important works and will point the way for the readers to make their own searches of the literature.

One of the earlier novels to incorporate folkloric elements is Cirilo Villaverde's *Cecilia Valdés or El Angel Hill: A Novel of Nineteenth-Century Cuba* (2005). Begun in Cuba in 1839, the novel went through various incarnations and was not completed until 1894, when Villaverde was in New York, exiled from his native Cuba. Considered by many to be Cuba's greatest nineteenth-century novel, the book incorporates mythic Cuban themes, local settings, and character types of the era. Today, many think that the character of the novel embodies the spirit of the Cuban people. Cecilia Valdés is the mixed-race child of a Spanish slave trader and a mulata. Having been removed from her mother, who is considered mentally ill, she falls in love with a white aristocrat, who is in fact her half brother. When he refuses to marry her and decides to marry someone else, she plots his death via a mulatto who is in love with Cecilia and will do what she asks. On her half brother's wedding day the mulato stabs him to death, thus avenging Cecilia. She is sent to the same asylum where her mother is, and the two are reunited. The novel takes up themes of slavery, incest, class, and the emergence of a mixed-race middle class. Cecilia Valdés, as a mulata, may be considered a metaphor for Cuba itself, and so the novel is really about the essence of Cuba. The theme of *Cecilia Valdés* reappears repeatedly in Cuban literature and in other artistic forms, most notably in the zarzuela of the same name by Gonzalo Roig.

In recent decades, two literary figures from the Caribbean, both writing in English, have won the Nobel Prize for Literature, Derek Walcott, originally from St. Lucia, in 1992 and V. S. Naipaul, originally from Trinidad and Tobago, in 2001. Two early works by Naipaul, *Miguel Street* (2002 [1959]) and *A House for Mr. Biswas* (1961) both written while he still lived in Trinidad, illustrate his use of folklore. *Omeros* (1990) by Derek Walcott is homage to his native St. Lucia.

Miguel Street is one of Naipaul's earliest works. It is a slice of life in a poor Port of Spain, Trinidad, neighborhood; the author describes the activities of the local characters who reside in the area. Of interest to the folklorist are the calypso lyrics that he intersperses from time to time as the story unfolds. No doubt, Naipaul heard these songs in his youth either on phonograph record or at performances.

On the surface, there does not seem to be much folklore in *A House for Mr. Biswas*. In what some critics consider to be his greatest work (and more than a few critics think he is the greatest writer in the English language alive today), however, Naipaul again creates his sardonic slice of life, exhibiting his well-known acerbic wit in this autobiographical novel of his youth spent in colonial Trinidad. This everyday-life folklore is supplemented by continual references to the Indian, especially Hindu, culture of the island, from the breakdown of the caste system to the wandering pundits to male-female relationships and marriage customs.

One need not look farther than to the description of Mr. Biswas's house at the opening of the book to get what may be one of the best accounts of folk architecture common in the islands. Built by a "solicitor's clerk who built houses in his spare time" (6), the house was made mainly

> from frames from the dismantled American Army camps at Docksite, Pompeii Savannah and Fort Read. The frames did not always match, but they enabled the solicitor's clerk to pursue his hobby with little professional help.
>
> On the ground floor of Mr Biswas's two-storey house the solicitor's clerk had put a tiny kitchen in one corner; the remaining L-shaped space, unbroken, served as drawingroom and diningroom. Between the kitchen and the diningroom there was a doorway but no door. Upstairs, just above the kitchen, the clerk had constructed a concrete room which contained a toilet bowl, a wash-basin and a shower; because of the shower this room was perpetually wet. The remaining L-shaped space was broken up into a bedroom, a verandah, a bedroom. Because the house faced west and had no protection from the sun, in the afternoon only two rooms were comfortably habitable: the kitchen downstairs and the wet bathroom-and-lavatory upstairs.
>
> In his original design the solicitor's clerk seemed to have forgotten the need for a staircase to link both floors, and what he had provided had the appearance of an afterthought. Doorways had been punched in the eastern wall and a rough wooden staircase—heavy planks on an uneven frame with one warped unpainted banister, the whole covered with a sloping roof of corrugated iron—hung precariously at the back of the house, in striking contrast with the white-pointed brickwork of the front, the white woodwork and the frosted glass of doors and windows. (7)

This passage is remarkably similar to the manner in which the old Carriacouan (and I suspect generic Caribbean) wood, or board, houses were constructed through the 1970s. The oddities that Naipaul claims in the above passage make sense when one realizes that old houses were routinely broken apart and built anew from the pieces in a different configuration on another lot. In Carriacou, the process was called a house break and is described in chapter 3 of this book.

Omeros may also be viewed on different levels. It is an epic poem modeled on the Homeric myths of the *Iliad* and the *Odyssey.* It is also bricolage, a fragmented description of traditional culture in St. Lucia spanning centuries of colonialism and the postcolonial period. Everyone on the island speaks standard West Indian English and English Creole, and about half the population speaks French Creole also, locally called Patois. Walcott refers to this multiculturalism; at times passages are written in Patois, usually followed by the same thing written in standard English or English Creole. Walcott, himself a mixture of the many races that make up the population of the island, is on an identity quest in *Omeros,* a word he designed to stand for the sea that surrounds the island (mer) as well as for mother (also mer), the island itself. But who is he; who is the Caribbean man and where is his place in the world? The answer is *Omeros,* St. Lucia, with the other Creoles of the island as they go about their daily, seemingly humdrum lives—lives that are in fact filled with Homeric struggles for existence and survival:

> This was the light that Achille was happiest in.
> When, before their hands gripped the gunwales, they stood
> For the sea-width to enter them, feeling their day begin. (9)

Although Naipaul and Walcott are the best-known and most-read authors from the English-speaking Caribbean, they represent a transition from the literature of the colonial and early postcolonial eras to the literature of today. Just as with the colonial authors, their literary models remained great European works, and their writing styles were squarely within a European literary framework. More recent authors, however, have moved away from simply putting this framework in a Caribbean setting. While continuing to owe a great debt to the whole stream of the development of literature within Spanish, French, or especially an English language patrimony, younger authors have captured the cadences of the Caribbean experience, especially its language and its culture. Note this use of language by Earl Lovelace, in *Salt* (1997), winner of the 1997 Commonwealth Prize:

> Two months after they hanged his brother Gregoire, king of the Deardnoughts band, and Louis and Nanton and Man Man, the other three leaders of African secret societies, who Hislop the governor claimed to be ringleaders of an insurrection that had a plan, according to the testimony of a mad white woman, to use the cover of the festivities of Christmas day to massacre the white and free coloured people of the island, Jo-Jo's great-grandfather, Guinea John, with his black jacket on and a price of two hundred pounds sterling on his head, made his way to the East Coast, mounted the cliff at Manzanilla, put two corn cobs under his armpits and flew away to Africa, taking with him the mysteries of levitation and flight, leaving the rest of his family still in captivity mourning over his selfishness, everybody putting in their mouth and saying, "You see! You see! That is why Black-people

children doomed to suffer: their own parents refuse to pass on the knowledge that they know to them." (3)

Lovelace sets the beginning of his novel in early-1800s Trinidad, when, in very brutal fashion, the British squashed a slave revolt on the island. This tale of flight, which happens after the failure of the revolt, is common in the West Indies. The story of the African's return home has been used in many variations in Caribbean literature and in at least one film (for a brief account of other uses of the tale see McDaniel 1998, 3). In this version of the story, those who are left behind to suffer in the Caribbean have eaten too much salt and are too heavy to levitate; they cannot follow Guinea John's flight back home.

Lovelace then goes on to weave a full account of those left behind, with the main characters, Bango Durity and Alford George, choosing alternative strategies to survive in the colony. Bango, a laborer and social critic, subverts racism and colonialism by embedding himself within the rich texture of the island's multicultural society. Lovelace's description of Bango's life exhibits a full range of local folklore. Alford, on the other hand, identifies with the Metropole, at first by being grounded in a colonial education and then by becoming a schoolteacher and a politician. Although the curse of salt was exhibited upon enslaved Africans, Lovelace metaphorically applies the notion to postcolonial Trinidad, where its diverse population from Africa and Asia must break its psychological bonds with Africa, India, and Great Britain so they can create a new, local identity.

Another folkloric use of salt is found in tales of the soucoyant. The soucoyant is a vampire that may be foiled by sprinkling salt on its skin, which it removes at night when it goes about its evil doings. It is well-known that a soucoyant cannot dress if its skin has been sprinkled with salt! However, before daybreak, to protect against a soucoyant's attack, one may sprinkle salt at the threshold of one's house; the soucoyant must count each grain before it can enter. Since it cannot finish the job until daylight, when the soucoyant again must put on its skin and return to normal life, the occupants are saved from having their blood sucked out of their bodies. A good review of the notion of "salt" in Caribbean folklore may be found at http://www.angelfire.com/wa2/margin/nonficSellmanSalt.html.

Other books by Lovelace also are rich with folkloric references to Trinidad. *The Dragon Can't Dance* (1979) is set during Carnival time, and one of his plays, *Jestina's Calypso* (1984) centers on a song, "Toco Jestina," Lovelace knew from his youth, growing up in Toco village. A repeated line is,

> Toco Jestina, who go marry to you
> Your face like a whale and you now come from jail.

The play is an exploration of issues of color, beauty, and identity and is written largely in vernacular language.

Caribbean Writers Abroad

The examples I chose to review in the previous section, *A House for Mr. Biswas* and *Omeros,* were written or conceived in original form while the authors were still living in the islands. I turn now to a handful of writers who either have been raised abroad or were born outside the Caribbean of Caribbean parents. It will not be possible even to begin to touch all such authors, and so a few representative samples will have to suffice.

Most small islands in the Caribbean cannot sustain a writer's life, and so many have chosen to live and work abroad, at least part of the time. One of the most important Caribbean writers was Haitian-born Jacques Stephen Alexis, who lived in France while attending medical school and traveled throughout Europe. His first novel, *Compère Général Soleil,* was written in draft form in 1949 and published in French in 1955. Now in an English-language edition, *General Sun, My Brother* (1999) is rich with characterizations of the local elite, of peasants, and Dominicans, who share the island of Hispaniola with Haitians. Alexis fills his novel with Haitian folklore, including use of the indigenous language of the Haitians, Kréyòl.

Audre Lorde was born in the United States to Caribbean parents. She had an important impact on both feminist and lesbian literatures in the United States. In her novel, *Zami: A New Spelling of My Name* (1982), she developed a sense of well-being as a lesbian, based in part on her search for her mother's Carriacouan roots. On Carriacou, which is part of the country of Grenada, the word *zami,* which means "friend" in Creole French (called Patois or "Broken French" in Carriacou), also means "lesbian" in Creole English. As Lorde came to know Carriacouan culture, she discovered that zami relationships were informally institutionalized as a folk custom, in part due to the large excess of adult women compared with men on the island.

Keith Warner, who has returned to Trinidad in retirement after a career teaching and writing in the Washington, D.C., area, has written about the use of calypso in Trinidad Literature (1982, 123–38).

John O. Stewart, also a Trinidadian, has taught for many years at the University of California, Davis. His background includes both literature and anthropology. Chapters of his book *Drinkers, Drummers, and Decent Folk* (1989), alternates ethnographic case studies with fiction. Together, they get at both objective and subjective truth about the islanders.

Paule Marshall was born in New York City of Barbadian parents. Her *Praisesong for the Widow* (1983) incorporates the common Caribbean myth of flight into the text, in a very different manner than Lovelace does in *Salt.* Avey Johnson, a black American from suburban New York City, is on a cruise in the Caribbean. While in Grenada she travels to the small island of Carriacou, where she soaks in her African roots by experiencing Afro-Caribbean culture, including the Big Drum Dance, the story of the flying African, and other customs. Lorna McDaniel, an ethnomusicologist, wrote an ethnography, entitled *The Big Drum Ritual of Carriacou: Praisesongs in Rememory of Flight* (1998), that was inspired by Marshall's novel, thus reversing the usual trend of fiction being based on fact. Two other writers have reached wider audiences in recent years, Edwidge Danticat of New York and Nalo Hopkinson of Toronto. Danticat was born in Haiti in 1969 and was raised there until she was 12 years of age. She then joined her parents in New York City, where she continues to live. She has written many novels and short stories, originally in her native Kréyòl while still a teenager in Haiti. Her later works are in English. While most of her writing concerns Haiti or Haitian émigrés in Brooklyn, one collection of short stories, *Krik? Krak!* (1996), stands out with respect to the use of folklore. Set in part in Haiti during the reign of dictator Jean-Claude Duvalier, the stories trace the Haitian boat people and how some settle in New York. The title refers to the tradition of storytelling in the Afro-French Caribbean, including Haiti, Martinique, Guadeloupe, Dominica, St. Lucia, and Carriacou. On these islands, krik? Krak! are folktales told at wakes or on other occasions to children or to anyone who may enjoy them. In one story, boat people flee Haiti and head toward the Bahamas. While under sail in rickety boats, some tell stories:

> We spent most of yesterday telling stories. Someone says, Krik? You answer, Krak! And they say, I have many stories I could tell you, and then they go on and tell these stories to you, but mostly to themselves. Sometimes it feels like we have been at sea longer than the many years that I have been on this earth. The sun comes up and goes down. (14)

Danticat has also written a memoir/travelogue of her first Carnival in Haiti, having been raised a Baptist and not allowed such festivities as a child. Her book is titled *After the Dance: A Walk through Carnival in Jacmel, Haiti* (2002).

Nalo Hopkinson is a Canadian science fiction writer. She was born in Jamaica in 1960 and lived in several West Island islands before settling with her family in Canada when she was 12 years of age. Her first novel, *Brown Girl in the Ring* (1998) is a science fiction novel set in a Toronto of the near future. The title itself refers to a popular children's folksong found in the English-speaking Caribbean:

> There's a brown girl in the ring, tra la la la la
> She's sweet like sugar and spice.

The song is also the title of a 1997 book of children's songs from Trinidad and Tobago, by Alan Lomax, J. D. Elder, and Bess Lomax Hawes, and of a CD of children's songs from the Caribbean by Lomax.

Moko Jumbies, St. Thomas carnival, U.S. Virgin Islands, May 2004. Photo: Kenneth Bilby.

In Hopkinson's novel, the Canadian government has abandoned the center of the city, and the remaining people are forced to live in chaos. The protagonist is Ti-Jeanne and her grandmother is Gros-Jeanne, who is a Vodou priestess. After the death of Gros-Jeanne, Ti-Jeanne, with the help of folk beliefs and bush medicine, is able to survive a series of trials, including the need to find a heart for a transplant for the premier of Ontario. The text is filled with allusions to Caribbean folk customs, and the dialogue is rich in vernacular speech.

Hopkinson's next novel was *Midnight Robber* (2000), a title taken from a Trinidad Carnival character whose roots go back to the Western cowboys that Trinidadians saw in films in the 1930s and adapted to Carnival. The midnight robber wears an exaggerated Mexican-style western hat and carries a gun and sometimes a whip. He "robs" fellow Carnival revelers and gives special speeches full of braggadocio. The novel unfolds with two narrators, one in vernacular speech and the other in standard English. It is the tale of Tan-Tan, a girl who pretends to be a midnight robber.

Garifuna masqueraders in Belize. Photo credit: Oliver Greene.

A third novel by Hopkinson is *Salt Roads* (2003), which has three main characters: Mer, a healer and slave in Haiti; Jeanne Duval, a dancer and courtesan of mixed African and French descent in Paris; and Meritet, an Ethiopian-Greek prostitute in fourth-century Egypt. A Haitian goddess, Ezili, who can move through time, works through the three women by traveling on the Salt Roads. Using the medium of Caribbean folklore, Hopkinson has created a novel that spans continents and leaps through centuries and cultures.

THEATER

Most Caribbean theater developed relatively late, in the nineteenth century, and Afro-Caribbean people were not usually directly involved in productions until well into the twentieth century. Folk themes show up first in localized vernacular theater, which sometimes evolved into "legitimate" theater in the twentieth century. A good overview of this process, listing both types of theater and individual actors and playwrights, is *The Cambridge Guide to African and Caribbean Theatre* (Banham, Hill, and Woodyard 1994, 159). This volume reviews plays from Spanish- and English-speaking islands but only contains a brief section on the French Caribbean. In the section on Cuba (159–67), the authors note that the person most responsible for the development of Cuban national theater was Francisco Covarrubias in the early nineteenth century. Covarrubias played the stereotyped, blackfaced character "negrito," an attempt to imitate folk, Afro-Cuban people's mannerisms, possibly even before a similar minstrelsy began in the United States. Moore covers more on this development in *Nationalizing Blackness* (1997), especially chapter 2 ("Minstrelsy in Havana: Music and Dance of the 'Teatro Vernáculo'"). In the nineteenth century and as recently as the early 1950s, there were few black Cuban actors, and Afro-Cuban roles were played by whites in blackface. There were classic stereotypes, "such as the *negrito, mulata,* and *gallego* [peasant Spaniard]" (45). The Teatro Vernáculo was a locale where music and dance were formalized into theatrical pieces. While formal theatrical productions were classics from Europe, a local Cuban theater aside from the Teatro Vernáculo developed in the 1940s (Cuba—E Theater and Film, http://encarta.msn.com/encyclopedia_761569844_5/Cuba.html).

Indigenous theater, with folk roots, began early in the twentieth century in Jamaica (Banham et al. 1994, 197–218). One of the most important performers and playwrights by midcentury was Louise Bennett (203), who was noted for her use of vernacular speech in her performances.

One the pioneers in twentieth-century theater in the eastern Caribbean was Errol Hill (Stone 1994). Hill's papers are online at http://ead.dartmouth.edu/html/ml77.html. His early play, *Man Better Man* (1964), concerns stickfighting in Trinidad, a kind of boxing in which two or more men hit each other with staves until one is felled or draws blood from his opponent. A very old folk custom in the Caribbean, it has central African, East Indian, and British historical antecedents. Hill's seminal book with respect to Caribbean folklore, *The Trinidad Carnival: Mandate for a National Theatre* (1997 [1972]), is the first major study on Trinidad Carnival and calypso, the music of Carnival. As was the case in Cuba, formal theater in Trinidad was based on foreign models, and European plays were produced. Hill argued for an indigenous theater, partly using Carnival as a model (114–19).

The Little Carib Theatre was Trinidad's first permanent arts venue. Beryl McBurnie established the Little Carib in Port of Spain in 1948, and it became a place for Creole arts, such as dance and steel-band presentations. The first stage presentation of a steel band, the Woodbrook Invaders Steel Orchestra—a performance that was actually recorded—was given at the Little Carib Theatre. The theater's clientele were the Trinidadian middle class and tourists. In 1959, Derek

Stickfighting in Martinique, postcard from the early 1900s.

Walcott extended the theater's mandate by founding the Little Theatre Workshop (http://www.ttw.org.tt/pastprod.html). Over the years, there have been many plays centering on Carnival activities or on other aspects of Trinidadian vernacular culture; the aforementioned *Jestina Calypso,* by Earl Lovelace, is one such example.

Folk theater, primarily from the English-speaking eastern Caribbean, has been well documented in the research of Roger Abrahams and by a group of scholars from the University of Puerto Rico (see especially Anonymous 2001). It is from such vernacular arts that playwrights have drawn themes and settings for their plays. A general trend in theater in the English-speaking Caribbean is to integrate more and more vernacular language, local settings, and thoroughly Creolize the play itself. Writers like Lovelace have moved away from the predominant use of standard English, as is found in Walcott and others, toward almost writing in English Creole as a distinct language. This trend also continues in vernacular theater by local playwrights, whose works are very close to their folk sources.

FILM

Caribbean folklore themes have been very common in films, nearly since the beginning of the medium. It is not possible to review all use of folklore themes in film, so I am going to review one film for each decade, beginning in the 1940s. This will simultaneously touch on Caribbean folklore in film while noting the changes in how folklore has been used over the years.

The most common theme putatively about Caribbean folklore in film, without a doubt, is what researcher Bob Corbett calls "Voodoo" and "Zombie" films (http://www.webster.edu/~corbetre/haiti/voodoo/zombilist.htm). Although based in the Haitian folk religion of Vodou and the zombie, or the "living dead," a relatively minor aspect of the religion, the terms have taken on lives of their own in Hollywood films and, indeed, in vernacular North American culture far removed from folklore origins. The image of the voodoo doll (in which one sticks pins to harm the person that the doll depicts); the zombie with arms outstretched, ready to strangle a fearful, hapless victim; the notion that voodoo is a false magic, a superstition; and even the sense that so-called voodoo economics is some sort of concocted economics that is false—all these notions tell us more about an American image of Vodou than they tell us about Haitian beliefs. Nevertheless, they "play off" the Haitian religion, so we need to know how and why the American view of the religion differs from the original.

The zombie film I have chosen to look at here is the classic *I Walked with a Zombie* (1943). Readers interested in the film as a horror classic should refer to the many Web sites that discuss it. I am concerned only with how the film relates to Caribbean folklore. The setting is the fictional Caribbean island of St. Sebastian. Like Walcott's *Omeros,* which is based on Homeric epics, *I Walked with a Zombie* is also a reformulated classic, in this case Charlotte Bronte's novel *Jane Eyre* (2003 [1847]). The plot has little to do with the real West Indies or Haitian zombies. Our folkloric interest is not the zombies, however, but the wonderful way the plot line is framed by Sir Lancelot's calypso, "Shame and Scandal in the Family." Lancelot (Lancelot Pinard) was born to an upper middle class family in Trinidad and moved to New York in the late 1930s. Originally intent on acting, he became a calypso singer—this would have been a forbidden occupation by his family back home—and performed in nightclubs in the city. The form of "Shame and Scandal" is based on traditional calypso. Pinard's original song itself has gone through many incarnations over the years, the most famous version of which is Lord Melody's (Fitzroy Alexander). Here is a case where a popular song, fit in the style of Trinidadian calypso, reenters the calypso tradition to become a legitimate vernacular song.

The next film of interest is *Island in the Sun* (1957), based on Alex Waugh's novel of the same name (1955), starred Harry Belafonte and Dorothy Dandridge. Set on the fictional island of Santa Marta (probably Grenada, where much of the movie was filmed), the plot concerns racism between the white and light-skinned elite on the island and the vast majority of laborers, who are of African descent. Belafonte plays labor leader David Boyeur, a character said to be modeled on Eric

Matthew Gairy, who later became the first prime minister of Grenada at the time of independence from Great Britain. Three aspects of the film relate to folklore. The beautiful photography of the island and its inhabitants throughout the film show evidence of local dress, architecture, sailing vessels, and other customs that, in passing, illustrate the folklore of the island. Next, this is the first major film in which the viewer can see and hear the steel band, which was invented less than 15 years earlier and which has become an important musical assemblage. Finally, Lord Burgess (Irving Burgess) wrote many of the songs that Belafonte sings. Although he was born in New York City, Burgess's mother was born in Barbados. He wrote or arranged many traditional West Indian songs, including the title song and "Lead Man Holler" (also in the film), which have the feel of traditional songs even though they are not.

Thunderball (1965) is the fourth of the many James Bond films. Part of the film is set in Nassau in the Bahamas, during a Jonkonnu celebration. Traditional players made their costumes for the film as Junkanoo is held on Boxing Day (December 26) and New Year's Day, not when the film was actually made. Jonkonnu, or "John Canoe," is a traditional celebration in the British Caribbean and elsewhere in the Americans. Costumed dancers, musicians and singers parade the streets, as in Nassau, or serenade from house to house or in public areas.

The Harder They Come (1973) is one of the first true West Indian films. Set in rural Jamaica and urban Kingston, the storyline tells of a young immigrant to the city, Ivan O. Martin (played by reggae star Jimmy Cliff), who tries to make it big. He records a hit 45 rpm record, but the profits go to crime bosses running the company, not to Ivan. The film presents a heightened sense of social realism, with its extreme social-class distinctions and the poverty of many urban residents. It centers on the underbelly of Jamaican society, including drug dealing, the seamy side of the record industry, Jamaican slums, and many songs by budding reggae singers, including, of course, Jimmy Cliff, Toots and the Maytals, and others. The film shows how traditional Jamaican culture becomes transformed into pop culture, first in Jamaica and then through the power of the film and the music, into a worldwide, mass media phenomenon.

Martiniquean Euzhan Palcy's first film was *Sugar Cane Alley* (1984). The film is set in Martinique in the 1930s, among a community of cane cutters and in sophisticated Fort of France. The storyline centers on relationships that young Jose has with his grandmother, an old man, and his best friend. The film opens with credits that run on top of Martiniquean postcards of the era. Postcards are a wonderful source for folklorists for many reasons. Of course, they were produced for tourists, but they often show many aspects of traditional culture. On a symbolic level, postcards may tell a deeper story of the relationship between tourism and the local culture and may present a harbinger for later bracketing of folklore for tourist consumption. The film also begins with an archaic beguine dance played on a piano, a dance and musical style that itself is based on folk themes. The intent of the beguine in the film, however, is to set the mood for urban Martinique, not the cane fields. The ambiance there is enhanced by a field song and by Krik?Krak! storytelling by the old man, Medouze, who tells Jose a version of the flying African myth. There are other folkloric or everyday-life references, including the workers in the field, the relationship between workers and the overseer, payday, the sheds where workers live, the torch lanterns, and more.

The last film I have selected is *Buena Vista Social Club* (1999). A documentary, the film traces the American guitarist and world-music aficionado Ry Cooder in his travels through Cuba in order to find musicians and singers from the island who were famous in the 1950s. It covers the old musicians' return to fame and their concertizing in the United States. In this better-than-average concert film, we get to see the back streets of Havana and meet some of the people who made several Cuban musical genres famous, such as singer Ibrahim Ferrer, pianist Rubén González, and singer and composer Eliades Ochoa. Each made important contributions to Cuban vernacular and popular music, especially to the bolero, the rumba, the son, and the chachacha.

THE INFLUENCE OF CARIBBEAN FOLK MUSIC AND DANCE ON STAGED DANCE AND CLASSICAL AND POPULAR MUSIC

The influence of Caribbean folk music and dance abroad has been slight in classical music but widespread in popular music. Similarly, Caribbean dance has had wide appeal in the last century, and many Caribbean dance styles have swept the globe. Unfortunately, information on the interrelationships between Caribbean folk genres and popular and classical music in both the Caribbean and elsewhere is widely scattered and found in bits and pieces in publications or Web sites that focus on other issues. In other words, it is necessary to dig to understand these relationships. However, several overviews of Caribbean music point to the seepage of folk music into popular styles and even into classical music. The best overall study of Caribbean music is Peter Manuel's *Caribbean Currents* (2006), which gives a regional overview with emphasis on folk and popular music. A quick overview of Afro-American music, centering on the Caribbean, is my own article "Music of the African Diaspora in the Americas" (2004). It sketches the influence of sacred folk music on popular music, especially the influence of Afro-Caribbean religions on such varied styles as salsa, reggae, and the Carnival music of Trinidad.

Dance

Although scholars usually separate music and dance, the two are often inseparable. Long out of print, Earl Leaf's *Isles of Rhythm* (1948) is one of the first books to trace dance styles of the Caribbean for a general audience. Leaf mostly visits tourist spots and describes staged shows that nevertheless are based on folk themes. He covers Cuba, Jamaica, Haiti, the Virgin Islands, Martinique, Trinidad, and briefly touches other places as well. The preface to the book was written by Katherine Dunham, who was a student of anthropologist Melville Herskovits as well as a dancer and choreographer. She researched dances in Haiti and elsewhere in the islands, and also wrote a book about her field experiences among the Jamaican maroons in which she collected ethnographic material for her staged dance routines (*Katherine Dunham's Journey to Accompong,* 1946). Lisa Lekis's *Folk Dances of Latin American* (1958) is still one of the best chronicles of dances that were performed in the mid-1950s and includes both folk and popular dance styles. In spite of the title, the book covers all the Caribbean. Lekis's book is an excellent snapshot of the sort of dances that formed the basis of the staged performances by Katherine Dunham, Beryl McBurnie, Massie Patterson, Josephine Premise, and Pearl Primus, all important dancers and choreographers who brought folk dance to the world stage.

Yvonne Daniel's *Rumba: Dance and Social Change in Contemporary Cuba* (1995) covers the gamut from traditional rumbas to staged performances of the dance, highlighting the rumba craze that spread throughout the world in the early 1930s. Another great book on Caribbean dance is Susanna Sloat's edited work *Caribbean Dance from Abakuá to Zouk* (2002). The book contains 23 articles that cover dance throughout the region. Unlike music scholars, who tend to focus on folk or popular music relatively narrowly, many dance researchers are dancers themselves and participate in dance companies that bring local folk dances to international communities. For example, in "Katherine Dunham's 'Tropical Revue,'" Veve A. Clark writes about Dunham's staged production of folk material. This article appears in a book co-edited by Sara E. Johnson (2006, 305–20). There are other articles that give an overview of the region (including Cuban dances), an article on Rex Nettleford's celebrated Jamaican Dance Theatre (Nettleford once staged a ballet on a song by early reggae singer Toots Hebert), more on Haitian and Dominican dance, and articles on dance styles from the eastern Caribbean stretching from Puerto Rico to Trinidad and Tobago.

Many important stage dancers and choreographers from the Caribbean sought to create formalized versions of folk dances of the islands, for the stage or on film. Perhaps the best way to find out about this aspect of Caribbean dance is to Google the names of dance pioneers. Here I will briefly mention a few; readers are urged to follow up with their own search using Internet sources. Beryl

McBurnie, before she established the Little Carib Theatre in Port of Spain, was as a dancer; her first production on the island was in 1940. Pearl Primus is another Trinidadian who became a famed stage dancer; she performed in New York City. Josephine Premise was an actor, singer, and dancer in New York, and she appeared in many West Indian productions in the city that were based on both folk themes and on Broadway dance styles. Massie Patterson, a Jamaican by birth, created her own dance company. Also a singer, she traveled the United States with Trinidadian composer, orchestra leader, and pianist Lionel Belasco.

Finally, there are many venues, especially clubs, restaurants, and cruise ships, throughout the Caribbean, in the United States, in Canada, and in Europe, that feature Caribbeanesque dance and music routines based on real or quasi-folk themes. These presentations are extremely wide ranging, from Desi Arnaz's dramatic staging of the Cuban song "Babalu," to a single Caribbean-like dance routine that may be featured in a club or at a theater-restaurant.

Folk Themes in Caribbean Classical Music

The impact that folk music has had on classical music, both in the Caribbean and abroad, has come primarily from the Greater Antilles, islands large enough to support a middle class and elite that patronized the concert hall and opera. The greatest impact has come from two sources, New Orleans and Cuba.

One may not think of New Orleans and its music as Caribbean, but historically, considering his Caribbean Spanish and French roots, it has been a bridge between the Caribbean and North America. Through about 1900, the cultural elite of New Orleans was French Creole, and New Orleans supported opera before most North American cities. A case can be made that New Orleans was a center of an indigenous Caribbean classical music that also included Cuba and Puerto Rico.

Perhaps the greatest composer of nineteenth-century North America was Louis Moreau Gottschalk (Starr 1995). Born and raised in New Orleans, Gottschalk's father was German and his mother was an elite Haitian. His grandmother and a black nurse, both of whom were born in Haiti, raised him. After the Haitian revolution at the beginning of the nineteenth century, many white and light-skinned Haitian estate owners dispersed. Some went to eastern Cuba, where they introduced their salon orchestra called orquesta Francesa. Others ended up in New Orleans. In New Orleans, social class in the early 1800s consisted of white or mostly white elite Creoles, a colored Creole middle class, and Afro-Caribbean slaves as well as a few North Americans. Gottschalk soaked up both the Creole and African music for which the city was famous, particularly the drum and ritual music that was played in Congo Square. Many of his classical pieces reflected these influences. His "Bamboula," written in 1844, was named after the bula, an African-style drum still found in parts of the Caribbean. As an adult, Gottschalk spent a time in Cuba, where he worked with local composers and musicians and added to the richness of Cuban classical music. Like his contemporary Frantz Liszt, Gottschalk was a prodigy. As an adult, he traveled the world, giving grandly bombastic concerts. Sometimes he would gather scores of pianos together on stage to play his compositions. He was both popular and controversial, and he was a major force in spreading composed versions of Afro-Caribbean music to Europe, the United States, and South America.

When Gottschalk was in Cuba in 1857, he directed a performance of his Third Symphony, "A Night in the Tropics." In addition to ten pianos that he brought from Santiago on the other end of the island, his orchestra included black tumba (drum) players. For the first time in such auspicious circumstances, Gottschalk presented what was essentially Creole classical music, combining European and African musical sensibilities.

Gottschalk's music fit into an existing strain of Cuban semiclassical music that was composed for the orquesta Francesa. Two Cuban composers, Manuel Saumell and José White, created contradanza compositions with an Afro-Cuban syncopation. Saumell was a pianist and wrote semiclassical pieces based on the contradanza, and White, a mulatto, wrote "La Bella Cubana," a habanera, one of the most popular pieces of the nineteenth century in Cuba (Sublette 2004, 150). The habanera rhythm, a version of the Cuban clave, was made famous in Bizet's light opera "Carmen," first performed in 1875. Semiclassical piano music, or music such as White's "La Bella Cubana," were not only popular in Cuba and in the Caribbean generally, but they represent a branch of a family of music that includes North American ragtime and, on the vernacular level, the roots of New Orleans jazz.

Ned Sublette has nicely summarized the musical mix in Cuba from which European and African musical sensibilities combined to create new classical and light classical music that has remained a part of the classical repertoire to this day:

> A well-established tradition of military wind bands playing regularly all across the length and breadth of the island; at the height of the popularity of Italian opera, the hemisphere's best company, as well as opera performances in many cities on the island; the largest theater in the hemisphere; in the cities, a substantial population of free people of color who dominated the profession of music; in the countryside, large numbers of newly arriving Africans who constantly refreshed the African musical and religious traditions; a deeply rooted tradition of popular poetry that emphasized the ability to improvise; a musical genre, the habanera, involving a syncopated bass and an orchestra that included rhythmic percussion, that had become popular across a wide part of the hemisphere (the contradanza-danza-habanera-tango complex would evolve into the danzón in Cuba, the tango in Argentina, and, under a different set of influences in the United States, would find its way into ragtime and the cakewalk); and a thriving tradition of comic music theater that had something in common with its U.S. Counterpart, the emerging minstrel show. (155)

In the 1930s, librettists Agustin Rodriguez and Jose Sanchez-Arcilla and composer Gonzalo Roig presented Cirilo de Villaverde's nineteenth century novel *Cecilia Valdés* as a zarzuela, or light opera. Roig was a violinist, bass player, and a symphony conductor. His zarzuela opened at the Teatro Marti in Havana in 1932 and went on to great success and many performances both in Cuba and in Latin America. The operetta is almost a perfect synthesis of European classical form and Afro-Cuban rhythms and includes a danzón, tangos, and other songs and instruments indigenous to the island.

Perhaps the most enchanting light classical music to have come out of Cuba in the nineteenth century, a style that has persisted to this day and influenced generations of musical configurations, is the danzón. A good source for understanding the Cuban danzón, and its Mexican spin-off, is "El Danzón en Cuba," in *De Cuba con Amor... El Danzón en Mexico* (Jara Gámez, Rodríguez Yeyo, and Zedillo Castillo 1994). The roots of the danzón were in the contradanza, which was similar to the square dance or the quadrille. The contradanza was popular in eastern Cuba and had been brought to the island by the Haitian elite and their slaves when they fled Haiti in the early 1800s. Miguel Failde Pérez, a man of mixed African and European descent, published the first danzón in 1879 (http://www.danzon.com/). The danzón was played by an orquesta Francesa, and the form of the dance was based on a syncopated version of the European rondo. This form eventually evolved and often contained a section, added by José Urfé in the early twentieth century, that was very reminiscent of the West African call-and-response melodic form, the estribillo. In the 1910s, Antonio María Romeu added a piano and flute to the configuration and renamed the orchestra the charanga. This style of orchestra changed throughout the twentieth century and adapted itself to various dance styles, including the mambo, chachacha, and the pachanga. Some important foreigners have composed danzones or danzón-like pieces, including Aaron Copeland and George Gershwin.

There are many important Cuban composers whose compositions bridged the gap between light classical pieces and popular music, including Ernesto Lecuona and Eliseo Grenet. All of them integrate European sensibilities with Afro-Cuban rhythms and melodic forms.

Puerto Rico has a deep and rich history of combining classical and folk music. Often, following Cuba, nineteenth-century Puerto Rican composers created the danza by combining contradanza melodies into one piece (Manuel 2006, 53–63). The most important period composers of danzas were Juan Morel Campos and Manuel Tavárez, whose music could be described broadly as syncopated Chopin (whose music was as French as it was Polish) for string orchestra. Delightful! Nineteenth-century Haitian classical music, for the most part, mirrored European styles but, coinciding with the American invasion and occupation of Haiti in 1915, African American composers in the United

States, as well as composers within the Haitian elite, created a classical music that incorporated Vodou themes derived from the folk culture of the Haitian peasants (Largey 2006, 3–4).

Pop Music

The greatest impact that Caribbean folklore has had outside the Caribbean itself has been in borrowing Caribbean popular music, which continues to be influenced by the vernacular music of the islands. New Orleans jazz, Cuban son, salsa, calypso, ska, reggae, dancehall, and konpa are some of the twentieth-century styles that have originated in the Caribbean region and have circled the globe. In recent years, there has been a plethora of excellent studies of each of these and related popular music, which I will now discuss.

Volume 2, *South America, Mexico, Central America, and the Caribbean,* of the omnibus encyclopedia *The Garland Encyclopedia of World Music* (Olsen and Sheehy 1998) contains many articles about music from most of the islands of the Caribbean as well as from mainland countries included within this handbook. While these articles focus on folk genres, one can find references to how those genres have influenced "popular music," which is listed in the index, including a very large subheading on the Caribbean. A brief overview of Caribbean music, "The Music of the Caribbean," is in this work and was written by Martha Ellen Davis (789–97). The same editors recently published a paperback edition on the music from Spanish-speaking countries included in that encyclopedia (*The Garland Handbook of Latin American Music,* 2000). Both massive encyclopedias are complete with CDs containing musical samples.

Jazz coalesced in New Orleans from marching bands and small, piano-based groups that played in bordellos and at other venues. I cannot trace the Caribbean influences on jazz here other than to suggest reading two books. These studies stress the vernacular origins of jazz in a city that mixed Creoles (black, white, and mixed-race), French-speaking Cajuns (the descendants of Acadians who fled British rule in the Canadian maritime provinces), and English-speaking whites and blacks, many of whom were the descendants of slaves. Ostransky points out in *Jazz City: The Impact of Our Cities on the Development of Jazz* (1978), that the local musical culture of the Creoles and the blacks is chiefly responsible for the development of jazz, especially when near century's end, segregationist laws, along with the closing of the red-light district, threw together dark- and light-skinned Creoles with English-speaking black Americans. This created a new cultural environment out of which jazz sprung. One view of how this happened is found in Alan Lomax's *Mister Jelly Lord* (1950), an "as told to" book based on the Library of Congress recordings that Lomax made with Jelly Roll Morton, a Creole pianist who played an archaic style of jazz that combined

Caribbean rhythms—Morton called it the "Spanish" tinge—with American ragtime. There is no more interesting firsthand account of how the aforementioned ethnic groups mixed to develop jazz, in spite of Morton's exaggerated claims of his own importance.

Twenty years ago, there were few studies of Caribbean music but quality ethnographies of Caribbean music from particular islands are now springing up with regularity. I will get to some of the most important new books in a moment, but now I want to review the few comprehensive studies of the Caribbean as a whole. The pioneer books that looked at the relationships between music in the Americas are John Storm Roberts' *Black Music of Two Worlds* (1998), *Latin Jazz* (1999a), and *The Latin Tinge* (1999b). Roberts, a music critic rather than an academic, examined the connection between Africa, where he had long experience, and African-influenced music of the Americas. He helped spread the concept within popular music of what is referred to as world music and was one of the first people to note the importance of clave rhythms in Latin music. A more recent study is Peter Manuel's *Caribbean Currents* (2006). This book covers the entire area and has a small section on Caribbean music abroad. Kenneth Bilby, probably the most knowledgeable scholar on Caribbean music, wrote the Jamaican chapter. Manuel's expertise is also important for our purposes, since he notes how popular music has been influenced by vernacular music. Manuel has written on the music of India and specializes in both Cuba and in Indian music in Trinidad. Finally, two of my essays in part trace the influence of folk music on popular music in the Caribbean: "West African and Haitian Influences on the Ritual and Popular Music of Carriacou, Trinidad, and Cuba" (1998) and "Music of the African Diaspora in the Americas" (2004). In these articles, I touch on how religious folk music has influenced popular music, such as its incorporation into Afro-Cuban music or Jamaican reggae.

Beginning in the mid-nineteenth century, folk music from Cuba has had a profound impact on popular music outside that country. In the nineteenth century, it was the habanera, which, as developed in Argentina, became the tango in the early twentieth century. In Cuba itself, Spanish- and African-based folk genres mixed and moved onto the world stage in a series of popular musical and dance styles. Some of these dances were based on Afro-Cuban modifications of the orquesta Francesa and the charanga, which evolved into a grouping of strings, flute, piano, string bass, guiro (a scrapper), and timbales (Afro-Cuban drums modeled after European military drums). The music was syncopated, and the rhythms were versions of clave: danzón, mambo, chachacha, pachanga.

Another Cuban configuration that went international was the conjunto. It originally consisted of Cuban folk instruments, such as the bongos, tres, guiro, marimbula (with metal strips attached to a wooden box that acts as a sounding board), and maracas (possibly also of American Indian origin). Some of these instruments gave way to or were supplemented by string bass (sub for the cajón), trumpet (added), saxophone (added), and guitar. The conjunto played Afro-Spanish Cuban music, such as the son, the rumba, the guaguanco, or the guaracha. In the 1940s, this grouping, with the saxophone added, was the basis of the Arsenio Rodriguez conjunto, which influenced the salsa band as it developed in New York City, where Rodriguez lived, played, and recorded for a time (García 2006). By the 1970s, this music was called salsa (meaning "sauce") and was the most important Latin musical style in New York, as played primarily by Puerto Rican and Cuban musicians. The style also spread to Mexico, Central America, and South America. Together with additions of Dominican merengue—itself influenced by the Cuban son (Austerlitz 1997), salsa, or its musical predecessors that originated in Cuban vernacular styles—salsa became a world music, rivaling rock, hip-hop, and reggae in some parts of the world for mass appeal. There are too many references to note here concerning this development, but a start in researching the subject may be found in books by Roberts, Sublette, and Moore. Salsa's greatest female singer, the late Celia Cruz, who incorporated elements from Santería into her musical performances, is the subject of Marceles's *Azúcar! The Biography of Celia Cruz* (2004).

There are too many studies of Latin music in New York to mention here, but a good review is Vernon W. Boggs's *Salsiology* (1992), which contains many articles, written by Boggs and others, about rumba, Puerto Rican influences on salsa, music venues in New York, musicians, and other topics. *Island Sounds in the Global City* (Allen and Wilcken 2001) has articles on Latin music in New York as well as Haitian and Trinidadian music in the city. The focus in both of these of these books is on how vernacular music from various places within the Caribbean becomes international in the environment of a large, metropolitan city where many different peoples meet and exchange musical ideas. Ruth Glasser's *My Music Is My Flag* (1995) not only notes the folk roots of popular music of Puerto Rico, it also traces the impact of Puerto Rican musicians on the Latin music scene in New York City, where they underwent influences from Cuban styles. Of special note is the coverage of Rafael Hernández and the Puerto Rican danza.

Two styles of popular music from the Dominican Republic are merengue (Austerlitz 1977) and bachata (Pacini Hernández 1995). The former is related to the Cuban son and has many rural and urban substyles. The latter is a more recent form of vernacular music that is popular in urban areas. Dominicans have brought both styles to New York City and elsewhere, where they have vied with salsa as the "sound" for immigrant Latin peoples.

These days, perhaps various incarnations of indigenous Jamaica music—mento, ska, reggae, and dancehall—are even more popular throughout the world than Afro-Cuban music. Each of these musical styles has vernacular roots. Mento is a traditional form of string band music that first became popular after World

War II (http://www.mentomusic.com/links.htm and http://homepages.nyu.edu/~dtn9606/mento.html). Mento has roots in Jonkonnu and quadrille music and was influenced by Trinidadian calypso; in fact, in the 1950s it was sometimes called calypso. Ska and reggae were popular dance music whose roots lie in the "sound systems" that Jamaicans developed in the 1950s, when disc jockeys traveled from town to town and gave open-air concerts of records—usually 45 rpm recordings—played one after the other. Sometimes they would add a patter to the recorded music. By the 1960s, original instrumental music, called versions, was recorded opposite a vocal selection, so that the DJ could talk over the music and segue into another selection. This was an origin of the now-worldwide DJ concept, which, after all, is really an early type of karaoke, which "democratized" the DJ concept by making anyone with guts enough to sing in front of peers and strangers into a karaoke machine.

Musically, ska and reggae have been influenced by many traditional and popular musical styles, including the music of the Rastafarians (a religion that originated in the 1930s that brings together traditional Jamaican customs, including music), Cumina, music of the maroons, and North American soul music. Dancehall evolved from reggae and dub music as played on sound systems. Dancehall is dance music played at all-night parties. The music is created by mixing recordings that DJs play, live patter, and live performers, blended into a seamless stream.

Discussions of Jamaican music can be found in Manuel (2006) (in the chapter written by Ken Bilby), Stolzoff (2000), and Hope (2006). Stolzoff briefly reviews earlier styles before focusing on dancehall, and Hope focuses exclusively on dancehall. There are very many books, articles, and Web sites devoted to the life and music of Bob Marley, arguably one of the two or three most well-known performers of the twentieth century. A good start on all things Marley is Timothy White's *Catch a Fire* (1992).

Music from Haiti and the French Caribbean has also made its mark on world music, although in recent decades not as much as music from Cuba or Jamaica. However, the impact of Trinidadian music that came out of the French Caribbean in the late 1700s is strong today—although, again, not as vast as reggae's influence. The spread of Afro-French music around the Caribbean goes like this. In the late 1700s, estate owners from the French Caribbean settled in Catholic Trinidad, where they formed a major part of rural, Creole culture on that island. Then, around 1800, there was a Haitian diaspora of slaves and estate owners who fled to Martinique, Guadeloupe, and eastern Cuba because of the slave rebellion in Haiti. Rural Haitian music centered on Vodou rites, while urban music centered on Carnival. The Haitian version of merengue is meringue, a Carnival music that has had an international influence.

Elizabeth McAlister's *Rara!* (2002) is the first book-length study of Haitian rara. The book is an interpretative ethnography of the Lenten Carnival bands that include vaccine (single-note trumpets made of hollowed-out bamboo) and other instruments, masquerades, and politically and sexually loaded songs filled with layers of meaning. In the chapter titled "Rara in New York City" (182–207), McAlister touches on rara in New York City, the development of "mizik rasin" which utilized drumming in Haitian pop music, and the creation of transnational alliances between rara musicians and other ethnic groups in the city, especially Jamaicans.

One of the best recent studies of popular music in Haiti is Gage Averill's *A Day for the Hunter, a Day for the Prey* (1997). Averill traces how vernacular and popular music in Haiti have developed in the twentieth century, in spite of a history of political repression; indeed, the music has expressed resistance to the political leadership. Some of the styles he discusses are traditional troubadour songs, konpa, and "roots music." A more recent synopsis, "Militarism in Haitian Music," by Averill and Yuen-Ming David Yih is found in *The African Diaspora: A Musical Perspective* (Monson 2000, 267–93). The article contains a great chart showing "the historical influence of the French military tradition on Haitian expressive culture" (272). The first book-length study of a popular music from the French West Indies, other than Haiti (and the first American ethnomusicological study to contain a CD), is Guilbault's *Zouk* (1993). Zouk is a mélange that has incorporated rhythms from Guadeloupian and Martiniquean drum and dance music. Zouk blends Afro-Caribbean, Indo-Caribbean, and European music. Popular music lyrics from the French islands of the Eastern Caribbean are the focus of Berrian's chapter on "Creole, Zouk, and Identity in Kassav's Optimistic Songs" (37–68), in her book *Awakening Spaces* (2000). She notes that Zouk music gained international prominence as played by "Kassav," a group of mostly Antillean musicians. Upon leaving the islands in the 1980s, the group made a big splash in Paris and in Africa. Berrian's study gives profiles of some of the Zouk composers and explains their lyrics in terms of political power and Creole identity.

In the last 90 years, vernacular and popular music from Haiti, Martinique, and Guadeloupe has feed into the mix of "world music," especially "Afropop" styles from central Africa. In some cases popular African and Caribbean music fused, as bands have exchanged musicians and as they perform together, especially in Europe. The best source for this development is the website for the syndicated public radio program, "Afropop Worldwide" (http://www.afropop.org/) or the Internet musical encyclopedia allmusic.com. Under the subheading "world" in the guide, one may quickly explore various world music styles and readily see the Caribbean connections to the international music scene. The Allmusic Guide includes essays on various genres but focuses mainly on specific artists and on CDs. Many popular music guides in book form that can be useful; for example, there is *World Music: The Rough Guide (Salsa to Soukous, Cajun to Calypso...The Complete Handbook)* (Broughton et al. 1994).

One other popular musical style has brought local, folk genres into the global popular mix and that is Trinidadian calypso. Historically, after Cuban music, the next important island to contribute to world music was Trinidad, not Jamaica or Haiti. Calypso moved from its island home as the Carnival music of Trinidad to many parts of the world by the 1910s, both as an influential style, but also as a part of the Trinidadian Carnival mix. The first syncopated black music from an English-speaking country was recorded in New York in 1912 by Lovey's Band from Trinidad (Spottswood and Hill 1989; Hill 1993). In the late 1920s, calypsonians recorded in New York, and some of those records were marketed in Ghana, where the Jacob Sam and the Kumasi Trio "covered" some of those recordings. Calypso was an important influence on the West African musical style called "highlife." A couple of decades later, in London, many musicians from the Caribbean, especially Trinidadians such as Lord Kitchener and Lord Beginner, mingled with West Africans and began to create new genres ("London Is the Place for Me 4"; see Noblett 2006). The internationalization of calypso has been documented nearly as thoroughly as Cuban music's spread from its home island. For example, *West Indian Rhythm* (Classic Calypso Collective 2006) is an encyclopedia of essays, song lyrics, reprints of old photographs, and 267 recordings on 10 CDs that documents calypsos recorded by the Decca company in Trinidad between 1938 and 1940. A close examination of this massive book and CD box set clearly illustrates the movement of calypso from a French Creole Carnival song to an international genre that both musically and lyrically contains cosmopolitan references to world events and a variety of musical styles. These styles include North American swing, the roots of the steel band, nineteenth-century Venezuelan string bands, Afro-Baptist songs, African songs, and many other types of music. By the late 1960s, these styles had coalesced into an international musical sound that sometimes fused with other Afropop styles. Other resources concerning the popularization of calypso include E. Hill (1997), Rohlehr (2004), D. Hill (1993), and Manuel (2006).

FESTIVALS

With the migration of Caribbean peoples outside their home islands, folk or local island festivals have circumnavigated the globe (see http://www.carnaval.com/main.htm for carnivals throughout the world, many of them in, or rooted in, the Caribbean). Such festivals have taken on new elements, especially in combining customs from various islands in a single event. One of the best places to see this process is New York City, whose Irish St. Patrick's Day parade, beginning in the nineteenth century, established a community parade as a vehicle for exhibiting the culture of immigrants and their ethnic identity. The major festivals in New York City that involve Caribbean peoples are the Puerto Rican Day Parade (http://www.nationalpuertoricandayparade.org/), the Dominican Day Parade (online English language newspaper, http://www.dominicantoday.com/app/frontpage.aspx, sometimes carries information on this event), and the largest of all, the West Indian Labor Day Parade (http://www.nationalpuertoricanday parade.org/; see also "Carnival: Community Dramatized," in Kasinitz 1992; Hill and Abrahamson 1979). The Trinidad-style Carnival has spread to over a hundred cities in Venezuela, North America, and Europe (see Nunley, "Festival Diffusion into the Metropole," in Nunley and Bettelheim 1988, 165–81). The Calle Ocho festival in Miami (Calle Ocho page is http://www.carnavalmiami.com/calle8/) is a complex street festival that was established by refugees from Cuba. Calle Ocho is now the single most important ethnic event in the city.

Each of these events mix Caribbean folk performances with typical New York, Miami, or other cities' local culture of street vending, glad-handing politicians, and the sort of activities one might find at any parade. The West Indian Labor Day is interesting because it mixes the customs of islands from the eastern Caribbean, Haiti, and Jamaica with a Trinidadian style Carnival form. In the week or so before Labor Day, thousands of West Indian-American and others converge on the City for converts, fashion shows, and other activities that cumulate with the Labor Day fete.

TOURISM AND FOLKLORE

Folk music and folk arts have been an integral part of the tourism industry in the Caribbean for over a hundred years; indeed, in some instances tourism has been responsible for modifying local customs, as experienced by islanders themselves. However, the local version of the custom often differs from the tourist version; both may have folk roots and both must be understood in the context of the performance, either a performance by local people put on by amateurs or professionals for tourists or a performance carried out by local people for themselves. Sometimes, as in the case of a very large festival—say, Carnival in Trinidad—the two are identical and the vast number of local participants overwhelms the relatively small numbers of tourists. In other instances—quadrille dances in some of the smaller islands of the eastern Caribbean, for example—the only venue where the custom remains may be in presentations for tourists, as local people no longer dance the quadrille for themselves. I have written a short article suggesting how music has been influenced by tourism (2002).

The presence of folk-related music and arts is overwhelming in the Caribbean tourist industry. Folklore is used to quickly give the tourist a sense of the place visited, either by including island music on cruise ships, in hotel entertainment, or in their advertisements on television or elsewhere. Caribbean actors, singers, and musicians entice North American tourists to come to the Caribbean, as island-based tourist industries vie for the money that the foreigners bring to their spot of sun, sand, and surf. Web sites maintained by Caribbean countries or by cruise lines, such as http://cruisereviews.com/, may be useful in documenting the interface between folklore and tourism. For example, particular cruises that that present Caribbean music or other folk arts, may be featured on cruise ship or country-based websites. Web sites also contains information on "shore excursions" that may include visits to folkloric groups. Many different Caribbean musical styles are played on cruise ships, in addition to the rock, rap, light classics, musicals, and so forth. Caribbean folklore is used to frame the tourist's trip, to give a sense of visiting a place different from home and to give the cultural flavor of the island.

In addition to tourism, folklore creates an image of Caribbean lifestyles through advertisements, films, novels written by people outside the islands, and in other media. As with the use of the ubiquitous voodoo stereotype, the Caribbean conjured up through such tactics may be based on folklore or it may be what Richard Dorson called "fakelore" (something that is said to be folklore but really is not). So-called Caribbean folklore in the hands of people outside the islands may be fakelore to Caribbean peoples. However, such fakelore becomes the image outsiders have of the Caribbean and it becomes folklore for the tourists; it is tourist folklore.

ART: PAINTING, PLASTIC ARTS, AND DESIGN

The last medium through which Caribbean folklore has spread outside the islands is art. This field is very large indeed, too large for me to cover adequately and well beyond my grasp of the subject. At every turn, Caribbean artists have utilized folkloric themes in their art. Caribbean artists range from professional (that is, formally trained in art) to folk (outsider or naïve artists), with many individuals falling between the two. Haitian artists have long enjoyed worldwide popularity. One book that traces the impact of Haitian art outside the home island is *Haitian Art in the Diaspora* (Viard 2003). This work includes a wide range of Haitian painters, both self- and formally trained. An earlier exhibition catalog is *Haitian Art* (Stebich 1978). This book includes articles and photographs of both plastic and graphic arts, mostly by naïve artists. *Memoria: Cuban Art of the 20th Century* (Veigas-Zamora et al. 2001) is an encyclopedia of Cuban plastic and graphic art, design, and photography of the last 50 years. In this massive volume on can find examples of Cuban folklore as seen by the artists. *AfroCuba: Works on Paper 1968–2003* is a catalog prepared by Judith Bettelheim (2005) for a gallery exhibition at San Francisco State University. It contains a variety of graphic arts by Cuban artists, together with brief biographies. Many of the paintings and other works presented in the catalog depict vernacular Cuban culture.

Folk artists are quite common in tourist locales; *The Mermaid Wakes* (Berg and Caliste 1989), with paintings by Canute Caliste of Carriacou, Grenada, is book of paintings by an outsider artist. His paintings hang in Europe and in the eastern United States.

There are other, diffuse examples of Caribbean creeping around the corners of worldwide mass-media-spread popular culture. There are the costumes of Peter Minshall, who designed the entertainment program for the Barcelona Olympics in 1992. Based on his annual Carnival masquerade bands, Minshall's masquerades are widely sought in North America and Europe. There is the multitalented Holder family, especially actor, painter, singer, musician, designer Jeffery. His

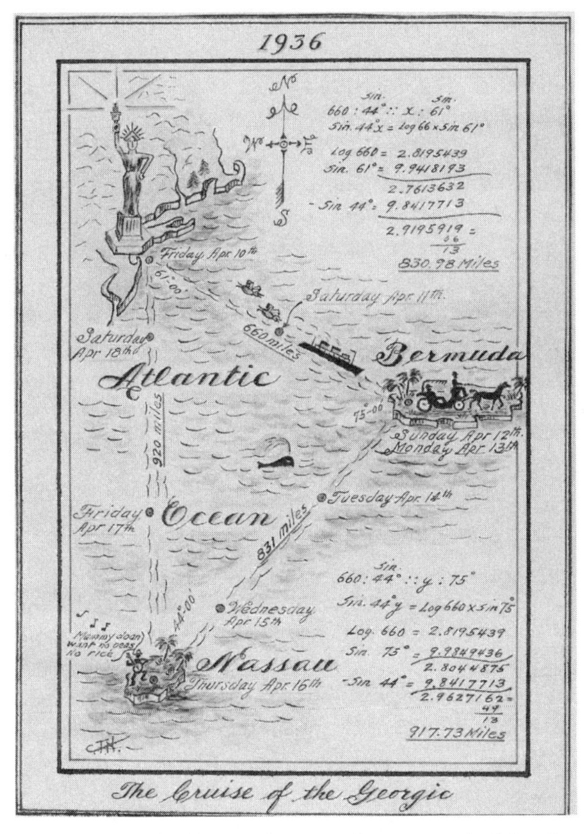

Tourist pen-and-ink map drawing of cruise to the West Indies, 1936.

masquerade designs were used in the move *The Wiz,* a black American version of *The Wizard of Oz.* Caribbean music—usually salsa or dancehall—is relatively common in television commercials. Finally, there are the little knickknacks that many tourists cherish—such as the "rumba box" from Jamaica—that seem to be sold at every airport on every island. Many, but not all, of these items are based on folkloric arts. I bought a set of papier-mâché statues of Santería Orisha (gods) in Cuba when I visited that island a decade and a half ago and I have my Cuban Eleguá on my desk. I pour libations of rum over it from time to time, especially when I think of a deceased friend from Mississippi whose license plate spelled out "Legba."

WORKS CITED

Abrahams, Roger D., with Nick Spitzer, John F. Szwed, and Robert Farris Thompson. 2006. *Blues for New Orleans: Mardi Gras and America's Creole Soul.* Philadelphia: U of Pennsylvania P.

Abrahams, Roger D., and John F. Szwed. 1983. *After Africa.* New Haven: Yale UP.

Alexis, Jacques Stephen. 1999. *General Sun, My Brother.* Trans. Carrol F. Coates. Charlottesville: U of Virginia P.

Allen, Ray, and Lois Wilcken, eds. 2001. *Island Sounds in the Global City: Caribbean Popular Music and Identity in New York.* Urbana: U of Illinois P.

Anonymous. 2001. *La Torre: Revista de la Universidad de Puerto Rico—El Caribe Anglófono Tercera Época,* no. 19 (January–March). (This issue of *La Torre* contains several articles on the folklore of the eastern Caribbean, especially on folk performance and masquerading.)

Austerlitz, Paul. 1997. *Merengue: Dominican Music and Dominican Identity.* Philadelphia: Temple UP.

Averill, Gage. 1997. *A Day for the Hunter, a Day for the Prey: Popular Music and Power in Haiti.* Chicago: U of Chicago P.

Banham, Martin, Errol Hill, and George Woodyard. 1994. *The Cambridge Guide to African and Caribbean Theatre.* New York: Cambridge UP.

Berg, Lora, and Canute Caliste. 1989. *The Mermaid Wakes: Paintings of a Caribbean Isle by Mr. Canute Caliste of Carriacou, Grenada.* London: Macmillan.

Berrian, Brenda F. 2000. *Awakening Spaces: French Caribbean Popular Songs, Music, and Culture.* Chicago: U of Chicago P.

Bettelheim, Judith. 2005. *AfroCuba: Works on Paper, 1968–2003.* San Francisco State University: distributed by U of Washington P.

Boggs, Vernon W. 1992. *Salsiology: Afro-Cuban Music and the Evolution of Salsa in New York City.* New York: Excelsior Music.

Booker, M. Keith, and Dubravka Juraga. 2001. *The Caribbean Novel in English: An Introduction.* Portsmouth, NH: Heinemann.

Brontë, Charlotte. 2003 (1847). *Jane Eyre.* Mineola, N.Y.: Dover.

Broughton, Simon, Mark Ellingham, David Muddyman, and Richard Trillo, eds. 1994. *World Music: The Rough Guide.* London: Penguin.
Burton, Richard D. E. 1993. "'Maman-France Doudou': Family Images in French West Indian Colonial Discourse." *Diacritics* 23, no. 3 (Autumn): 69–90.
Cable, George W. 1959. *Creoles and Cajuns: Stories of Old Louisiana.* Garden City, N.Y.: Doubleday Anchor.
Carpentier, Alejo. 1989. *La Mùsica en Cuba.* Havana: Editorial Pueblo y Educación.
———. 2001. *Music in Cuba.* Ed. Timothy Brennan and trans. Alan West-Durán. Minneapolis: U of Minnesota P.
Clark, Veve and Sara E. Johnson, eds. 2006. *Kaiso! Writings by and about Katherine Dunham.* Madison: U of Wisconsin P.
Classic Calypso Collective, ed. 2006. *West Indian Rhythm: Trinidad Calypsos on World and Local Events Featuring the Censored Recordings, 1938–1940,* Bear Family Records, BCD 16623. (Book and 10-CD box set.)
Cuba—E Theater and Film, http://encarta.msn.com/encyclopedia_761569844_5/Cuba.html.
Daniel, Yvonne. 1995. *Rumba: Dance and Social Change in Contemporary Cuba.* Bloomington: Indiana UP.
Danticat, Edwidge. 1996. *Krik? Krak!* New York: Vintage.
———. 2002. *After the Dance: A Walk through Carnival in Jacmel, Haiti.* New York: Crown Journeys.
Dunham, Katherine. 1946. *Katherine Dunham's Journey to Accompong.* New York: Henry Holt.
Equiano, Olaudah. *The Life of Olaudah Equiano or Gustavus Vassa, the African.* 1789. 2 vols. with a new intro. by Paul Edwards. London: Dawsons of Pall Mall, 1969.
Fanon, Frantz. 1967. *Black Skin, White Masks.* Trans. Charles Lam Markmann. New York: Grove Press.
Figueredo, D. H., ed. 2006. *Encyclopedia of Caribbean Literature.* Vols. 1 and 2. Westport, Conn.: Greenwood Press.
García, Arsenio. 2006. *Arsenio Rodríguez and the Transnational Flows of Latin Popular Music.* Philadelphia: Temple UP.
Gates, Henry Louis, Jr., ed. 1987. *The Classic Slave Narratives.* London: Mentor.
Georges, Robert A., and Michael Owen Jones. 1995. *Folkloristics: An Introduction.* Bloomington: Indiana UP.
Glasser, Ruth. 1995. *My Music Is My Flag: Puerto Rican Musicians and Their New York Communities, 1917–1940.* Berkeley: U of California P.
Guilbault, Jocelyne. With Gage Averill, Édouard Benoit, and Gregory Rabess. 1993. *Zouk: World Music in the West Indies.* Chicago: U of Chicago P.
Hill, Donald R. 1993. *Calypso Calaloo: Early Carnival Music in Trinidad.* Gainesville: U of Florida P. (Book with CD.)
———. 1998. "West African and Haitian Influences on the Ritual and Popular Music of Carriacou, Trinidad, and Cuba." *Black Music Research Journal* 18, no. 1/2 (Spring/Fall): 183–201.

———. 2002. "Music for Tourists in the Twentieth-Century Caribbean." *El Caribe Anglófono: Tercera Época* (La Torre: Revista de la Universidad de Puerto Rico) 7, no. 25 (July–September).

———. 2004. "Music of the African Diaspora in the Americas" In *Overviews and Topics.* Vol. 1 of *Encyclopedia of Diasporas: Immigrant and Refugee Cultures around the World,* ed. Melvin Ember, Carol R. Ember, and Ian Skoggard, 363–73. New York: Kluwer Academic/Plenum.

———, and Robert Abramson. 1979. "Play Mas' in Brooklyn." New York: *Natural History* (August).

Hill, Errol. 1997. *The Trinidad Carnival: Mandate for a National Theatre.* London: New Beacon. (Orig. pub. 1972.)

Hill, John Errol (ed.), Joel Oliansky, and Oliver Hailey Gassner. 1964. *The Yale School of Drama Presents: Man Better Man; Here Comes Santa Clause; Hey You, Light Man!* New York: E.P. Dutton.

Hope, Donna P. 2006. *Inna di Dancehall: Popular Culture and the Politics of Identity in Jamaica.* Kingston, Jamaica: U of the West Indies P.

Hopkinson, Nalo. 1998. *Brown Girl in the Ring.* New York: Warner.

———. 2000. *Midnight Robber.* New York: Warner.

———. 2003. *The Salt Roads.* New York: Warner.

Jara Gámez, Simón, Aurelio Rodríguez Yeyo, and Antonio Zedillo Castillo. 1994. "El Danzón en Cuba." *De Cuba Con Amor...El Danzón en México,* 201–53. México, D. F.: Grupo Azabache.

Kasinitz, Philip. 1992. *Caribbean New York: Black Immigrants and the Politics of Race.* Ithaca, N.Y.: Cornell UP.

Largey, Michael. 2006. *Vodou Nation: Haitian Art Music and Cultural Nationalism.* Chicago: U of Chicago P.

Leaf, Earl. 1948. *Isles of Rhythm.* New York: A. S. Barnes.

Lekis, Lisa. 1958. *Folk Dances of Latin America.* New York: Scarecrow Press.

Lomax, Alan. 1950. *Mister Jelly Roll.* New York: Universal Library of Grosset & Dunlap.

———. 1997. *Brown Girl in the Ring.* Rounder Records, RDCD1716.

Lomax, Alan, J. D. Elder, and Bess Lomax Haws. 1997. *Brown Girl in the Ring: An Anthology of Song Games from the Eastern Caribbean.* New York: Pantheon.

Lorde, Audre. 1982. *Zami: A New Spelling of My Name.* Freedom, Calif.: Crossing Press.

Lovelace, Earl. 1979. *The Dragon Can't Dance.* London: Andre Deutsch.

———. 1984. *Jestina's Calypso and Other Plays.* London: Heinemann.

———. 1997. *Salt.* New York: Persea.

Manuel, Peter (with Kenneth Bilby and Michael Largey). 2006. *Caribbean Currents: Caribbean Music from Rumba to Reggae.* Philadelphia: Temple UP.

Marceles, Eduardo. 2004. *Azúcar! The Biography of Celia Cruz.* Trans. Dolores M. Koch). New York: Reed Press.

Marshall, Paule. 1983. *Praisesong for the Widow.* New York: Plume.

McAlister, Elizabeth. 2002. *Rara! Vodou, Power, and Performance in Haiti and Its Diaspora.* Berkeley: U of California P.

McDaniel, Lorna. 1998. *The Big Drum Ritual of Carriacou: Praisesongs in Rememory of Flight.* Gainesville: U of Florida P.

Monson, Ingrid. 2000. *The African Diaspora: A Musical Perspective.* New York: Routledge.

Montejo, Esteban. 1968. *The Autobiography of a Runaway Slave.* Ed. Miguel Barnet, trans. Jocasta Innes. New York: Pantheon.

Moore, Robin D. 1997. *Nationalizing Blackness: Afrocubanismo and Artistic Revolution in Havana, 1920–1940.* Pittsburgh: U of Pittsburgh P.

Naipaul, V. S. 1959 (2002). *Miguel Street.* New York: Vintage.

———. 1961. *A House for Mr. Biswas.* New York: Knopf.

Noblett, Richard, with Mark Ainley. 2006. "London Is the Place for Me 4: African Dreams and the Piccadilly High Life." Honest Jons Records, HJR CD 25. Compact disc notes.

Nunley, John W., and Judith Bettelheim. 1988. *Caribbean Festival Arts: Each and Every Bit of Difference.* Seattle: U of Washington P.

Olsen, Dale A., and Daniel E. Sheehy, eds. 1998. *South America, Mexico, Central America, and the Caribbean.* Vol. 2 of *The Garland Encyclopedia of World Music.* New York: Garland Publishing.

———. 2000. *The Garland Handbook of Latin American Music.* New York: Garland Publishing.

Ortiz, Fernando. 1995. *Cuban Counterpoint: Tobacco and Sugar.* Durham, N.C.: Duke UP.

Ostransky, Leroy. 1978. *Jazz City: The Impact of Our Cities on the Development of Jazz.* Englewood Cliffs, N.J.: Prentice Hall.

Pacini Hernández, Debora. 1995. *Bachata: A Social History of a Dominican Popular Music.* Philadelphia: Temple UP.

Price, Richard. 2002. *First-Time: The Historical Vision of an African American People.* 2nd ed., with a new preface by the author. Chicago: U of Chicago P.

Roberts, John Storm. 1998. *Black Music of Two Worlds: African, Caribbean, Latin, and African-American Traditions.* New York: Schirmer.

Roberts, John Storm. 1999a. *Latin Jazz: The First of the Fusions—1880s to Today.* New York: Schirmer.

———. 1999b. *The Latin Tinge: The Impact of Latin Music on the United States.* New York: Oxford UP.

Rohlehr, Gordon. 2004. *A Scuffling of Islands: Essays on Calypso.* San Juan, Trinidad: Lexicon Trinidad.

Sloat, Susanna, ed. 2002. *Caribbean Dance from Abakuá to Zouk.* Gainesville: U of Florida P.

Spottswood, Richard, and Don Hill. 1989. *Calypso Pioneers.* Rounder Records, CD 1039.

Starr, S. Frederic. 1995. *Bamboula! The Life and Times of Louis Moreau Gottschalk.* New York: Oxford UP.

Stebich, Ute. 1978. *Haitian Art.* New York: Brooklyn Museum and Harry N. Abrams.

Stewart, John O. 1989. *Drinkers, Drummers, and Decent Folk: Ethnographic Narratives of Village Trinidad.* Albany: State University of New York Press.

Stolzoff, Norman C. 2000. *Wake the Town and Tell the People: Dancehall Culture in Jamaica.* Durham, N.C.: Duke UP.

Stone, Judy S. J. 1994. *Studies in West Indian Literature: Theatre.* London: Macmillan.

Sublette, Ned. 2004. *Cuba and Its Music: From the First Drums to the Mambo.* Chicago: Chicago Review Press.

Thompson, Robert Farris. 1984. *Flash of the Spirit.* New York: Vintage.

Veigas-Zamora, Jose, Cristina Vives Gutierrez, Aldolfo V. Nodal, Valia Garzon, and Dannys Montes de Oca. 2001. *Memoria: Cuban Art of the 20th Century.* Los Angeles: International Arts Foundation.

Viard, Emile. 2003. *Haitian Art in the Diaspora.* Quebec [?]: Vie et Arts.

Villaverde, Cirilo. 2005. *Cecilia Valdés or El Angel Hill: A Novel of Nineteenth-Century Cuba.* New York: Oxford UP.

Walcott, Derek. 1990. *Omeros.* New York: Farrar, Straus and Giroux.

Warner, Keith Q. 1982. *Kaiso! The Trinidad Calypso: A Study of the Calypso as Oral Literature.* New York: Three Continents Press.

Waugh, Alec. 1955. *Island in the Sun: A Story of the 1950's Set in the West Indies.* New York: Farrar, Straus and Cudahy.

White, Timothy. 1992. *Catch a Fire: The Life of Bob Marley.* New York: Henry Holt.

Films

Buena Vista Social Club. 1999. Directed by Wim Wenders and produced by Ulrich Felsberg and Deepak Nayar.

The Harder They Come. 1973. Directed and produced by Perry Henzell.

I Walked with a Zombie. 1943. Directed by Jacques Tourneur and produced by Val Lewton. RKO Pictures.

Island in the Sun. 1957. Directed by Robert Rossen and produced by Darryl Zanuck and based by the novel of the same name by Alec Waugh (1955).

Sugar Cane Alley. 1984. Directed by Euzhan Palcy and produced by Sumafa-ORCA-N.E.F. Diffusion.

Thunderball. 1965. Directed by Terence Young and produced by Kevin McClory.

Web Pages

http://www.danzon.com/
http://www.afropop.org/

http://www.allmusic.com
http://www.carnaval.com/main.htm
http://www.carnavalmiami.com/home.html and http://www.carnavalmiami.com/calle8/ (Calle Ocho festival in Miami [The generic Web site for Cuban activities and the Calle Ocho page])
http://cruisereviews.com/
http://www.dominicantoday.com/app/frontpage.aspx (The Dominican Day Parade [This online English-language newspaper sometimes carries information on this event.])
http://ead.dartmouth.edu/html/ml77.html (Errol Hill's papers)
http://www.mentomusic.com/links.htm and http://homepages.nyu.edu/~dtn9606/mento.html)
http://www.nationalpuertoricandayparade.org/ (The Puerto Rican Day Parade and The West Indian Labor Day Parade)
http://www.ttw.org.tt/pastprod.html (Derek Walcott and Little Carib Workshop)
http://www.webster.edu/~corbetre/haiti/voodoo/zombilist.htm (Voodoo and zombie films)

Glossary

For Readers: This glossary gives minimal definitions and is not meant to be complete. A good way to use it is to Google the term you are interested in and then, using the guide in the Web Pages appendix, assess the quality of the fuller information you find on the Web concerning the term. You will be richly rewarded: some of these terms yield hundreds of hits, especially if it is a sacred word or if it refers to a form of popular music.

Abakuá (also called Ñáñigo). A male secret society in Cuba, known for its machismo and for its ritual music.

Aché. In the *Yoruba* religion, a vital or life force found in gods, or *Orishas.*

Acrolect. The formal or standard form of a language.

Afrocentrism. A wide variety of scholarly and emotional approaches to cultural heritage ranging from a recognition of African cultural heritage in the Americas to claims that most important civilizations in the Atlantic region and Europe have an African origin.

Aguinaldo. Nativity songs in the Spanish-speaking Caribbean and on the mainland.

All-rounder. A term borrowed from the game of cricket, in the British Caribbean, an all-rounder is someone who is capable of doing many different things well.

Anancy (Annancy, Nancy, Brer Rabbit). Trickster spider or, in the United States, rabbit of a cycle of folktales, most of which originated in Ghana among the Akan people. These stories are widespread in the Caribbean.

Arará. See *Rada.*

Arnaz, Desi (1917–1986). Cuban-born American dancer, singer, actor, and television star and producer. While he did not introduce Cuban rhythms to the United States, his rendition of Margarita Lecuona's "Babalu," a fanciful takeoff of a Santería ceremony, helped continue the Cuban craze and fed stereotypes of the "mysterious" Afro-Cuban religion while at the same time presenting a popularization of folkloric material.

Arsenio. See *Rodriguez, Arsenio.*

Babalawo. A spiritual leader or priest in the *Yoruba* faith.

Bachata. A topical song style that originated in the Dominican Republic.

Baha. A bamboo trumpet in the southeastern Caribbean.

Balakadri. See *Quadrille.*

Bamboula. The name of a Caribbean drum and of one of *Gottschalk's* most famous compositions. Also, a generic name for a nineteenth-century Afro-Caribbean dance and drum. In Guadeloupe, bamboulas were fetes for enslaved people. See also *Bula.*

Basilect. Informal speech. In Creole languages this is often considered a different language than the standard or *Acrolect* form of speech.

Batá. A set of three, hour-glass-shaped drums that originally were played in *Yoruba* sacred ceremonies but now are commonly added to Latin orchestras.

Beguine. A Martiniquean popular music in the first half of the twentieth century that was based on folk drum music from the nineteenth century.

Belair (Bélè in the French Creole–speaking Caribbean). A common name given to a group of nineteenth-century topical songs in the Eastern Caribbean, many of which are still performed.

Bélè. See *Belair.*

Belief. A notion held to be true, and which may be true but has not been proved to be so. Belief forms the basis of religion and is a guide to secular affairs as well.

Benoit, Rigaud (1911–1986). Former cobbler and shoemaker, he became one of Haiti's most famous *Outsider Artists.*

Bazile, Castera (1923–1966). Haitian *Outsider Artist* and muralist.

Big Drum Dance (Nation Dance). A folk ritual held to honor the ancestors that was once common in the Grenadines and Grenada but now is found mostly in Carriacou, Grenada.

Black-and-white minstrels. In Trinidad's Carnival and elsewhere in the West Indies, serenaders who apply white and black paint to their faces and sing late-nineteenth-century minstrel songs of U.S. origin. Probably modeled after American minstrels who toured the islands at that time. Also called "Yankee Minstrels" or the "Yankee Band."

Blackface. Masking by putting black soot or some other substance on one's face. Although the custom predates modern *slavery* in Europe, in the Caribbean and elsewhere it is associated with minstrelsy, where white people put on the masquerade and mimicked supposed characteristics of people of African descent. By the late nineteenth century there were also Afro-American versions of blackface vaudeville. In the Caribbean, two common blackface characterizations were the Cuban negrito, a stock player in the Teatro Vernáculo (vernacular theater), and the Yankee Band, in which Black Trinidadians put on both black and white face to mimic North American minstrels and Yankees in general.

Board house. The name for wood-plank, folk houses in Carriacou that were popular in the 1960s through the 1970s, after Hurricane Janet.

Boas, Franz (1858–1942). German-born American anthropologist and folklorist. Boas was one of the founders of the American Folklore Society in 1888. He also helped tie together four disciplines that were taught separately in Europe—physical anthropology, anthropological linguistics, cultural anthropology, and anthropological archaeology—into a single scholarly department.

Bolero. In Cuba and Mexico and elsewhere in Latin America, a ballad played to guitar or orchestral accompaniment.

Bomba. In Puerto Rico, a style of dance and song with drum accompaniment.

Bongo(s). A wake dance in Trinidad and Tobago, and a similar dance elsewhere in the Lesser Antilles. *Bongos* refers to a set of two small Cuban drums that are attached and played while grasped between one's knees. See *Kumina.*

Boula. A drum used in Haitian *Vodou.*

Botanicas. Herbal stores where medicines, magical substances, and statues of Santería gods may be purchased.

Bricolage. Using some idea or object that was intended for one purpose, for a different purpose. In Caribbean folklore this term helps explain the creativeness, adaptability, and resourcefulness of Creole culture and its delightful fusion of unlike parts.

Brujería. The name for witchcraft in Cuba and other Spanish-speaking countries of the Americas.

Bula. An Afro-Caribbean drum that plays basic rhythms. See also *Bamboula.*

Bura (Burra). A neo-African drum style in Jamaica; also the name applied to any drum music of African origin.

Burrokeet. A masquerade in the Caribbean islands in which a person wears a donkey and rider costume.

Bush medicine. A system of folk medicine utilizing herbs and other wild plants for curing ailments.

Cabildos. Associations of enslaved Africans and Creoles in Cuba that were based on the ethnic identity of the members. At times, the Cuban state and the Catholic Church allowed slaves to create entertainment on special occasions.

Cable, George W. (1844–1925). American writer and novelist who wrote about New Orleans and Creole life.

Calabar. A region and city in southeast Nigeria from where slaves were shipped to the Americas. The *Abakuá* secret society in Cuba likely began in Calabar.

Calaloo (Callaloo, Callooloo). A soup made with dasheen leaves, okra, and crab or pigtail.

Calinda. See *Kalinda.*

Caliste, Canute (Emmanuel Calliste, 1914–2005). Boat builder, carpenter, shipwright, violinist, and *Outsider Artist* who gained fame in Europe and the United States for his paintings of folklife on his native island of Carriacou, Grenada.

Call-and-response. A family of melodic styles that includes a lead voice and a chorus; although the form is common throughout the world, the character this melodic type takes in the Caribbean suggests an African origin.

Calle Ocho. A Cuban American street festival in Miami.

Calypso. A topical, Carnival song that developed in Trinidad around 1900 and has undergone many changes and spawned many related styles in the last hundred years.

Caribbean. As a geographic area, the Caribbean includes the islands that front or are within the Caribbean Sea and the Bahamas. "Caribbean," or Creole, culture extends to Charleston; certain peoples of the sea islands of South Carolina and Georgia; and New Orleans and its immediate environs. In Central America Caribbean peoples also live in Belize (especially the Garifuna) and other countries along the Caribbean coast. In South America, the countries of Guyana, Surinam, and French Guinea are also considered Caribbean in culture.

Carnival. In the Caribbean countries with a Catholic population, a celebration that takes place just before the beginning of Lent.

Carpentier, Alejo (1904–1980). Swiss-born Cuban author, ethnomusicologist, and intellectual.

Carr, Andrew. Trinidadian scholar and writer who documented French Creole and African culture of the island.

Cassava (Yucca). A starchy root that is a Caribbean staple and is made into breads and cakes; it is the basis of tapioca.

Cecilia Valdés. Title of Cirilo de Villaverde's epic nineteenth-century Cuban novel about race, class, and romance. The theme was used for composer *Gonzalo Roig's zarzuela.*

Chachacha. A Cuban dance, backed by a *charanga* orchestra that burst on the international scene in the early 1950s.

Chac-chac (maracas). A small gourd shaker filled with corn or pebbles.

Changüi. A type of song and dance of the *guajiros* in eastern Cuba.

Charanga (Orquesta Francesa). A small orchestra with violin(s), flute, string bass, paila or timbales, güiro, and, by the early 1900s, piano. It was an indoor version of the Cuban orquesta tipica, which excluded the piano but had brass and reed instruments.

Chronemics. The cultural use of time.

Chutney. A sweet and spicy jam that originated in India and is popular in the Caribbean.

Chutney calypso. A type of *calypso* in Trinidad and Guyana in which songs once part of a woman's celebration of marriage are now sung in public at competitions, just like other forms of calypso.

Clarke, John Henrik (1915–1998). Leading scholar and spokesperson for the pan-Africanist, Afrocentric position concerning the diaspora of Africans throughout the Americas. Both revered for his championing of Afrocentrism and criticized for his lack of scholarly rigor.

Clave. "Key" in Spanish, this is a family of Afro-Cuban and other rhythms in the Americas that is based on two beats followed by three beats, or vice versa.

Combite. A voluntary work group in Haiti. In Carriacou, a simplified version is called a helping.

Comparsas. Large groups of masqueraders and revelers in Cuban Carnival.

Conga. A rhythm and style of dance for Carnival in eastern Cuba.

Congo. In the Caribbean, the names given to an ethnic group whose ancestors were enslaved in the Congo. In Cuba, people from the Congo are called Bantus.

Congo Square. At the southern edge of what is now Louis Armstrong Park in New Orleans, this was an open area where slaves were allowed to congregate, play music, and have other entertainment, through the early 1800s.

Conjunto. A small musical group made up of different instruments in different places. In Cuba, a conjunto group originally played *rumbas* and *sons* and consisted of stringed and percussion instruments. Later a trumpet was added and, by the 1940s, a saxophone was added.

Contradance. A dance that was popular from the late eighteenth century in which male and female couples faced each other in a line before executing a set series of movements.

The Converted. An Afro-Protestant faith in St. Vincent that is closely related to the *Spiritual Baptists* of Trinidad.

Coolie. In the Eastern Caribbean, a derogatory word to describe a person of Asian Indian descent.

Covarrubias, Francisco (1775–1850). Playwright and actor who developed Cuba's national theater. He played the black faced negrito character, whose antics were stereotyped and allegedly those of enslaved Afro-Cubans.

Craft. Making an object by hand, from raw materials, to completion.

Creole (Kwéyòl). Caribbean people, their culture, or vernacular language, whose ancestors came from Africa, Europe, or both.

Creole Guyanais. Creole French as spoken in French Guiana.

Creole language. A language that combines two or more historically unrelated languages. Creole languages are full languages and may be spoken from birth, unlike true *pidgin* languages, which may not have complete grammars. Creole French and English Creole are two important Creole languages in the Caribbean. There is dispute among linguists whether there are true Spanish Creole languages.

Cromanti (Kromanti, other spellings). Ancestral name for people in the Caribbean and the Americas who were enslaved in the Gold Coast (now Ghana) in the eighteenth and nineteenth centuries.

Cruz, Celia (1925–2003). Cuban-born American singer, perhaps Cuba's greatest singing star, who toured the world spreading Cuban and New York–style salsa. She began her singing career with La Sonora Matancera in Cuba but moved to the New York area after the establishment of communism in Cuba.

Cuatro (Quatro). In Puerto Rico, an instrument with four or more sets of doubled strings. In the southeastern Caribbean and in Venezuela, a small four-stringed instrument.

Culture. Knowledge and learned behavior that is shared by a group of people.

Cumina. A *Yoruba*-influenced Jamaican Afro-Caribbean religion that dates from the second half of the nineteenth century.

Curandero. One who deals with bush medicine in Spanish-speaking countries in the Americas. Similar to a bush doctor in the English-speaking Caribbean.

Curry. A powder that combines many spices. Originally used in India, curry is common in Caribbean cuisine.

Dahomey. Former name of the modern nation of Benin.

Damballa. *Fon* God that is found in Haitian *Vodou* and in other Afro-Caribbean religions.

Dancehall. A type of Jamaican musical and dance experience that evolved out of *reggae* and *sound systems* into a high-tech performance involving scores of singers, disc jockeys, sound technicians, and others in sometimes very large groups.

Danza. A Puerto Rican indoor dance that is similar to the Cuban *danzón.*

Danzón. A syncopated rondo in Cuba created in the last third of the nineteenth century that brought together different contradance movements into a single piece. By the early twentieth century it was the favorite form of indoor dance. Danzones were played by *charangas,* or orquestas Francesa, and were also very popular in Mexico.

Day of the Kings. See *Día de Reyes.*

Débòt. A drum dance in St. Lucia.

Décima. A type of Spanish poetic music that is widespread in the Americas.

Día de Reyes (Day of Kings). Through 1880, a "holiday" for enslaved and free Afro-Cubans to celebrate the Adoration of the Three Magi that included music, dancing, and other forms of feasting.

Dilogún. A type of *Yoruba* divination found in Cuba that involves casting shells.

Diwali (Divali, the Festival of Lights). A Hindu celebration of Lord Rama's return from a long exile. Diwali is found in Indian communities throughout the Caribbean, especially in Guyana and Trinidad, where it is a national holiday. Non-Hindus also participate.

Djab. French Creole for devil.

Doudou. In French Creole, "darling." Also, a Creole lover of a mainland French man (see *matador*).

Dreadlocks. A hairstyle of long strands of knotted hair worn by *Rastafarians* or simply as a fashion statement.

Dub. In Jamaica, a form of music in which an instrumental rendition of a record is made so that it can be mixed with other tunes or a disc jockey may talk or sing over it.

Dunham, Katherine (1909–2006). Black American dancer, choreographer, author, and ethnographer who popularized African and African American (including Caribbean) dance in the Americas and Europe on stage, in films, in clubs, and in other venues.

Eleguá (*Ishu* in Yoruba, and *Llegba or Legba* in English and in *Kwéyòl*). The trickster god in various *Yoruba-* and *Fon-*based faiths.

Elliott, Ebenezer "Pa Neezer" (deceased). A famous *Obeahman* from south Trinidad who was sought by clients for cures or for other magical purposes.

Folk (vernacular) architecture. Buildings made by ordinary people, as opposed to formally trained architects. Such structures often conform to traditional styles and tend to change little over time.

Folklore. The culture of everyday life as well as traditional knowledge and activities learned partly by listening, watching, and imitating a person who carries out the tradition rather by than primarily learning formal and storable information outside of memory, such as from books, film, or sound recordings.

Folktale. A traditional story or narrative told to entertain or teach a moral point, especially at wakes or other periodic events.

Equiano, Olaudah (Gustavus Vassa) (c. 1745–c. 1797). Born in Benin (now Nigeria), Equiano was enslaved, lived in *slavery* in the West Indies and elsewhere, bought his freedom, and wrote a sensational, imaginative narrative of his ordeals in English in 1789.

Ethnic group. People who share an identity and customs, either real or perceived, and who see themselves or are seen by outsiders as a group.

Ethnography. A scholarly description of the way of life of a group of people. Much of contemporary folklore ethnography is humanistic and interpretative in that it uses subjective techniques, such as literary style, and may interject the researcher as an "actor" in the study. Other folkloric ethnography is more objective and seeks to discover information that may be compared with other cultures as a part of social science.

Everyday life. Ordinary or mundane activities carried out by anybody, as well as extraordinary activities in which people participate.

Fanon, Franz (1925–1961). A Martiniquean psychiatrist and author who championed anticolonial and antiracist causes. He had served with distinction in the French army in World War II and later trained as a psychiatrist. He practiced in Algeria, then a French colony, but was expelled because of his support of freedom for the Algerians.

Failde Pérez, Miguel. Late-nineteenth-century Cuban composer credited with the first published *danzón.*

Folk community. Originally, people who live as a group, regularly meet, and collectively share traditional customs on a daily basis; a traditional culture. The concept has expanded to include people who may occasionally meet, such as an occupational or interest group, who nonetheless share values and experiences in face-to-face settings or through media (e.g., e-mail friends or groups, pen pals, "telepals," conference goers, family reunions, etc.).

Folklife. The folklore of everyday life.

Fon. A major ethnic group in Benin whose religion forms an important part of Haitian *Vodou.*

Foulard. The classic head tie for French Creole women during the colonial era.

Gallego. In Cuba, a peasant or poor person of Spanish descent.

Garifuna. People of Native American and African descent who originally lived in St. Vincent when enslaved Africans freed themselves by settling among the Indians. Later, they fought the British, who removed them from the island and settled them on an island off Central America. Today, they are found in pockets along the Caribbean coast of Central America. Formerly they were called Black Caribs.

Garvey, Marcus (1887–1940). Jamaican founder of the Universal Negro Improvement Association, a black pride and self-help organization with many businesses that gained wide appeal in New York and elsewhere in the Americas after World War I. Today, Garvey is admired by both *Rastafarians* and by many mainstream Jamaicans.

Geertz, Clifford (1926–2006). One of the most prominent anthropologists in the United States during his lifetime. He moved cultural anthropology away from social science and materialism toward a more subjective approach to the discipline. He was especially influential in developing interpretative *ethnography* as opposed to a fact-based, objective *ethnography.*

Goombay. A drum with a stretched skin covering a square or circular wooden frame. Also, a festival in the Bahamas.

Globalization. The internationalization of economics (production, distribution, and consumption of goods and services) or, more broadly, the spread of culture across national boundaries.

Gottschalk, Louis Moreau (1829–1869). The New Orleans–born Gottschalk was a virtuoso pianist and bombastic concertizer and composer of classical music in both the Western and *Creole* traditions.

Grenet, Eliseo (1893–1950). The most famous of three musical brothers, whose 1927 arrangement of the traditional song "Ay, Mamá Inés" became world famous. He is also responsible for spreading the *conga* in the early 1930s.

Guaguanco. An African-derived Cuban rhythm and dance that is one of several types of *rumbas.*

Guajiro. A Cuban peasant.

Guaracha. Originating in Cuban comic theater, this song and dance form contains a *call-and-response* melodic structure that combines African with Spanish origins.

Guayabera (or "shirt jacket" in the English-speaking Caribbean). A fancy shirt with two rows of pleated material down the front.

Guiro. A Caribbean musical instrument made from a gourd with a grooved surface that is rubbed with a stick or a piece of iron.

Gullah (a somewhat derogatory name for Gullah is "Geechee"). The name given to the people of African descent who live along the southeast coast of the United States, centering on the Georgia and South Carolina Sea Islands. Their language and culture tie them to Caribbean peoples and to people from West Africa, especially Sierra Leone.

Gwoka. "Big Drum" in English, this is a style of drumming music in Guadeloupe.

Habanera. A Cuban rhythm that dates at least from the middle 1800s. A form of clave and related to the Argentinean tango.

Helping. See *Combite.*

Herskovits, Melville (1895–1963) and Frances (d. 1972). A student of Franz Boas, Herskovits was an early champion of "Africanisms," the retention and reformulation of African cultural traits in the Americas. Although his concept of Africanisms was controversial from the beginning, more recently many scholars have moved away from a strict search for Africanisms to examining Caribbean culture as a created whole made up of many, disparate parts. Frances coauthored several books with her husband and was said to be a better ethnographer.

Hill, Errol (1921–2003). Trinidadian scholar, actor, playwright, director, theater historian, and author of first major study of Trinidad Carnival.

Hosay (called Tadja in Guyana). A Shiite Muslim ritual and festival, versions of the Muḥarram, commemorating the death and martyrdom of *Husayn,* son of Fatima, who was the daughter of the Prophet Mohammed. It is found in the Caribbean where there are people of Indian descent. In Trinidad the celebration is ecumenical, and non-Muslims, including *Creoles,* join in the procession of the Tadjas, replicas of Husayn's tomb.

Houdini (Wilmoth Houdini, Wilmoth Hendricks Edgar, Leon Sinclair, King Houdini) (1895–1973). A calypso singer from Trinidad who took his stage name after the magician. He was the first major singer to leave the island and settle in New York City, where he made many records from 1928 until about 1950.

Houngan (papaloi). A priest in the *Vodou* faith.

Hounfour (hunfor, humfort). The temple in the *Vodou* faith.

House break. In Carriacou, taking apart a *board house* and moving all or part of it to another location.

Husayn. Grandson of the Prophet Muhammad.

Hyppolite, Hector (1894–1948). Haiti's most famous *Outsider Artist* in the first half of the twentieth century.

Ifá. *Yoruba* (Lucumí) divination in Cuba.

Indenture. In some parts of the Caribbean, a form of labor that replaced *slavery* when it was abolished. Typically an indentured laborer would work for a number of years and receive payment at the end of the contracted period. Then the indentured person was free to return to his or her home country or stay on the island where he or she worked.

Interpretative ethnography. See *Ethnography.*

Jibaro. A Puerto Rican peasant whose image is of a simple but wise person, the real soul of the islanders.

John Canoe. See *Jonkonnu.*

Jonkonnu (JonKanoo, John Canoe). A Christmastime masquerade, music, or street festival that once spread from parts of the southern United States to Guyana. Jonkonnu combines British-style folk plays (mumming) with West African–influenced sacred masquerades.

Juan Bobo. The name of a Puerto Rican cycle of folktales. Juan Bobo is depicted as a seemingly simple *Jibaro,* or peasant, who nevertheless usually wins out in the end.

Kadans. A Haitian dance that became popular in Martinique.

Kalinda (Calinda). A centuries-old dance that was popular throughout the Caribbean area and into North America from the eighteenth century. From the late nineteenth century, the term refers to a song for stickfighting.

Kélé. A drum-based *Yoruba* ritual in St. Lucia.

Kinesics. Cultural communication by using gestures.

Kongo. See *Congo.*

Konpa. A Haitian popular music.

Krik? Krak! A folktale and the tag opening line for tales from the French Creole–speaking areas of the Caribbean. The story teller says "Krik?" and the audience says "Krak!" and then the story proceeds. If the audience attention wanes, then the story teller says "Krik?" again and demands a return "Krak!" before continuing.

Kromanti. See *Cromanti.*

Kumina. An Afro-Jamaican drum-based ritual, also known as the Bongo Nation.

Kwadril. See *Quadrille.*

Kwéyòl. See *Creole.*

Lajabless. A female "devil" with one cloven hoof that chases young men at night, seeking to do them harm.

La Rose and La Marguerite Societies. In St. Lucia, two groups that compete against each other in an annual festival, through their dances and songs.

Latifundia. In Cuba, very large sugar plantations in the mid-nineteenth century that utilized slave labor.

Lecuona, Ernesto (1895–1963). Cuban composer, pianist, and songwriter. As much as any classically trained Cuban musician, Lecuona was responsible for spreading Cuban vernacular music, in popular or light classical forms, throughout the world, both in his compositions and in the recordings by his group.

Legba. See *Eleguá.*

Leggo. In Trinidad, a litany-style topical song for outdoor festivals. In Carriacou, a season of the year when the crops have been harvested and the animals have been released ("leggo season"). See also *Road march.*

Lekis, Lisa (1917–1995). Mississippi-born sociologist, dance authority, and dancer. The first scholar to systematically catalog the dances of the Caribbean and the Americas.

Léwòz. "The rose" in English, this is a style of outdoor music in Guadeloupe.

Little Carib Theatre. A theatrical venue established by *Beryl McBurnie* in Port of Spain, Trinidad, in 1948 and expanded by Derek Walcott with the Little Theatre Workshop in 1959. In the Little Carib and the Little Theatre Workshop, many arts were honed, from socially acceptable steel bands to small orchestra and theater performances.

Loa (Lwa). A god in the *Vodou* faith.

Lomax, Alan (1915–2002). American ethnomusicologist, writer, and producer of radio, television, and film on vernacular music of the world. In 1933 he made pioneering field recordings in the Bahamas and Haiti in the 1930s and in the Eastern Caribbean in 1962.

Loogarou. In the French-speaking Caribbean, a vampire that emanates fire from its eyes as it flys about, searching for a human or animal to suck its blood.

Lorde, Audre (1934–1992). Feminist and gay-rights author and poet, whose mother was born in Carriacou, Grenada. Lorde wrote *Zami,* about lesbianism and her Caribbean roots.

Lord Melody (Fitzroy Alexander) (1926–1988). One of Trinidad's most important calypsonians of the mid-twentieth century, famed for his self-deprecating wit and his insult songs against the Mighty Sparrow.

Lucumí. See *Santería.*

McBurnie, Beryl (1914–2000). Founder of the *Little Carib Theatre* in Port of Spain Trinidad in 1948, which she ran for decades. A dancer and choreographer, she supported local musicians and artists, including steel bands, calypso, dance orchestras, and playwright and poet Derek Walcott. Her theater was used as the *mas* camp for Peter Minshall's Carnival band, Zodiac, his first in 1978.

Madras. Eighteenth- and nineteenth-century *Creole* woman's dress, consisting of a skirt over many petticoats.

Magic. Manipulation of a supernatural power for an individual's benefit.

Malinowski, Bronislaw (1884–1942). Polish-born British social anthropologist who developed a theory of society regarding primary institutions created by groups of people to satisfy basic biological "needs." Malinowski was especially important in creating an ethnographic technique that involved cutting oneself off, as much as possible, from one's own culture and learning the language and culture of the people being studied by living with them for one or more years at a stretch.

Mambo (mamaloi). A priestess in the *Vodou* faith; also, an Afro-Cuban dance.

Manding (Mandingo, Mandinka, Mande). Name for people who were enslaved in the Caribbean and whose ancestors originally lived in the ancient Mali Empire in West Africa.

Manman. A large drum used in Haitian *Vodou.*

Maracas. See *chac-chac.*

Marimbula. A Cuban lamellaphone made from a hollow wooden box to which large metal strips are attached. The player sits on the box and plunks the metal strips.

Maroon (from the Spanish cimmaron). A person who escaped from *slavery* in the Americas and the Caribbean and joined with others to form an ecumenical African-like society. Also, the name given to a cooperative work group or an annual community ritual in Carriacou, Grenada.

Mas. Masquerade. To "play mas" is to participate in masquerading through the streets during Carnival.

Matador. A prostitute, a madam, a kept woman, or a strong woman who may take on a male lover. Similar to a *doudou,* who, in the French-speaking Caribbean is a Creole woman who takes a mainland French lover.

Mazouk. In the French Caribbean, a Creolized European mazurka; by the late twentieth century Mazouk evolved into *Zouk.*

Mento. A Jamaican vernacular topical music that peaked in popularity in the 1940s and 1950s.

Merengue (meringue in Haiti). A style of popular music in the Dominican Republic.

Mermaid. In Caribbean folklore a mythological half-fish, half-woman who lives in sea lagoons and who receives sacrifices. She may bring good fortune. Historically, Caribbean mermaids seem to combine European and West African origins, especially the water spirit Mami Wata whose shrines are found throughout West Africa.

Mesolect. Speech that is a transitional form between the standard form of the language *(Acrolect)* and the completely informal form of the language *(Basilect).*

Midnight Robber. A Carnival character in Trinidad with a broad sombrero who carries one or two pistols or a whip and spiels a patter of braggadocio.

Mitchell, Joseph (1908–1996). Writer for newspapers and the *New Yorker* magazine in a style of social realism that presaged the gonzo journalism of the 1960s. Mitchell had sympathy for ordinary people that was readily apparent in his articles, especially in "Houdini's Picnic," one of the great ethnographic descriptions of a West Indian community event in the late 1930s.

Moko Jumbies. Stilted masqueraders in the West Indies of an African origin.

Montejo, Esteban (1860–1973). Author of a narrative, as written down and edited by Miguel Barnet. Montejo was a slave in Cuba into his early adult years, was a fugitive for a time, and fought in the War of Independence against Spain. His account is full of folkloric customs, especially music.

Morel Campos, Juan (1857–1896). Student of *Manuel G. Tavárez* and composer of Puerto Rican *danzas.*

Morton, Ferdinand "Jelly Roll" (late nineteenth century–1941). *Creole* American pianist, composer, orchestra leader, and pioneer of New Orleans jazz. He recorded his reminiscence for Alan Lomax at the Library of Congress in Washington, D.C., in 1938.

Muḥarram. A Shiite Islamic observance that commemorates the death of Muhammad's grandson *Husayn.*

Mulata. A woman of mixed African and European descent; a seductive character in folk theater and literature in the Caribbean.

Myth. The grounding for belief and customs (as revealed in stories, place names, proverbs, etc.) of traditional ideas that explain the origins of a people and their rightful place in their cultural and physical environment.

Ńáñigo. See *Abakuá.*

Nation. "Nation" is a name commonly given to a putative African group in the Caribbean. For Nation Dance see *Big Drum Dance.*

Negrito. In Cuba, a stereotyped blackfaced character in vernacular theater who mimicked what were supposed to be Afro-Cuban mannerisms.

Neoteric. Cultures, such as in the Caribbean, whose people and whose traits were, in large part, imported from some other part of the world (e.g., in the case of the Caribbean, Caribbean cultures are newly created mixtures of Western European and West African cultures and less influenced by Native Americans).

Nyabinghi. The central ritual in the *Rastafarian* faith.

Ọba. A mythological character and the name of a *Yoruba* king. Ọba is also the name of a major river in Nigeria and the name of a wife of Shango.

Obatala (Obatalá). Creator god in various *Yoruba* faiths in the Caribbean.

Obeah (Obi). The name for magic in parts of the Caribbean. The word is of *Fon* origin.

Obeahman. A person who practices obeah, usually for a client's fee.

Ochun. See *Ọshun.*

Ogan. A drum used in Haitian *Vodou.*

Ogun (Ogoun, Ogou). God of iron and ironworkers in *Yoruba* faiths in the Caribbean.

Orisha (Oricha). The name for gods in the *Yoruba* religion. Also, in some parts of the Caribbean, the name given to the Lucumí religion.

Orquesta Francesa. See *Charanga.*

Ortiz, Fernando (1881–1969). Cuban scholar who came to champion "Afrocubanismo." Ortiz published more about Afro-Cuban customs than any other researcher.

Ọshun. *Yoruba* goddess of love, wealth, and intimacy and the name of a river in Nigeria.

Outsider Artist. An imprecise term to describe folk artists whose work is "unschooled" or "naïve."

Ọya. The goddess of the River Niger and the *Yoruba* god of wind and fertility.

Pachanga. A dance craze in Cuba and New York in the early 1960s.

Pan. An individual steel "drum" or an entire "steel" orchestra.

Papaloi. See *Houngan.*

Paralinguistics. Nonlinguistic sounds that convey meaning in a culture, such as the way words are spoken and not the meaning of the words themselves.

Parang. In Trinidad, Christmas-season serenades with songs about the Nativity. In Carriacou, an October topical song competition based roughly on the Trinidadian model.

Parsons, Elsie Clews (1874–1941). Anthropologist and folklorist who pioneered the collecting of folklore in the Caribbean and elsewhere in the Americas.

Patterson, Massie. West Indian singer, songwriter, and concert performer. Collaborated with calypso entrepreneur and orchestra leader Lionel Belasco.

Perez, Ralph. Puerto Rican "artist and repertoire" man who worked for Decca records gathering talent, especially in the Caribbean, for the company to record.

Petro. A Haitian cult that is part of the *Vodou* faith, said to have originated in Haiti.

Pidgin. An argot or vocabulary with minimal grammar that is used to communicate by people who speak different languages. When a pidgin becomes the first language of children, it contains full grammar and is considered to be a *Creole* language.

Pierrot (Paywo, "clown," or Pays Roi, "country king"). A classical Carnival character dressed in a jersey made with small triangles of cloth, in the center of which is a heart containing mirrors. In Carriacou, Pierrots gather to perform *Shakespeare Mas* on Carnival Tuesday.

Pinard, Lancelot "Sir Lancelot" (1903–2001). Trinidad-born calypso singer who gained fame performing at the Village Vanguard in New York City and later went on to sing and act in many Hollywood films.

Plena. A topical song that was popular in Puerto Rico from the late 1920s through about 1950.

Pocomania (Pukkumina). See *Revivalism.*

Postmodernism. Wide-ranging theories that reject modernism, with its reliance on science and its romantic literature. In folklore, postmodernism is the theory behind interpretative *ethnography.*

Premise, Josephine. American dancer and singer of Haitian descent who was a major stage actor in New York and elsewhere from the 1940s through the 1980s.

Pretender (Lord Pretender, Aldric Adrian Farrell) (1917–2002). Born in Tobago of Trinidadian parents, Pretender recorded first for RCA Victor's Bluebird Records in 1937 and went on to become one of great composers of "extempore" calypso (verses partly made up on the spot to fit a selected subject).

Primus, Pearl (1919–1994). Trinidadian-born dancer, choreographer (in the manner of *Katherine Dunham*), college instructor, and scholar who helped to popularize West Indian dance styles through her performances and her teaching.

Proxemics. The cultural use of space.

Punto. A group of Spanish lyrical musical styles that is widespread in the Americas.

Quadrille (balakadri or kwadril in French Creole). In the Caribbean, a series of dances of European origin in which four couples execute a series of steps, often accompanied by a string band and sometimes by drums.

Quatro. See *Cuatro.*

Ramayana. An ancient Sanskrit text that tells of the birth and travels of Lord Rama, the seventh incarnation of Lord Vishnu. In Guyana, Trinidad, and elsewhere in the Caribbean where there are Indian populations it is celebrated with folk plays concerning the adventures of Lord Rama.

Rada (Arará, other spellings). A port in Benin through which slaves were exported to the Americas. The name given to such people, many of whom were *Fon.* A Haitian cult that is a part of the *Vodou* faith.

Rara. A band that plays for the Haitian Carnival of the same name.

Rastafarians. Adherents of a religion first practiced in Jamaica that is founded on the divinity of the former emperor of Ethiopia, Haile Selassie, the Bible, and on a fusion of Jamaican religions.

Reggae. A form of Jamaican popular music that developed in the late 1960s from various indigenous folk sources as well as North American popular music.

Revivalism. An Afro-Christian religion in Jamaica that is sometimes called Pocomania.

Riddim. A basic rhythmic line in Jamaican music; similar to *Toque.*

Rites of passage. The movement of a person from one stage in life to another, beginning with a culturally defined "baptism" and ending with funerary rites.

Road march. The term that replaced *leggo* to depict litany-style songs played for Carnival in Trinidad and at other outdoor festivals. Originally, road marches were played for steel bands.

Rodriguez, Arsenio (1911–1970). Cuban *tres* musician, composer, and *conjunto* leader. Considered one of the greatest tres players of all time, he was very influential in the development of *salsa* music.

Romeu, Antonio María (1876–1955). Cuban orchestra leader who made many recordings of the *danzón* in the first decades of the twentieth century. It is said that he is responsible for adding piano to the *charanga.*

Roig, Gonzalo. Composer of many *danzones* and of the *zarzuela Cecilia Valdés.*

Roti. In the Caribbean region, an Indian bread filled with curried potato, chicken, beef, or other ingredients.

Rumba. Several related Cuban dances that developed in the slums of Havana and the docks of Matanzas in the late nineteenth century. The original folk styles became popularized in a dance craze in the early 1930s. As a musical form, the rumba influenced Congolese popular music by midcentury.

Salsa. "Sauce" in Spanish, the term became associated with the Afro-Cuban music that incubated in the 1940s and 1950s in New York City but came into its own as a major world music in the 1970s.

Salt. Condiment with great symbolic significance. The most widespread tale associates eating too much salt with becoming too heavy to fly back to Africa to escape *slavery.*

Santería. A Caribbean religion, especially prominent in Cuba, that combines aspects of *Yoruba* and Roman Catholic faiths, especially in the treatment of Catholic Saints as *Yoruba* gods. The more *Yoruba* version of the religion is known as Lucumí in Cuba.

Saramaka. A group of *maroons* who live in Suriname.

Saumell, Manuel (1817–1870). Nineteenth-century Cuban composer who wrote Creolized contradances.

Segon. A drum used in Haitian *Vodou.*

Seis. A type of poetry that is sung to string accompaniment. Originally from Spain and North Africa, the form is widespread in the Americas.

Selassie, Haile (Ras Tafari) (1892–1975). Former emperor of Ethiopia whose struggle against Italian occupation at the opening of World War II and whose long rule from 1930 to 1974 inspired some Caribbean people, especially the *Rastafarians* in Jamaica, to see him as divine.

Shango (Sango, Saugo, Sobo). The *Yoruba* sky god of thunder and lightning and formerly the name given to the Orisha religion of Trinidad.

Shakespeare Mas (Speech Mas, Pierrot Mas). In Carriacou, a masquerade on Carnival Tuesday in which participants wearing a *Pierrot* outfit and a cape shout speeches at opponents. Some of the speeches are based on Shakespeare's *Julius Caesar,* while others are based on British heroes or are traditional braggadocio.

Shanto. The name created by vaudevillian Bill Rogers for a style of Guyanese music in the 1930s and 1940s that is similar to Trinidadian calypso with a dash of British music-hall music thrown in.

Shouters. See *Spiritual Baptists.*

Ska. A dance and song style that was first popular in Jamaica in the 1960s and has had off-again-on-again popularity worldwide ever since.

Slackness. Rude or overtly sexual behavior and the name for a style of *Dancehall* music.

Slash-and-burn agriculture. A form of horticulture in which, after harvest, the remaining brush is burned off to clear the land for the next crop and to provide nutrients to the soil. This anthropological definition of the agricultural practice, which may be destructive to the environment when used by a large or dense population of farmers, should not be confused with the same phrase that refers to the military tactic, a "scorched earth" policy of ethnic cleansing, in which people are moved off the land by burning or otherwise destroying everything in sight.

Slavery. When someone is, by law, "owned" as property and therefore may be bought and sold. See also *Indenture.*

Soca. "Soul calypso," a kind of calypso that developed in the 1970s that is dance oriented and usually contains sexy lyrics.

Son. A topical song that developed in central and eastern Cuba in the first two decades of the twentieth century. The son became the most representative song form on the island through the early 1950s. It was played with a small conjunto configuration.

Sorcery. The use of spells or materials to magically cause good or harm to someone.

Soirée. In nineteenth-century Guadeloupe, dances for elite estate owners.

Sound systems. In the 1950s in Jamaica, outdoor music players consisting of one or more record turntables, multiple speakers, and a microphoned disc jockey singsonging a patter that creates segues between recordings. Later, this influenced both the development of rap in the United States and *Dancehall* in Jamaica.

Speech Mas. See *Shakespeare Mas.*

Spiritual Baptists. A religion in Trinidad that combines African and Protestant beliefs. Once derisively called the Shouters for their sometimes flamboyant singing style.

Steel band. A configuration of instruments often made from 55-gallon oil drums that are cut to different sizes. Notes are pounded out along the top of each *pan* so that in concert, scores of instruments create a robust music.

Superstition. Irrational belief. This is an archaic opinion once held by folklorists and the lay public alike that some people were governed by false beliefs. Actually, much of what we all do is based on opinions that are either emotionally based, rendering empirical proof irrelevant, or that may not be provable. Seen this way, much of human behavior is necessarily "superstitious."

Syncretism. A term championed by Melville Herskovits to describe the process by which elements from two or more cultures are fused into a single cultural trait. For example, the adoration of Santa Barbara as a Catholic saint or as a Santería *Orisha* (god).

Tadja (Tadjahs). The Guyanese version of the ritual that is called *Hosay* in Trinidad. It is also the name for the ceremonial tomb of *Husayn* that is displayed during the celebration.

Tango. Early-twentieth-century Argentinean dance based, in part, on the nineteenth-century Cuban *habanera* rhythm.

Tassa. The drums used for the *Hosay* festival in Trinidad.

Tavárez, Manuel G. (1842 or 43–1883?). Composer of Puerto Rican *danzas.*

Tea meeting. A folk play and musical performance once held in Nevis. Full of grandiloquent characterizations and boisterous speech.

Temne. The name for people in the Caribbean whose ancestors were enslaved in Sierra Leone.

Toque. A rhythm in Afro-Cuban music. Certain toques are often associated with particular gods in Afro-Cuban Santería.

Tonada. A style of Spanish verse that is sung widely in the Americas.

Tradition. The part of culture that is handed down through the generations and is thought to be relatively unchanged in the process.

Transculturalism. A term coined by *Fernando Ortiz* to refer to cultural exchange between two or more groups of people.

Transnationalism. A culture that exists as a functioning unit in two or more countries, as individuals from the culture move from country to country and from community to community.

Tres. A Cuban instrument played by *guajiros* and usually made of three sets of doubled strings on a guitarlike wooden body.

Tumba Francesa. An Afro-Caribbean configuration found in eastern Cuba that was brought to the island by slaves from Haiti and their owners at the time of the Haitian revolution. The drum ("tumba") assemblage is played for contradances.

Turner, Lorenzo (1895–1972). Major scholar of the Gullah people and their language; he also conducted fieldwork in Brazil and West Africa.

Vassa, Gustavus. See *Olaudah Equiano.*

Vernacular. Originally referring to informal speech or dialect, the word now includes everyday activities or folklife as opposed to "cultivated" activities.

Villaverde, Cirilo (1812–1894). Cuban author of *Cecilia Valdés,* an epic novel of colonial Cuba.

Vodou. Along with Catholicism, the major religion of Haiti, based, in part on *Fon* religion.

Wanga. See *Obeah.*

Waterman, Richard (1914–1971). Ethnomusicologist who developed an influential system of describing African components in the music of the Americas.

West Indies. For the purposes of this handbook, the West Indies include the islands or countries of the Caribbean except the islands where Spanish is spoken (Cuba, Puerto Rico, and the Dominican Republic). However, a more inclusive definition of the West Indies would include all the islands of the Caribbean region, and a less inclusive definition would exclude Haiti.

White, José (1835–1918). A prodigy and a discovery of *Gottschalk's,* White was a Cuban violinist and composer.

Williams, Eric Eustace (1911–1981). Historian and politician who served as Trinidad and Tobago's first prime minister from 1956 to 1981, as the two-island nation moved from being a British colony to being an independent nation.

Witchcraft. The use of a supernatural force by a member of society to cause harm to a person or to the group as a whole.

World Music. A name commonly applied to a very large variety of popular musical styles that mix formerly disparate musical styles, such as French Caribbean and Congolese *rumba,* both of which are in part developed from Cuban *rumba.*

Yemaja (Emanja). A goddess of the sea in several *Yoruba*-based faiths.

Yoruba. A very large group of people who live in southwestern Nigeria. Many of their customs, in modified form, are found in the Caribbean—especially their religion, which is variously called Santería, Lucumí, or, formerly, *Shango.*

Zami. "Friend" in Kwéyòl, but in Carriacou, Grenada, it also means "lesbian."

Zapateo. A dance of Spanish origin that is found in Cuba and Mexico and elsewhere in Spanish-speaking America.

Zarzuela. Light opera in Spain and in Cuba.

Zombie. In Haitian *Vodou,* the body of a dead person who has been possessed by someone for a nefarious purpose. In Grenada, a lesbian (see *Zami*).

Zouk. A late-twentieth-century, electrified version of *Mazouk.*

Bibliography

BOOKS AND ARTICLES

Aarne, Antti, and Stith Thompson. 1964. *The Types of the Folktale: A Classification and Bibliography.* Helsinki: Tampere.

Abrahams, Roger D. 1983. *The Man-of-Words in the West Indies: Performance and the Emergence of Creole Culture.* Baltimore: Johns Hopkins UP.

———. 1992. *Singing the Master: The Emergence of African-American Culture in the Plantation South.* New York: Penguin. (Although not on the Caribbean, this book by Abrahams, who is such an important Caribbeanist folklorist, is included here. This book on Afro-American folk culture of the nineteenth century informs Caribbean folklore.)

———. 2002. "Nevis and St. Kitts: Tea Meetings, Christmas Sports, and The Moonlight Night." In *Caribbean Voyage, the 1962 Field Recordings.* Rounder Records, 82161–1731–2. Compact disc notes.

———, with Nick Spitzer, John F. Szwed, and Robert Farris Thompson. 2006. *Blues for New Orleans: Mardi Gras and America's Creole Soul.* Philadelphia: U of Pennsylvania P.

——— and John F. Szwed. 1983. *After Africa.* New Haven: Yale UP. (Classic reference on eighteenth- and nineteenth-century folklore from English-speaking authors.)

Aching, Gerard. 2002. *Masking and Power: Carnival and Popular Culture in the Caribbean.* Minneapolis: U of Minnesota P.

Alexis, Jacques Stephen. 1999. *General Sun, My Brother.* Trans. Carrol F. Coates. Charlottesville: U of Virginia P. (This book by an early Haitian author is full of folkloric settings.)

Allen, Ray, and Lois Wilcken, eds. 2001. *Island Sounds in the Global City: Caribbean Popular Music and Identity in New York.* Urbana: U of Illinois P.

Allsopp, Richard. 1996. *Dictionary of Caribbean English Usage.* New York: Oxford UP.

Anonymous. 2001. *La Torre: Revista de la Universidad de Puerto Rico—El Caribe Anglófono Tercera Época,* no. 19 (January–March). (This issue of *La Torre* contains several articles on the folklore of the eastern Caribbean, especially on folk performance and masquerading.)

Anonymous. 2002. *Captive Passage: The Transatlantic Slave Trade and the Making of the Americas.* Washington, D.C.: Smithsonian Institution Press. (This book contains a lot of graphics and text detail on the Middle Passage.)

Anthony, Michael, and Andrew Carr, eds. 1975. *David Frost Introduces Trinidad and Tobago.* London: Andrew Deutsch (Includes articles by Andrew Carr on Carnival, Derek Walcott on Port of Spain, Brinsley Samaroo on East Indian culture, and many more.)

Austerlitz, Paul. 1997. *Merengue: Dominican Music and Dominican Identity.* Philadelphia: Temple UP.

Averill, Gage. 1997. *A Day for the Hunter, a Day for the Prey: Popular Music and Power in Haiti.* Chicago: U of Chicago P.

——— and Lois Wilcken. 1998. "Haiti." In Olsen and Sheehy, *South America, Mexico, Central America, and the Caribbean.*

Banham, Martin, Errol Hill, and George Woodyard. 1994. *The Cambridge Guide to African and Caribbean Theatre.* New York: Cambridge UP.

Barnet, Miguel, ed. 1968. *The Autobiography of a Runaway Slave; Esteban Montejo.* Trans. Jocasta Innes. New York: Pantheon.

Barrett, Leonard. 1976. *The Sun and the Drum: African Roots in Jamaican Folk Tradition.* Kingston, Jamaica: Heinemann.

———. 1997. *The Rastafarians.* Boston: Beacon Press.

Bascom, William. 1980. *Sixteen Cowries: Yoruban Divination from Africa to the New World.* Bloomington: Indiana UP.

Bauman, Richard. 1978. *Verbal Art as Performance.* Rowley, Mass.: Newbury House.

———, ed. 1992. *Folklore, Cultural Performances, and Popular Entertainments: A Communications-Centered Handbook.* New York: Oxford UP.

Béhague, Gerald, ed. 1984. *Performance Practice: Ethnomusicological Perspectives.* Westport, Conn.: Greenwood Press.

———. 1992. "Music Performance." In Bauman, *Folklore, Cultural Performances, and Popular Entertainments.*

Bennett, Herman L. 2005. *Africans in Colonial Mexico: Absolutism, Christianity, and Afro-Creole Consciousness, 1570–1640.* Bloomington: Indiana UP.

Berg, Lora, and Canute Caliste. 1989. *The Mermaid Wakes: Paintings of a Caribbean Isle by Mr. Canute Caliste of Carriacou, Grenada.* London: Macmillan.

Berger, Harris M., and Giovanna P. Del Negro. 2004. *Identity and Everyday Life: Essays in the Study of Folklore, Music, and Popular Culture.* Middletown, Conn.: Wesleyan UP.

Berrian, Brenda F. 2000. *Awakening Spaces: French Caribbean Popular Songs, Music, and Culture.* Chicago: U of Chicago P.

Besson, Gérard, 2001. *Folklore and Legends of Trinidad and Tobago.* Trinidad: Paria Publishing. (This book is part of a multimedia trilogy. It may be purchased together with a CD: Besson, Gerard, comp. 2002. *Spirits of Trinidad and Tobago.* Angostura. [Stories from Paramin Village]. There is also a DVD of related material: 2006. *Trinidad and Tobago Folklore—A Documentary Film.* Trinidad: S.D.L. Productions, in association with Sonaris.)

Bettelheim, Judith, ed. 2001. *Cuban Festivals: A Century of Afro-Cuban Culture.* Princeton, N.J.: Markus Wiener.

———. 2005. *AfroCuba: Works on Paper, 1968–2003.* San Francisco State University: distributed by U of Washington P.

Bierhorst, John, ed. 2002. *Latin American Folktales: Stories from Hispanic and Indian Traditions.* New York: Pantheon.

Bilby, Kenneth. 2005. *True-Born Maroons.* Gainesville: U of Florida P.

Black, Clinton V. 1966. *Tales of Old Jamaica.* London: Collins.

Boggs, Vernon W. 1992. *Salsiology: Afro-Cuban Music and the Evolution of Salsa in New York City.* New York: Excelsior Music.

Booker, M. Keith, and Dubravka Juraga. 2001. *The Caribbean Novel in English: An Introduction.* Portsmouth, NH: Heinemann.

Boulton, Laura. 1969. *The Music Hunter: The Autobiography of a Career.* Garden City, N.Y.: Doubleday. (Boulton was a pioneering field ethnomusicologist who made some recordings in the Caribbean.)

Brandon, George. 1983. *The Dead Sell Memories: Santeria from Africa to the New World.* Bloomington: Indiana UP. (Covers Santería in Cuba.)

Broughton, Simon, Mark Ellingham, David Muddyman, and Richard Trillo, eds. 1994. *World Music: The Rough Guide.* London: Penguin.

Brown, David H. 2003. *Santería Enthroned: Art, Ritual, and Innovation in an Afro-Cuban Religion.* Chicago: U of Chicago P.

Brown, Karen McCarthy. 1991. *Mama Lola: A Vodou Priestess in Brooklyn.* Los Angeles: U of California P.

Burton, Richard D. E. 1993. "'Maman-France Doudou': Family Images in French West Indian Colonial Discourse." *Diacritics* 23, no. 3 (Autumn): 69–90.

———. 1997. *Afro-Creole: Power, Opposition, and Play in the Caribbean.* Ithaca, N.Y.: Cornell UP.

Cable, George W. 1959. "The Dance in Place Congo." In *Creoles and Cajuns: Stories of Old Louisiana,* ed. Arlin Turner. Garden City, N.Y.: Doubleday Anchor Books. (Orig. pub. in *Century Magazine,* February and April 1886.)

Chamoiseau, Patrick. 1994. *Creole Folktales.* New York: The New Press. (This is a translation from French into English by Linda Coverdale of a *Au temps de l'antan.* Chamoiseau is considered to be one of the great writers from the French-speaking Caribbean.)

Carpentier, Alejo. 1989. *La Mùsica en Cuba.* Havana: Editorial Pueblo y Educación.

———. 2001. *Music in Cuba.* Ed. Timothy Brennan, trans. Alan West-Durán. Minneapolis: U of Minnesota P.

Cartey, Wilfred. 1991. *Whispers from the Caribbean: I Going Away, I Going Home—A Critical Review of the Works of Caribbean Novelists.* Los Angeles: Center for Afro-American Studies, UCLA. (This is a narrative review of mostly works in English written just before there was an explosion in West Indian writing, by a Trinidadian author.)

Chevannes, Barry. 1998. *Rastafari and Other African-Caribbean Worldviews.* New Brunswick, N.J.: Rutgers UP.

Clark, Veve. 1982. "Katherine Dunham's Tropical Revue." *Black American Literature Forum* 16, no. 4 (winter): 142–152.

Clark, Veve and Sara E. Johnson, eds. 2006. *Kaiso! Writings by and about Katherine Dunham.* Madison: U of Wisconsin P.

Clarke, Sebastian. 1981. *Jah Music: the Evolution of the Popular Jamaican Song.* London: Heinemann.

Classic Calypso Collective, ed. 2006. *West Indian Rhythm: Trinidad Calypsos on World and Local Events Featuring the Censored Recordings, 1938–1940.* Bear Family Records, BCD 16623. (Book and 10-CD box set.)

Clement, Paul C. 1999. *Petite Martinique: Traditions and Social Change.* New York: Vantage.

Clements William M. 2006. *North and South America.* Vol. 4 of *The Greenwood Encyclopedia of World Folklore and Folklife.* Westport, Conn.: Greenwood Press. (In regard to the Caribbean, this volume covers Cuba, Haiti, the Caribs of Dominica, and Jamaica.)

Cohen, Ronald D., ed. 2003. *Alan Lomax: Selected Writings 1934–1997.* New York: Routledge. (Includes one article on Lomax's historic recording trip to the Caribbean in 1962.)

Comitas, Lambros. 1968. *Caribbeana, 1900–1965: A Topical Bibliography.* Seattle: U of Washington P. (This omnibus Caribbean bibliography contains a large section entitled "Elements of Culture" that covers the same material found in this handbook, except it was compiled over 40 years ago.)

Conyers, James L., Jr., and Julius E. Thompson, eds. 2004. *Pan African Nationalism in the Americas: The Life and Times of John Henrik Clarke.* Trenton, N.J.: Africa World Press.

Courlander, Harold. 1960. *The Drum and the Hoe: Life and Lore of the Haitian People.* Berkeley: U of California P.

———. 1996. *A Treasury of Afro-American Folklore: The Oral Literature, Traditions, Recollections, Legends, Tales, Songs, Religious Beliefs, Customs, Sayings, and Humor of Peoples of African Descent in the Americas.* New York: Smithmark.

Cowley, John. 1991. "Carnival and Other Seasonal Festivals in the West Indies, U.S.A. and Britain: A Selected Bibliographical Index." Bibliographies in Ethnic Relations No. 10, University of Warwick: Centre for Research I Ethnic Relations.

———. 1996. *Carnival Canboulay and Calypso: Traditions in the Making.* New York: Cambridge UP.

Creel, Margaret Washington. 1988. *"A Peculiar People:" Slave Religion and Community-Culture among the Gullahs.* New York: New York UP.

Crowley, Daniel J. 1966. *I Could Talk Old-Story Good: Creativity in Bahamian Folklore.* Berkeley: U of California P.

———, ed. 1977. *African Folklore in the New World.* Austin: U of Texas P.

Dance, Daryl C. 1988. *Folklore from Contemporary Jamaicans.* Knoxville: U of Tennessee P.

Daniel, Yvonne. 1995. *Rumba: Dance and Social Change in Contemporary Cuba.* Bloomington: Indiana UP.

Danticat, Edwidge. 1996. *Krik? Krak!* New York: Vintage.

———. 2002. *After the Dance: A Walk through Carnival in Jacmel, Haiti.* New York: Crown Journeys.

de Certeau, Michel. 1984. *The Practice of Everyday Life.* Berkeley: U of California P.

———, Luce Giard, and Pierre Mayol. 1998. *Living and Cooking.* Vol. 2 of *The Practice of Everyday Life.* Minneapolis: U of Minnesota P.

Deacon, Desley. 1997. *Else Clews Parsons: Inventing Modern Life.* Chicago: U of Chicago P. (Parsons was one of the first anthropologists to document folktales in field settings in the Caribbean.)

De Verteuil, Anthony. 1984. *The Years of Revolt: Trinidad, 1881–1888.* Port of Spain, Trinidad: Paria. (This is the first major study to cover the Canboulay and Hosay disturbances of the 1880s.)

Dirks, Robert. 1987. *The Black Saturnalia: Conflict and Its Ritual Expression on British West Indian Slave Plantations.* Gainesville: U of Florida P.

Dormon, James H., ed. 1996. *Creoles of Color of the Gulf South.* Knoxville: U of Tennessee P.

Dudley, Shannon. 2003. *Carnival Music in Trinidad.* New York: Oxford UP.

Dundes, Alan, comp. 1976. *Folklore Theses and Dissertations in the United States.* Austin: U of Texas P. (Contains a few dissertations on Caribbean folklore, which may be located in the subject index.)

Dunham, Katherine. 1946. *Katherine Dunham's Journey to Accompong.* New York: Henry Holt.

———. 1969. *Island Possessed.* Chicago: U of Chicago P.

Edwards, Jay D. 1983. "The First Comparative Studies of Caribbean Architecture." *New West Indian Guide*, 173–200. (This review article contains many references.)

Elder, J. D. 1965. *Song Games from Trinidad and Tobago.* N.p.: Publications of the American Folklore Society.

Equiano, Olaudah. 1789. *The Life of Olaudah Equiano or Gustavus Vassa, the African.* 2 vols., with a new intro. by Paul Edwards. London: Dawsons of Pall Mall, 1969.

Fales-Hill, Susan. 2004. *Always Wear Joy: My Mother Bold and Beautiful.* New York: HarperCollins, Amistad. (This is a biography of Josephine Premice, as recounted by her daughter.)

Fanon, Frantz. 1967. *Black Skin, White Masks.* Trans. Charles Lam Markmann. New York: Grove Press.

Fayer, Joan, and Joan McMurray. 1999. "The Carriacou Mas as Syncretic Artifact." *Journal of American Folklore* 112: 58–73.

Fernández Olmos, Margarite, and Lizabeth Paravisini-Gebert, eds. 2001. *Healing Cultures: Art and Religion as Curative Practices in the Caribbean and Its Diaspora.* New York: Palgrave.

———. 2003. *Creole Religions of the Caribbean: An Introduction from Vodou and Santería to Obeah and Espiritismo.* New York: New York UP.

Fernandez, Raul A. 2006. *From Afro-Cuban Rhythms to Latin Jazz.* Berkeley: U of California P.

Figueredo, D. H. 2006. *Encyclopedia of Caribbean Literature.* Vols. 1 and 2. Westport, Conn.: Greenwood Press.

García, Arsenio. 2006. *Arsenio Rodríguez and the Transnational Flows of Latin Popular Music.* Philadelphia: Temple UP.

Gaskin, Molly R. 2006. *Medicinal Plants of Trinidad and Tobago and the Caribbean.* Trinidad: Pointe-a-Pierre Wild Fowl Trust. (This book contains descriptions of herbs and associated cures. It also includes photos of some of the herbs.)

Gates, Henry Louis, Jr., ed. 1987. *The Classic Slave Narratives.* London: Mentor.

Georges, Robert A., and Michael Owen Jones. 1995. *Folkloristics: An Introduction.* Bloomington: Indiana UP.

Georgia Writer's Project—Savannah Unit of the Work Projects Administration. 1940. *Drums and Shadows: Survival Studies among the Georgia Coastal Negroes.* Athens: Brown Thrasher Books and U of Georgia P. (This book is included in this list because it contains interviews, conducted in the 1930s, with very old people who recount the slavery and postslavery era. Those old cultures bear a similarity to nineteenth-century Caribbean cultures.)

Gilroy, Paul. 1993. *The Black Atlantic: Modernity and Double Consciousness.* Cambridge, Mass.: Harvard UP.

Glasser, Ruth. 1995. *My Music Is My Flag: Puerto Rican Musicians and Their New York Communities, 1917–1940.* Berkeley: U of California P.

Green, Garth L., and Philip W. Scher, eds. 2007. *Trinidad Carnival: The Cultural Politics of a Transnational Festival.* Bloomington: Indiana UP.

Green, Thomas A., ed., 1997. *Folklore: An Encyclopedia of Beliefs, Customs, Tales, Music, and Art.* Santa Barbara, Calif.: ABC-CLIO.

Guilbault, Jocelyne. With Gage Averill, Édouard Benoit, and Gregory Rabess. 1993. *Zouk: World Music in the West Indies.* Chicago: U of Chicago P.

Hall, Stuart. 1996. "The Question of Cultural Identity." In Stuart Hall, David Held, Don Hubert, and Kenneth Thompson, eds., *Modernity: An Introduction to Modern Societies.* London: Blackwell.

Harris, Joel Chandler. 1965. *Uncle Remus.* Intro. by Stella Brewer Brookes. New York: Schocken Books. (Orig. pub. 1880. Chandler's Uncle Remus tales are the southern American equivalent to Caribbean Nancy stories.)

Henry, Frances, ed. 1969. *McGill Studies in Caribbean Anthropology,* Occasional Paper Series, No. 5. Montreal: Centre for Developing-Area Studies, McGill U.

———. 2003. *Reclaiming African Religions in Trinidad: The Socio-Political Legitimation of the Orisha and Spiritual Baptist Faiths.* Kingston, Jamaica: U of the West Indies P.

Herskovits, Frances and Melville. 1934. *Rebel Destiny,* New York: McGraw-Hill Book Co.

Herskovits, Melville. 1937. *Life in a Haitian Valley.* New York: Garden City, N.Y.: Doubleday.

———. 1941. *The Myth of the Negro Past.* Boston: Beacon Press.

———. 1947. *Trinidad Village.* New York: Alfred A. Knopf.

Hill, Donald R. 1973. "'England I Want to Go': The Impact of Migration on a Caribbean Community." Ph.D. diss., Indiana U.

———. 1977. *The Impact of Migration on the Metropolitan and Folk Society of Carriacou, Grenada.* Vol. 34, part 2, of the Anthropological Papers of the American Museum of Natural History, 193–391. New York: American Museum of Natural History.

———. 1993. *Calypso Calaloo: Early Carnival Music in Trinidad.* Gainesville: U of Florida P. (Book with CD.)

———. 1998. "West African and Haitian Influences on the Ritual and Popular Music of Carriacou, Trinidad, and Cuba." *Black Music Research Journal* 18, no. 1/2 (Spring/Fall): 183–201.

———. 2002. "Music for Tourists in the Twentieth-Century Caribbean." *El Caribe Anglófono: Tercera Época* (La Torre: Revista de la Universidad de Puerto Rico) 7, no. 25 (July–September).

———. 2004. "Music of the African Diaspora in the Americas." In *Overviews and Topics.* Vol. 1 of *Encyclopedia of Diasporas: Immigrant and Refugee Cultures around the World,* ed. Melvin Ember, Carol Ember, and Ian Skoggard, 363–73. New York: Kluwer Academic/Plenum.

———, and Robert Abramson. 1979. "Play Mas' in Brooklyn." *Natural History* (August).

———, Maureen Warner-Lewis, John Cowley, Lise Winer, eds. 1998. "Peter Was a Fisherman: The 1939 Trinidad Field Recordings of Melville and Frances Herskovits." Vol. 1. Rounder Records, CD 1114.

———, and Lise Winer, eds. 2003. "'Rastlin' Jacob—The Music of the Spiritual Baptists of Trinidad: The 1939 Trinidad Field Recordings of Melville and Frances Herskovits." Rounder Records, CD 1115.

Hill, Errol. 1997. *The Trinidad Carnival: Mandate for a National Theatre.* London: New Beacon Books. (Orig. pub. 1972.)

Hill, John Errol (ed.), Joel Oliansky, and Oliver Hailey Gassner. 1964. *The Yale School of Drama Presents: Man Better Man; Here Comes Santa Clause; Hey You, Light Man!* New York: E.P. Dutton.

Hope, Donna P. 2006. *Inna di Dancehall: Popular Culture and the Politics of Identity in Jamaica.* Kingston, Jamaica: U of the West Indies P.

Hopkinson, Nalo. 1998. *Brown Girl in the Ring.* New York: Warner.
———. 2000. *Midnight Robber.* New York: Warner.
———, ed. 2003a. *Mojo Conjure Stories.* New York: Warner.
———. 2003b. *The Salt Roads.* New York: Warner.
Horowitz, Michael M., ed. 1971. *Peoples and Cultures of the Caribbean: An Anthropological Reader.* Garden City, N.Y.: Natural History Press.
———. 1992. *Morne-Paysan: Peasant Village in Martinique.* Prospect Heights, Ill.: Waveland Press.
Houk, James T. 1995. *Spirits, Blood, and Drums: The Orisha Religion in Trinidad.* Philadelphia: Temple UP.
Hunton, Alphaeus, and John Henrik Clarke, eds. 1964. "The People of the Caribbean Area," Special volume of the journal *Freedomways: A Quarterly Review of the Negro Freedom Movement* 5, no. 3, Summer.
Ibekwe, Patrick. 1998. *Wit and Wisdom of Africa: Proverbs from Africa and the Caribbean.* Oxford: New Internationalist Publications.
Jara Gámez, Simón, Aurelio Rodríguez Yeyo, and Antonio Zedillo Castillo. 1994. "El Danzón en Cuba." *De Cuba Con Amor... El Danzón en México*, 201–253. México, D. F.: Grupo Azabache.
Kasinitz, Philip. 1992. *Caribbean New York: Black Immigrants and the Politics of Race.* Ithaca, N.Y.: Cornell UP.
Kephart, Ronald F. 2000. *"Broken English": The Creole Language of Carriacou.* New York: Peter Lang.
Korom, Frank J. 2003. *Hosay Trinidad: Muharram Performances in an Indo-Caribbean Diaspora.* Philadelphia: U of Pennsylvania P.
Kubik, Gerhard. 1999. *Africa and the Blues.* Jackson: U of Mississippi P. (Covers the African roots of Mississippi Delta blues but is of interest for Kubik's method, which could be applied to Caribbean music.)
La Guerre, John, ed. 1974. *Calcutta to Caroni: The East Indians of Trinidad.* Bristol: Longman Caribbean.
Largey, Michael. 2006. *Vodou Nation: Haitian Art Music and Cultural Nationalism.* Chicago: U of Chicago P.
Leaf, Earl. 1948. *Isles of Rhythm.* New York: A. S. Barnes. (Broad-based popular study of Caribbean dance and performance.)
Lekis, Lisa. 1958. *Folk Dances of Latin America.* New York: Scarecrow Press.
Lévi-Strauss, Claude. 1966. *The Savage Mind.* Chicago: U of Chicago P.
Lewis, Oscar. 1966. *La Vida: A Puerto Rican Family in the Culture of Poverty.* New York: Random House.
Liverpool, Hollis "Chalkdust." 2003. *From the Horse's Mouth: Stories of the History and Development of the Calypso.* Diego Martin, Trinidad: Juba.
———. 2001? *Rituals of Power and Rebellion: The Carnival Tradition in Trinidad and Tobago, 1763–1962.* Chicago: Research Associates School Times Publications and Frontline Distribution International.

Livingston, James T. 1974. *Cuban Rhythms: The Emerging English Literature of the West Indies.* New York: Washington Square Press.

Lomax, Alan. 1950. *Mister Jelly Roll.* New York: Universal Library of Grosset & Dunlap. (This book is an "as told to" biography of Jelly Roll Morton, famed New Orleans pianist and Creole.)

———. 1997. *Brown Girl in the Ring.* Rounder Records, RDCD1716. (Caribbean children's songs.)

———, J. D. Elder, and Bess Lomax Haws. 1997. *Brown Girl in the Ring: An Anthology of Song Games from the Eastern Caribbean.* New York: Pantheon.

Lorde, Audre. 1982. *Zami: A New Spelling of My Name.* Freedom, Calif.: Crossing Press. (Lesbian view of women's rights, which briefly discusses that issue in Carriacou.)

Lovelace, Earl. 1978. *The Schoolmaster.* Portsmouth, NH: Heinemann.

———. 1979. *The Dragon Can't Dance.* London: Andre Deutsch.

———. 1982. *The Wine of Astonishment.* Oxford: Heinemann. (A novel about a Trinidadian stickfighter.)

———. 1984. *Jestina's Calypso and Other Plays.* London: Heinemann.

———. 1997. *Salt.* New York: Persea.

Manuel, Peter (with Kenneth Bilby and Michael Largey). 2006. *Caribbean Currents.* Philadelphia: Temple UP.

Marceles, Eduardo. 2004. *Azúcar! The Biography of Celia Cruz.* Trans. Dolores M. Koch. New York: Reed Press.

Marshall, Paule. 1983. *Praisesong for the Widow.* New York: Plume.

Mason, Michael Atwood, and Charles Greg Kelley. 1990. "Folk Religions of the African Diaspora." Special Issue of *Folklore Forum* 23, no. 1/2.

McAlister, Elizabeth. 2002. *Rara! Vodou, Power, and Performance in Haiti and Its Diaspora.* Berkeley: U of California P.

McDaniel, Lorna. 1998. *The Big Drum Ritual of Carriacou: Praisesongs in Rememory of Flight.* Gainesville: U of Florida P.

Métraux, Alfred. 1972. *Voodoo in Haiti.* New York: Schocken Books.

Mintz, Sidney W. 1974. *Caribbean Transformations.* Chicago: Aldine.

———. 1987. *Sweetness and Power: The Place of Sugar in Modern History.* New York: Penguin.

Mitchell, Joseph. 2001. "Houdini's Picnic." In Mitchell, *McSorley's Wonderful Saloon,* 253–66. New York: Pantheon Books. (Article about calypsonian Wilmoth Houdini at a New York party in the late 1930s.)

Monson, Ingrid. 2000. *The African Diaspora: A Musical Perspective.* New York: Routledge.

Montejo, Esteban. 1968. *The Autobiography of a Runaway Slave.* Ed. Miguel Barnet, trans. Jocasta Innes. New York: Pantheon.

Moore, Robin. D. 1997. *Nationalizing Blackness: Afrocubanismo and Artistic Revolution in Havana, 1920–1940.* Pittsburgh, Pa.: U of Pittsburgh P.

Murphy, Joseph M. 1988. *Santería: An African Religion in America.* Boston: Beacon Press.

Naipaul, V. S. 1959 (2002). *Miguel Street.* New York: Vintage. (A novel about a Trinidadian community.)

———. 1961. *A House for Mr. Biswas.* New York: Alfred A. Knopf, a division of Random House. (A novel about an iconoclastic Asian Trinidadian.)

Nettleford, Rex. M. 1974. *Mirror Mirror: Identity, Race, and Protest in Jamaica.* Kingston, Jamaica: William Collins & Sangster.

Nicholls, Robert W. 1998. *Old-Time Masquerading in the U.S. Virgin Islands.* St. Thomas: Virgin Islands Humanities Council.

Noblett, Richard. With Mark Ainley. 2006. "London Is the Place for Me 4: African Dreams and the Piccadilly High Life," Honest Jons Records, HJR CD 25. Compact disc notes. (Music of England-based West Indian singers.)

Nunley, John W., and Judith Bettelheim. 1988. *Caribbean Festival Arts: Each and Every Bit of Difference.* Seattle: U of Washington P.

Okpewho, Isidore, Carole Boyce Davies, and Ali A. Mazrui, eds. 2001. *The African Diaspora: African Origins and New World Identities.* Bloomington: Indiana UP. (Contains articles by the Prices and one by Keith Warner on film, as well as other articles that touch on identity and folklore.)

Olsen, Dale A., and Daniel E. Sheehy, eds. 1998. *South America, Mexico, Central America, and the Caribbean.* Vol. 2 of *The Garland Encyclopedia of World Music.* New York: Garland Publishing.

———. 2000. *The Garland Handbook of Latin American Music.* New York: Garland Publishing.

Orovio, Helio. 2004. *Cuban Music from A to Z.* Durham, N.C.: Duke UP.

Ortiz, Fernando. 1981. *Los Bailes y el Teatro de los Negros en el Folklore de Cuba.* Havana: Editorial Letras Cubanas.

———. 1984. "La Clave Xilofonica de la Musica Cubana: Ensayo Etnográfico." Havana: Editorial Letras Cubanas.

———. 1986. *Los Negros Curros.* Havana: Editorial de Ciencias Sociales. ("Los negros curros" were "street dandies" in early-nineteenth-century Havana.)

———. 1995a. *Cuban Counterpoint: Tobacco and Sugar.* Durham, N.C.: Duke UP. (Orig. pub. as *Contrapunteo Cubano del Tabaco y el Azúcar,* 1940.)

———. 1995b. *Los Negros Brujos.* Havana: Editorial de Ciencias Sociales. (Discusses witchcraft in Cuba.) (Orig. pub. 1906.)

Ostransky, Leroy. 1978. *Jazz City: The Impact of Our Cities on the Development of Jazz.* Englewood Cliffs, N.J.: Prentice Hall. (Covers jazz in selected cities, including New Orleans, from a social and cultural point of view.)

Owens, Joseph. 1976. *Dread: The Rastafarians of Jamaica.* Kingston, Jamaica: Sangster.

Pacini Hernández, Debora. 1995. *Bachata: A Social History of a Dominican Popular Music.* Philadelphia: Temple UP.

Pollitzer, William S. 2005. *The Gullah People and Their African Heritage.* Athens: U of Georgia P. (Orig. pub. 1999.)

Price, Richard, ed. 1973. *Maroon Societies: Rebel Slave Communities in the Americas.* Garden City, N.Y.: Doubleday Anchor Books Edition.

———. 1990. *Alabi's World.* Baltimore: Johns Hopkins UP.
———. 1995. *Enigma Variations: A Novel.* Cambridge, Mass.: Harvard UP.
———. 1998. *The Convict and the Colonel.* Boston: Beacon Press.
———. 2001. The Miracle of Creolization: A Retrospective." *New West Indian Guide* 72: 233–55.
———. 2002. *First-Time: The Historical Vision of an African American People, Second Edition With a New Preface by the Author.* Chicago: U of Chicago P.
———, and Sally Price. 1992. *Equatoria.* New York: Routledge.
———, and Sally Price. 2003. *The Root of Roots: Or, How Afro-American Anthropology Got Its Start.* Chicago: Prickly Paradigm Press / U of Chicago P.
Price, Sally. 1984. *Co-wives and Calabashes.* Ann Arbor: U of Michigan P. (In the course of describing the lives of women among the Saramaka, Price also covers folklore, including songs and artifacts.)
———, and Richard Price. 1999. *Maroon Arts: Cultural Vitality in the African Diaspora.* Boston: Beacon Press.
Primiano, Leonard Norman. "Folklife." In *Folklore: An Encyclopedia of Beliefs, Customs, Tales, Music, and Art,* ed. Thomas A. Green, 322–31. Oxford: ABC-CLIO.
Ramnarine, Tina K. 2001. *Creating Their Own Space: The Development of an Indian-Caribbean Musical Tradition.* Kingston, Jamaica: U of the West Indies P.
Redfield, Robert, 1989. *The Little Community and Peasant Society and Culture.* Midway Reprint. Chicago: U of Chicago P.
Regis, Louis. 1999. *The Political Calypso: True Opposition in Trinidad and Tobago, 1962–1987.* Gainesville: U of Florida P.
Richardson, Bonham C. 2004. *Igniting the Caribbean's Past: Fire in British West Indian History.* Chapel Hill: U of North Carolina P. (Although this is not a book on folklore, fire figures prominently in many incidents enshrined in West Indian tales and songs, especially with respect to burning the sugarcane fields, Carnival, and the Trinidad water riots of 1903, all of which Richardson covers. Richardson takes an interesting ecological approach to fire-related rituals.)
Riggio, Milla C. 1998. *TDR: Special Expanded Issue—Trinidad and Tobago Carnival. Drama Review: The Journal of Performance Studies,* 42, no. 3 (Fall).
———. 2004. *Carnival: Culture in Action—The Trinidad Experience.* Worlds of Performance. New York: Routledge.
Roberts, John Storm. 1998. *Black Music of Two Worlds: African, Caribbean, Latin, and African-American Traditions.* New York: Schirmer.
———. 1999. *The Latin Tinge: The Impact of Latin Music on the United States.* New York: Oxford UP.
Rodman, Selden. 1948. *Renaissance in Haiti: Popular Painters in the Black Republic.* New York: Pellegrini & Cudahy. (Rodman—1909–2002—was a poet, anthologist, and art critic who championed Haitian outsider art in Haiti the late 1940s and early 1950s.)
Rohlehr, Gordon. 1990. *Calypso and Society in Pre-Independence Trinidad.* Trinidad: Self-published.

———. 2004. *A Scuffling of Islands: Essays on Calypso.* San Juan, Trinidad: Lexicon Trinidad.

Rubin, Vera, and Lambros Comitas. 1975. *Ganja in Jamaica.* The Hague: Mouton.

Sanabria, Harry. 2007. "Food, Cuisine, and Cultural Expression." In *The Anthropology of Latin America and the Caribbean.* New York: Pearson.

Scher, Philip W. *Carnival and the Formation of a Caribbean Transnation.* Gainesville: U of Florida P, 2003.

Schoemaker, George H. 1990. *The Emergence of Folklore in Everyday Life.* Bloomington, Ind.: Trickster Press.

Sloat, Susanna, ed. 2002. *Caribbean Dance from Abakuá to Zouk.* Gainesville: U of Florida P.

Smith, M. G. 1962. *Kinship and Community in Carriacou.* New Haven, Conn.: Yale UP.

Soles, Diane. 2000. "The Cuban Film Industry: Between a Rock and a Hard Place." In *Cuban Transitions at the Millennium*, ed. Eloise Linger and John Cotman, 123–35. Argo, Md.: International Development Options.

Spottswood, Richard, and Don Hill. 1989. *Calypso Pioneers.* Rounder Records, CD 1039.

Starr, S. Frederic. 1995. *Bamboula! The Life and Times of Louis Moreau Gottschalk.* New York: Oxford UP.

Starr, S. Frederic, ed. 2001. *Inventing New Orleans: Writings of Lafcadio Hearn.* Jackson: U of Mississippi P.

Stebich, Ute. 1978. *Haitian Art.* New York: Brooklyn Museum and Harry N. Abrams.

Stephens, Patricia. 1999. *The Spiritual Baptist Faith.* London: Karnak House.

Stewart, Gary. 2000. *Rumba on the River: A History of the Popular Music of the Two Congos.* New York: Verso.

Stewart, John O., ed. 1983. *Bessie Jones: For the Ancestors—Autobiographical Memories.* Chicago: U of Illinois P. (Bessie Jones was the last of the Georgia Sea Island Singers.)

———. 1989. *Drinkers, Drummers, and Decent Folk: Ethnographic Narratives of Village Trinidad.* Albany: State U of New York P.

———. 1998. *Looking for Josephine and Other Stories.* Toronto: TSAR. (Through short stories, anthropologist John Stewart illustrates the culture and folklore of Trinidad.)

Stewart, Sue. 1999. *¡Musica! The Rhythm of Latin America: Salsa, Rumba, Merengue, and More.* San Francisco: Chronicle Books.

Stolzoff, Norman C. 2000. *Wake the Town and Tell the People: Dancehall Culture in Jamaica.* Durham, N.C.: Duke UP.

Stone, Judy S. J. 1994. *Studies in West Indian Literature: Theatre.* London: Macmillan.

Stone, Ruth M., ed. 2002. *The World's Music: General Perspectives and Reference Tools.* New York: Routledge. (This encyclopedia contains a section on Caribbean and Latin music, including a list of films and videos.)

Stuempfle, Stephen. 1995. *The Steelband Movement: The Forging of a National Art in Trinidad and Tobago.* Philadelphia: U of Pennsylvania P.

Sublette, Ned. 2004. *Cuba and Its Music: From the First Drums to the Mambo.* Chicago: Chicago Review Press.

Szwed, John F., and Roger D. Abrahams. 1978. *The West Indies, Central and South America.* Part 3 of *Afro-American Folk Culture: An Annotated Bibliography of Materials from North, Central and South America and the West Indies.* Philadelphia: Institute for the Study of Human Issues.

Taylor, Patrick. *Nation Dance: Religion, Identity, and Cultural Difference in the Caribbean.* Bloomington: U of Indiana P.

Thomas, Jeffrey, comp. 1992. *Forty Years of Steel: Annotated Discography of Steel Band and Pan Recordings, 1951–1991.* Westport, Conn.: Greenwood Press.

Thompson, Robert Farris. 1984. *Flash of the Spirit: African and Afro-American Art and Philosophy.* New York: Vintage.

Thompson, Stith. 1955. *Classification of Narrative Elements in Folk Tales, Ballads, Myths, Fables, Mediaeval Romances, Exempla, Fabliaux, Jest-Books, and Local Legend.* Bloomington: Indiana UP.

Torres, Arlene, and Norman E. Whitten, Jr., eds. 1998. *Eastern South America and the Caribbean.* Vol. 2 of *Blackness in Latin America and the Caribbean: Social Dynamics and Cultural Transformations.* Bloomington: Indiana UP.

Trouillot, Michel-Rolph. 1983. "The Production of Spatial Configurations: A Caribbean Case." *New West Indian Guide* 57, no. 3/4: 215–29.

Upton, D. and J. M. Vlach, eds. *Common Places: Readings in American Vernacular Architecture.* Athens: U of Georgia P.

Veigas-Zamora, Jose, Cristina Vives Gutierrez, Aldolfo V. Nodal, Valia Garzon, and Dannys Montes de Oca. 2001. *Memoria: Cuban Art of the 20th Century.* Los Angeles: International Arts Foundation.

Viard, Emile. 2003. *Haitian Art in the Diaspora.* Quebec[?]: Vie et Arts.

Villaverde, Cirilo. 2005. *Cecilia Valdés or El Angel Hill: A Novel of Nineteenth-Century Cuba.* New York: Oxford UP.

Vlach, J. M. 1975. "Sources of the Shotgun House: African and Caribbean Antecedents for Afro-American Architecture." Ph.D. diss., Indiana U.

Walcott, Derek. 1990. *Omeros.* New York: Farrar, Straus and Giroux.

Walker, Clarence E. *We Can't Go Home Again: An Argument about Afrocentrism.* New York: Oxford UP.

Warner, Keith Q. 1982. *Kaiso! The Trinidad Calypso: A Study of the Calypso as Oral Literature.* New York: Three Continents Press.

Warner-Lewis, Maureen. 1996. *Trinidad Yoruba: From Mother Tongue to Memory.* Tuscaloosa: U of Alabama P.

Waterman, Richard. 1943. "African Patterns in Trinidad Negro Music." Ph.D. diss., Northwestern U.

Waugh, Alec. 1955. *Island in the Sun: A Story of the 1950's Set in the West Indies.* New York: Farrar, Straus and Cudahy.

Westmorland, Guy T., Jr. 2001. *West Indian Americans: A Research Guide.* Westport, Conn.: Greenwood Press.

White, Timothy. 1992. *Catch a Fire: The Life of Bob Marley.* New York: Henry Holt.

Wilson, Peter J. Crab. 1973. *Antics: The Social Anthropology of English-Speaking Negro Societies of the Caribbean.* New Haven, Conn.: Yale UP.

———. 1974. *Oscar: An Inquiry into the Nature of Sanity?* Prospect Heights, Ill.: Waveland Press. (This is a partly autobiographical work about Oscar Bryan, an individualist from Providencia Island.)

Web Resources

Web sites change by the nanosecond, and our swath of Caribbean folklore is broad. Although I have told myself a million times not to exaggerate, there must be millions of Web sites out there that touch on Caribbean folklore. These facts conspire against creating a "complete" and "authoritative" directory of sites. The best I can do is to point readers in a direction and let you jump in. To paraphrase Lao Tse, the way I set out below is not *the* way.

First, I will suggest how one may evaluate Web sites. Next, I will list Web sites with "accurate" information or links to information relevant to Caribbean folklore. Finally, I will suggest some nontraditional ways one may use the Internet to collect traditional but "virtual" folklore. That is, the last group of sites is the digital age's version of folk communities—sites that, when accessed, allow one to be "in the e-field," doing "e-ethnography." It is just as if one is in a community on a Caribbean island observing or participating in a ritual or watching someone cook traditional food. The only difference is that actually being there is better.

HOW TO EVALUATE THE QUALITY OF WEB SITES

Evaluating information-based Web sites for accuracy is difficult. Free encyclopedias, such as Wikipedia (http://www.wikipedia.org/), are seductively easy to use and sometimes may offer solid and even insightful information. Web sites created by fans of some particular folk genre, by branches of Caribbean governments, or even by commercial entities, especially those that sell music or books, may all be helpful. Nevertheless, all, in one way or another, may fall victim to pitfalls.

Here are some ideas for assessing a Web site.

1. Many Web sites plagiarize from one another. An error, such as incorrectly listing someone's date of birth, may be stamped out a hundred times inaccurately, in each case leading back to an original source that is wrong.
2. Web sites may oversimplify and thereby give a false impression.
3. One should quickly check four or five sources that seem independent from each other in their source information. It they agree on some issue but state it differently, then there is a greater likelihood that the information is correct. However, if they use the exact phrase used by another site—reviews of CDs are especially prone to this fault—beware.
4. Web sites with a url ending in ".edu" may be good sources. I have found Web sites created by units of colleges and universities—such as Caribbean studies, folklore, or anthropology departments—to be better on average than, say, commercial Web sites. Sometimes one is able to find a professor who has gone to the trouble of describing, outlining, or otherwise detailing some aspect of Caribbean folklore in a very meticulous way, suggesting that they know what they are talking about. (Sometimes, however, fans of a particular folk genre can do even better. Check out http://www.cuatro-pr.org/ to see an excellent site developed by enthusiasts.)
5. Know the difference between an artistic or humanistic use of folklore on a Web site and one that is objective. Both have their value; a poet's Web site may yield a deep understanding of some bit of folklore where the facts cannot. However, one should also have an objective grounding in the folklore.
6. Check out the presence of links on the Web page, as well as their quality.
7. Use http://alexa.com/ to evaluate URLs by reading reviews of the Web site and its potential value.
8. I found out about alexa.com from http://www.lib.berkeley.edu/TeachingLib/Guides/Internet/Evaluate.html. This is an excellent tool for Web site evaluation from a top university, the University of California at Berkeley.

INSTITUTIONAL SITES

These Web sites are generic sites for academic disciplines that relate to folklore, not just Caribbean folklore. They occasionally have something on the Caribbean but are useful more particularly for getting a feel for how folklorists, ethnomusicologists, and others go about doing folklore research. One may then apply that spirit to Caribbean material one finds elsewhere, especially through the links that are found on most of these Web sites. This section is organized by institution, location, formal name of the unit to which the url refers, and finally the url.

Columbia College, Chicago. Center for Black Music Research (CBMR): http://www.cbmr.org/. CBMR conducts research on black music, defined in the traditional and widest possible manner. In the last two decades it has become the major focus for research into Caribbean music in the United States, especially from the point of view of ethnomusicologists and anthropologists. In addition to having permanent and part-time scholars, either in Chicago or in the Virgin Islands, which is used as its Caribbean base, it has research fellowships and a growing archive of recordings and printed matter.

Indiana University, Bloomington. The Department of Folklore and Ethnomusicology at Indiana University: http://www.indiana.edu/~folklore/. This joint department is the home of both the Folklore and Ethnomusicological Institutes and is affiliated with the IU Archives of Traditional Music.

Indiana University, Bloomington: The Indiana University Archives of Traditional Music: http://www.indiana.edu/~libarchm/index.html. This archive houses the largest university-based traditional archives in the United States and includes many Caribbean recordings, dating from the early 1900s to the present.

Indiana University, Bloomington. The Society for Ethnomusicology: http://webdb.iu.edu/sem/scripts/home.cfm. This is the home location for the most important ethnomusicological journal in the United States, with worldwide connections.

Library of Congress, Washington, D.C. The Folklife Center: http://www.loc.gov/folklife/. The Folklife Center of the Library of Congress contains a very large collection of documents and historical recordings, including the Alan Lomax recordings from the 1930s and from 1962.

Memorial University of Newfoundland and Labrador, St. John's, Newfoundland. The Department of Folklore: http://www.mun.ca/folklore/about/. Although not strong in Caribbean folklore, Memorial University is one of the few universities that offers a Ph.D. in folklore.

The New York Public Library, New York City. The Schomburg Center for Research in Black Culture: http://www.nypl.org/research/sc/sc.html. Located in Harlem, the Schomburg is a branch of the New York Public Library. With the exception of the Library of Congress, the Schomburg Center probably has more items of interest to Caribbean folklore researchers than any other institution in the United States. It houses some of the papers of John Henrik Clarke and Melville and Frances Herskovits, and it contains a very large library of Caribbean music.

Ohio State University, Columbus. American Folklore Society: http://afsnet.org/. Founded in 1888, this is the oldest folklore institution in the United States with worldwide interests.

Smithsonian Institution, Washington, D.C. Smithsonian Folkways/Smithsonian Global Sound: http://www.smithsonianglobalsound.org/ An excellent site for finding world music, especially Caribbean music. In addition to having Moe Asch's old Folkways recordings and Emory Cook's Cook Records, among the finest commercial recordings of world music (including many Caribbean issues) available for online copying, it also has been active in sponsoring new field recordings. The site grows almost daily and includes some of the best field recordings of Caribbean materials, including some collected by Ken Bilby. By accessing Smithsonian Global Sound, a researcher can quickly assemble a CD or iPod full of Caribbean vernacular music, including the annotated notes, some by noted scholars, from the original albums.

University of California at Berkeley. The Folklore Program: http://ls.berkeley.edu/dept/folklore/graduate.html. This program includes a concentration in Latin America and the Caribbean and is also strong in ethnomusicology. The Folklore Archive contains a half million items, including some from Creole cultures.

University of California at Los Angeles: The Department of Ethnomusicology at the University of California at Los Angeles: http://www.ethnomusic.ucla.edu/. This department focuses on performance of world music, especially from the Pacific region, and on ethnographic scholarship. However, the Ethnomusicological Archive contains material from the Spanish-speaking Caribbean.

University of Pennsylvania, Philadelphia: Folklore and Folklife: http://www.sas.upenn.edu/folklore/. The program in Folklore and Folklife is affiliated with the Center for Folklore and Ethnography. UP contains folklore and ethnomusicology notes and recordings from Jamaica and the Eastern Caribbean.

University of Texas, Austin: The Américo Paredes Center for Cultural Studies (APCCS), http://www.utexas.edu/cola/centers/culturalstudies/about/. This interdisciplinary department was formerly called the Center for Intercultural Studies in Folklore and Ethnomusicology. It is strong in Chicano studies but also Latin America and the Caribbean.

WEB SITES ABOUT PIONEERING RESEARCHERS AND CARIBBEAN WRITERS

These Web sites are listed in alphabetical order and include only deceased scholars. No comments are made about scholars who are extensively covered in the Handbook, but a few who were only briefly mentioned or not mentioned at all are annotated, complete with birth and death dates, if known.

Lydia Cabrera (1910–1984). The Lydia Cabrera Collection, University of Miami Libraries, Coral Gables, Florida: http://imls.library.miami.edu/chcdigital/chc0339/chc0339_find.shtml. With the exception of Fernando Ortiz, Lydia Cabrera has written more about Cuban music than any other scholar. Her research is in Spanish and until recently has been hard to find. However, the University of Miami Libraries hold her collection and are in the process of organizing it for both Spanish and English speakers. From this URL one may also link to the libraries' Cuban Heritage Collection.

Caribbean Writers: http://core.ecu.edu/engl/deenas/caribbean/carbwtrs.htm. This Web site gives short biographies of selected writers as well as photographs, major works, and a few links.

Melville J. and Frances S. Herskovits. Melville J. Herskovits Library of African Studies, Northwestern University: http://www.library.northwestern.edu/africana/herskovits.html and the Melville J. and Frances S. Herskovits Collection, Schomburg

Center, New York Public Library: http://www.nypl.org/research/sc/WEBEXHIB/legacy/a.htm.

Errol Hill, The Papers of Errol G. Hill in the Dartmouth College Library: http://ead.dartmouth.edu/html/ml77.html. This site is one of the best examples of archival presentation of the Library's holdings on a subject that I've seen. You will know right where to go to find the information on Hill that you need.

Zora Neale Hurston. Zora Neale Hurston, Dept. of English, University of Minnesota: http://voices.cla.umn.edu/vg/Bios/entries/hurston_zora_neale.html.

Alan Lomax. The Association for Cultural Equity: http://www.culturalequity.org/index.html. At this printing the Association for Cultural Equity is reconstructing its Web site. The new Web page is expected in July 2007. Please note that many Lomax materials are in the process of being accessed into the Alan Lomax Collection, Folklife Center of the Library of Congress: http://www.loc.gov/folklife/lomax/. More on Lomax's Caribbean recordings may be found at the Alan Lomax Collection, Rounder Records: http://www.rounder.com/series/lomax_alan/.

Fernando Ortiz. Fernando Ortiz Foundation: http://www.fundacionfernandoortiz.org/fortiz.htm. Studies from the Schomburg Center that are dedicated to Fernando Ortiz are found on this Web site: http://digital.nypl.org/schomburg/ortiz/ortizfront.htm

Elsie Clews Parsons. The "Elsie Clews Parsons Papers," The American Philosophical Society, Philadelphia: http://www.amphilsoc.org/library/mole/p/parsons.htm

Selden Rodman (1909–2002). Guide to the Selden Rodman Papers, Yale University: http://mssa.library.yale.edu/findaids/stream.php?xmlfile=mssa.ms.0871.xml. A short biography and a guide to the collected papers of Selden Rodman, North American poet, anthologist, and champion of Haitian outsider art.

Lorenzo Turner. Lorenzo D. Turner papers 1915–1973, Melville J. Herskovits Library of African Studies, Northwestern University: http://findingaids.library.northwestern.edu/fedora/get/inu:inu-ead-afri-0023/inu:EADbDef11/getDescriptiveSummary

The Andrew Pearse Papers are housed in the Special Collections section of Universtiy of West Indies, St. Augustine, Trinidad: http://www.mainlitwwi.tt/divisions/wi/collsp/specialcoll.htm

TOPIC WEB SITES

General Caribbean

The Society for Latin American and Caribbean Anthropology—A Section of the American Anthropological Association: http://www.aaanet.org/slaa/

Journals

Anthurium, A Caribbean Studies Journal: http://scholar.library.miami.edu/anthurium/home.htm. This electronic journal is published by the University of Miami and contains folkloric material as well as all things Caribbean.

Calabash, an electronic journal from New York University on Caribbean arts and humanities: http://www.nyu.edu/calabash/index.shtml

Callaloo is a humanistic journal of Caribbean literature and poetry and may be accessed in an e-version through various subscription-based databases and search engines: http://muse.jhu.edu/journals/callaloo/

Caribbean Quarterly is a journal of Caribbean Arts that features a lot of folklore-related articles. Access is subscription based through databases and search engines.

The Journal of Folklore Research at Indiana University: http://www.indiana.edu/~jofr/

Journal of Pidgin and Creole Languages, published at Ohio State University: http://www.ling.ohio-state.edu/~jpcl/. This succinct site has important links, especially one to the Society for Pidgin and Creole Linguistics (the Society for Caribbean Linguistics).

Journal of West Indian Literature, published at the Cave Hill Campus, University of the West Indies, http://www.cavehill.uwi.edu/fhe/hum/publications/JournalsJWIL.htm

The New West Indian Guide is very strong on folklore and the arts. This Web site has a list of all articles, book reviews, and so forth and is quite handy: http://www.kitlv.nl/nwig-56–77–1982–2003.html

Small Axe is a good general journal on the Caribbean: http://www.smallaxe.net/

La Torre: Revista de la Universidad de Puerto Rico, from the Universidad de Puerto Rico is a journal published in both Spanish and English and often includes articles concerning the folklore of the Eastern Caribbean.

Wadabagei: A Journal of the Caribbean and Its Diasporas publishes works by Caribbean scholars on a wide range of subjects: http://www.lexingtonbooks.com/Journals/wadabagei/Index.shtml

Africanisms and Afrocentrism

Africanisms in material culture: http://www.ulib.iupui.edu/subjectareas/aas/survivals.html

Article presenting an Afrocentric viewpoint, with a long bibliography: http://www.geocities.com/Athens/Academy/8919/structure.htm

Article criticizing Afrocentrism: http://www.butterfliesandwheels.com/printer_friendly.php?num=3

Religion and Magic

A site on Mami Wata (Mammy Water), from the point of view of devotees: http://mamiwata.com/mami.html

An essay entitled "A Study in Salt," by Tamara Kaye Sellman: http://www.angelfire.com/wa2/margin/nonficSellmanSalt.html.

This Web site covers many different religions, including those in the Caribbean: http://www.religioustolerance.org/

Carnival

This Web site, with its worldwide links, seems sufficient to cover Caribbean Carnivals: http://www.carnaval.com/main.htm

West Indian Carnival in Brooklyn Resources, compiled by the Brooklyn Public Library: http://www.brooklynpubliclibrary.org/explore_topic_detail.jsp?subjectpageid=1128

Caribbean Music at Home and in the Diaspora

Afropop Worldwide is the premier site for music of the African diaspora and is especially strong in Caribbean musical styles in various parts of the world: http://www.afropop.org/

Musical Traditions is a British-based electronic journal and commercial CD site that has many scholarly articles on Caribbean music: http://www.mustrad.org.uk/

Dr. John Aske of the Department of Foreign Languages of Salem State College in Massachusetts developed an excellent Web site on Latin Music. It is especially strong on the Spanish-speaking countries in the Caribbean and Latin music in the diaspora: http://www.lrc.salemstate.edu/aske/latmusic.htm

This atlas, or encyclopedia, of plucked instruments includes instruments from a few Spanish-speaking countries in the Caribbean. It is also useful on the topic of string instruments from Venezuela and the islands off the Venezuelan coast and in the southern part of the Eastern Caribbean: http://www.atlasofpluckedinstruments.com/central_america.htm

Although this is a commercial site, it is great for salsa. Descarga is in the process of reissuing on CD recordings from the New York City–based Fania label: http://www.descarga.com/cgi-bin/db

The Allmusic guide has essays and reviews of many Caribbean CDs, though its focus is more on music criticism than on academic scholarship: http://www.Allmusic.com

Caribbean Food

The Caribbean Food Emporium is a commercial site that has books for sale, information, and good links: http://www.caribbeanfoodemporium.co.uk/descriptions.htm

Sites Dedicated to Locations: New Orleans and the East Coast of the United States

U.S. southeast coast sea islands. This Web site is maintained by a Gullah woman: http://www.netpro1000.com/sites/lsimmons/index.asp. It contains many links.

Southern Florida. The Historical Museum of South Florida often has exhibits and Web-based information on Caribbean folk culture and cultures of the Caribbean diaspora: http://www.hmsf.org/

Bahamas

Created by the Bahamas Ministry of Tourism, within this site are pages, such as "local customs," that give information on folklore.

Great Britain

One interesting site about Caribbean peoples in the British Isles is http://www.movinghere.org.uk. Once at the site one can find histories of migrants from the Caribbean, festivals, etc.

Cuba

A Web site dedicated to Afro-Cuban culture: http://www.afrocubaweb.com/default.htm

This commercial site established by David Brown lists botanicas and sells ritual objects and recordings about Afro-Cuban religion: http://www.folkcuba.com

This site is similar to folkcuba.com, is headed by Jorge L. Rodriguez, and has links to other sites: http://afrocuba.org/

Florida International University's Cuban collection, certainly one of the best of its kind anywhere in the world, is especially strong in recorded commercial music and photographs of musicians from Cuba (the Cristobal Diaz Ayala collection): http://library.fiu.edu/latinpop/index.cfm

Created by María Teresa Linares, one of the leading authorities on Cuban music, this site is in Spanish: http://www.musica.cult.cu/documen/musicampesina.htm

Cuban theater: http://encarta.msn.com/encyclopedia_761569844_5/Cuba.html

A Web site on the danzón: http://www.danzon.com/

Jamaica

There are many ska, reggae, and dancehall sites. The best bet is to look around and follow the rules for assessing sites spelled out previously.

This site comes recommended by Norman Stolzoff, dancehall authority. It is a clearinghouse of all things reggae, with many links: http://niceup.com

This is the Web page for the National Library of Jamaica and has many good links: http://www.nlj.org.jm/docs/history.htm

This mento Web site has links to other mento Web sites: http://www.mentomusic.com/links.htm

Dan Neely's home page is very strong on the topic of mento: http://homepages.nyu.edu/~dtn9606/

Hispaniola (Haiti and the Dominican Republic)

Haiti, including folklore and the arts: http://www.webster.edu/~corbetre/haiti/haiti.html

This Web site promotes Dominican culture: http://www.elcaballotours.com/dominicain_republic_art_culture_en.html

Ivan Erickson is a Dominican American who makes Carnival masks: http://www.dominicanmasks.com/

Puerto Rico

This is one of the best Web sites on a Caribbean folk genre—in this case, the Puerto Rican Cuatro and related instruments. It contains original research and many links: http://www.cuatro-pr.org/

This Web site is mostly in Spanish but has a few pages in English. It covers the Puerto Rican danza: http://www.ladanza.com/

Eastern Caribbean—French language

This is a course at Harvard on French Caribbean literature: http://hcl.harvard.edu/research/guides/courses/2006spring/french196/specialized.html

This nice bibliography of writers and theater in Francophone Caribbean is written in English and French: http://www.libraries.rutgers.edu/rul/rr_gateway/research_guides/latin/carribean.shtml

Trinidad

Trinidad artist: http://brianwongwon.blogspot.com/

Interesting Trinidad site about art and more: http://thebookmann.blogspot.com/

A Trinidad carnival Web site that is just "ok": http://www.visittnt.com/todo/events/carnival2002/carnival/traditionalcharacters.htm

A site on Hosay: http://www.der.org/films/hosay-trinadad-review.html

England-based contemporary calypso researcher: http://www.calypsoarchives.co.uk/

This is one of the oldest and best Web sites on calypso. It was established by a Nigerian émigré and criminal defense lawyer based in Washington D.C., G. Godwin Oyewole: http://www.kaiso.net/

Asian Indians

Web site on Indians in the diaspora that includes a few articles on the Caribbean: http://www.sscnet.ucla.edu/southasia/diaspora/freed.html

Maroons

Web site of Richard and Sally Price: http://www.richandsally.net/index.htm

This site is from the Smithsonian Institution and has information and many links on maroons: http://www.folklife.si.edu/resources/maroon/presentation.htm

Collecting Caribbean Folklore on the Web

As I was preparing this handbook, I noticed that the Web is not just a source for information about Caribbean folklore, it is also a source of Caribbean folklore. There are many ways the Web may be used for this purpose, and I have thought of a few of them. For example, one may search through sites in which individuals post short videos, and sometimes long ones, on a whim or in earnest. The first site that comes to mind for this is youtube.com. For example, among all the junk, I found a nice short video entitled "Trinidad and Tobago Tassa Divali." What makes the one-minute-plus video interesting is that the drummers are in an upscale shopping mall, and as they wander through a dining area people react to the complex rhythms. Under "salsa" there are many videos, including several from the World Salsa Championship. In one, a young brother-sister team of dancers is announced as "half Korean/half Salvadorian." Yes, Caribbean dance is world dance. Also found on youtube.com was "Obatala Santería Yoruba Baba," in which dancers and drummers performed on stage while one dancer simulated possession.

Check also http://myspace.com/, http://www.dailymotion.com/us, or http://www.stickam.com/.

Mass-media database. To use for Caribbean folklore, search for an island or a genre: http://www.archive.org/

Internet Radio

There are Internet radio stations around the world, but especially from the Caribbean, and the BBC quite often broadcasts Caribbean-related material. For the BBC Caribbean go to this Web site: http://www.bbc.co.uk/caribbean/institutional/weather.shtml

E-mail, E-mail Groups, Blogs, Conversation Threads, or Just Plain Google

Sometimes you can just e-mail a friend who lives in or is from a Caribbean country. Via e-mail, I was given a great recipe for "jacks broth," a cure-all and aphrodisiac soup with small "jacks," a sardine-like fish, and okra. I have not tried it yet, however, since I cannot get any jacks. E-mail groups can help bring together people with similar interests. I have also Googled conversation threads in which expatriate Carriacouans are reminiscing about their homeland, including stories about magic, supernatural creatures, and other memories of home. Blogs may give "raw" information on Caribbean folklore. The quickest way I have found to find a blog is to type into a search engine the work "blog" together with the topic I want to search, in quotation marks. For example, in Google, the terms "'blog' 'Caribbean folklore'" yielded 154 hits. Finally, you could simply use any number of search engines—my favorites are Google, Copernic, and Yahoo—and just type away. Soon they may lead you to some fresh source of information, relatively firsthand (what would be called a "primary source" in the pre-high-tech era) on some tidbit of Caribbean folklore. One should also check family reunion and Caribbean country Web sites. Reunions can be found by simply typing some generic Caribbean family name into a search engine, along with "family reunion." If that generates too many hits, also put an island into the search.

For example, http://www.spiceislandertalkshop.com/talkshop/ is a message stream from Grenada. And here is a family Web site, from Carriacou (Grenada): http://carriacoufamilywebsite.com/.

Folklore in Caribbean Newspapers: Both Traditional Folklore Research and E-Folklore Sites

Following a grand British tradition, Caribbean newspapers in English, at least from the late eighteenth century, have been rich in folkloric material, especially about the vicissitudes of everyday life. Someone stole a cow, a person is accused of holding an illegal drum dance, a topical song is written parodying a prime minister: all these topics have been covered in detail in the Caribbean press. Most English-speaking islands have their own newspapers, and most of the larger newspapers have Web versions. The site http://www.escapeartist.com/media9/media9.htm lists some Caribbean newspapers, and Yahoo's site, http://www.google.com/Top/Regional/Caribbean/News_and_Media/Newspapers/ lists more. Another site, http://caribbeannewspapers.com/, is also useful. Alternatively, you can search a particular newspaper, such as the *Jamaica Gleaner* (http://www.jamaica-gleaner.com/), one of the oldest in the Caribbean. Look at current issues for modern traditions, or carry out a search of the newspaper using ProQuest, which is digitizing newspapers and other printed materials in searchable PDF files. The *Gleaner* is in the ProQuest system, but in order to use ProQuest one must either pay for the service or attend or be affiliated with a school or other institution that subscribes.

Folklore from Cruise Ship Web Sites

One of my favorite ways to get tourist lore on Caribbean topics is to look at cruise ship Web sites. Princess Cruises is one such site: http://www.princess.com/.

CONCLUSION

Folklorists have used library research as well as field studies to carry out their projects. Most likely some folklore Ph.D. student is, right now, preparing a dissertation in folklore, perhaps Caribbean folklore, using exclusively virtual ethnography culled from the Internet.

Index

About the Author

DONALD R. HILL is Professor of Anthropology and Africana and Latino Studies at State University College at Oneonta. He has been a Curator of Education at the American Museum of Natural History, and his previous books include *Calypso Calaloo: Early Trinidadian Carnival Music* (1993), and *The Impact of Migration on the Metropolitan and Folk Society of Carriacou, Grenada* (1977).